International Politics of Energy Interdependence

International Politics of Energy Interdependence

The Case of Petroleum

Nazli Choucri
Massachusetts Institute of Technology

with Vincent Ferraro

Lexington Books
D.C. Heath and Company
Lexington, Massachusetts
Toronto London

Library of Congress Cataloging in Publication Data

Choucri, Nazli.
International politics of energy interdependence.

Bibliography: p.
Includes index.
1. Petroleum industry and trade. 2. Power resources. 3. International economic relations. 4. World politics—1965- I. Ferraro, Vincent, joint author. II. Title.
HD9560.6.C5 338.2'7'282 74-31716
ISBN 0-669-98293-8

Published simultaneously in Canada.

Printed in the United States of America.

International Standard Book Number: 0-669-98293-8

Library of Congress Catalog Card Number: 74-31716

Contents

List of Figures

List of Tables

Preface

The energy problem is basically a political one—it emanates from disputes over who controls energy transactions, what the rules of the game will be, who gains and who loses, and at what costs to whom. To consider the energy issue in its purely economic guise is to distort its underlying nature and to obscure both the definition of the problem and the search for solutions. This book emphasizes the political elements of an issue that has to date been treated as overwhelmingly economic in nature. It is a study of the evolving crisis and of the changing structure of petroleum transactions; of the antagonistic stands among players in the energy game as well as their common interests; of the strength of countries that have caused the present energy situation to become one of crisis, and of the forces that will tear those countries apart. In short, it is a study of the factors that render incomplete, if not misleading, a purely economic assessment of the energy crisis and the prospects for solutions.

The central concern of this book is with the worldwide interdependence generated by increased petroleum trade and higher prices, and the constraints on the international behavior of virtually all nations. The conflicts over price, distribution, and regulation of market shares in petroleum transactions—undoubtedly critical factors in posing a crisis for oil-importing nations—are symptomatic of more basic underlying political differences. The dispute between importers and exporters of crude petroleum is one of domination and control. The emphasis on control is designed to complement economic perspectives on energy transactions with political ones, and not to argue that politics can explain the crisis completely.

Part I serves as an introduction to the analysis of petroleum politics by delineating the structure of the world petroleum market over the past 25 years and describing the changing power relationship among various parties to petroleum transactions. New sources of petroleum, which may change these relationships, are identified and their potential effect upon the world market is evaluated, as is the possible impact of alternative sources of energy.

Part II begins with an analysis of the economic implications of the post-1973 increases in petroleum prices and the potential impact on the oil-importing nations, and then examines the political factors that impinge upon the cohesion of the oil-exporting states. To date, most analyses of the Organization of Petroleum Exporting Countries have focused on its economic features. This book is designed to provide political correctives for economic assumptions, and to introduce a distinctly political dimension in the assessment of economic strategies.

Part III speculates about the implications of alternative sources of energy for the nature of interdependence among producers and consumers of energies other than petroleum. This "epilogue," by necessity halting and tentative, seeks to identify what we have learned from our experience with petroleum that might assist our understanding of the future.

This book is written as a commentary on, and extension of, investigations in three related research projects: First is the study on evolving patterns of global interdependence undertaken for the U.S. State Department jointly by Hayward R. Alker, Jr., Lincoln P. Bloomfield, and myself. I have drawn extensively on Volume II of the four volume final report of this study entitled *Analyzing Global Interdependence* (M.I.T.: Center for International Studies, 1974). Second is the ongoing study of the long-range resource availability in the United States, directed by Dennis Meadows, supported by a grant from the National Science Foundation (Research Applied to National Needs) for an interdisciplinary analysis of specific resource-related problems. Work done in the course of preparing the final report of political aspects of this project, entitled *Energy Problems and International Politics: A Simulation Model of Exchange, Price, and Conflict* (M.I.T.: Center for International Studies, January 1976) is closely related to the investigations reported in this book. Third is another ongoing inquiry into the relationship of resource constraints and foreign policy, also supported by the National Science Foundation (Political Science). These three projects have provided the incentive for writing this essentially interpretive study of petroleum politics.

I am indebted to many colleagues, research assistants, and students at M.I.T. and elsewhere. Without their assistance, suggestions, comments, criticisms, and corrections, this book would have never been finished. The comments and criticism of Lincoln P. Bloomfield and Hayward R. Alker, Jr. have been invaluable, as have the suggestions of Ted Greenwood, Howard Margolis, Davis Bobrow, Dennis Meadows, Howard Beckman, Dennis Pirages, David Kay, and Jerome Rothenberg. Ann Alker, Amelia C. Leiss, Priscilla Mandrachia, and Dovianna Barrens made useful suggestions on earlier drafts.

The research assistance of Ernest Evans, Beth Gould, Ijaz Gilani, Brian Pollins, D. Scott Ross, and Richard Samuels is noted with appreciation. Gilani has played a large role in the analysis of Middle East politics and Samuels made important contributions in the course of collecting facts and figures for the analysis of the disbursement of petroleum revenues.

The discussions and debates at the World Oil Project seminars of the Energy Laboratory at M.I.T. during the summer of 1975 provided useful insight and evidence into the issues at hand, as have the sessions of the Conference on Depletable Resources sponsored by the National Science Foundation, held at The Brookings Institution in early June 1975.

But it is to M.A. Adelman and R.S. Eckaus that I owe the greatest debt of all. Professor Adelman tried to educate me on the intricacies of the world petroleum market and prevented me from holding some of the more naive misconceptions. Professor Eckaus with great patience and sharp criticism made invaluable suggestions throughout.

Vincent Ferraro's role in this study has been extensive from the start. His contributions include general research assistance, data collection, editorial suggestions, footnote preparations, bibliographical compilation, and substantive additions. His work, competence, and reliability made him a most valuable collaborator.

Nazli Choucri

Cambridge, Massachusetts
October 1975

Part I:
Introduction: Global Energy Transactions

1 The Petroleum Market and Alternative Sources of Energy

By now the dramatic worldwide growth in energy usage is well recognized. The almost perfect positive correlation between gross national product and per capita energy use (calculated on a cross-section comparison of 96 nations) attests to the criticality of energy to industrial processes.[1] In fact, energy use is often employed as an indicator of industrial productivity, based on the observation that the higher a nation's productivity, the greater its energy requirements. This chapter describes recent trends in energy flows, examines the structure of the world petroleum market, identifies new sources of petroleum, and describes the major characteristics of other sources of energy.

The average rate of growth in worldwide energy consumption over the past decade was 6.0 percent per year. The United States has averaged 3.1 percent per year growth in the demand for energy throughout the past 20 years. It is the world's largest producer of energy, but also its largest consumer. The fact that the country's domestic consumption exceeds its present production, contributing to a dramatic increase in net energy imports over the past few years, is a major political issue. Forty percent of United States energy needs are met through liquid fuels; dependency on imports of liquid fuels has increased steadily from 11 percent in 1955 to 35 percent in 1973.[2] And the demand for "clean" energy, resulting from environmental concerns, has tended to contribute further to policies of importation rather than exploitation of indigenous resources.

The dependency on energy imports varies from state to state. Although Europeans are highly dependent on foreign sources for liquid fuel, they are almost totally self-sufficient in solid fuels. In Japan the situation is dramatic: the country depends entirely on foreign sources for energy resources. By contrast, the USSR is one of the world's net energy exporters, although it produces and consumes only a fraction of the energy processed by the United States. In 1972 the USSR produced 37 percent less energy than did the United States, and consumed 52 percent less. This difference accords the USSR a certain flexibility in energy policy that is not shared by other nations. Of the major powers, the People's Republic of China alone seems to have developed a balanced energy budget, consuming as much as is produced domestically. At this stage China may be developing its petroleum resources primarily for export, perhaps to the same degree as the USSR; but Chinese policies and prospects are still unclear.

Energy Interdependence

The flow of energy across national boundaries has become an important political issue, which has dramatically drawn our attention to the particular patterns of interdependence that result from energy transactions. Such interdependence has been molded as much by the energy requirements of the advanced industrial nations as by the desire of the resource-rich, less developed nations to exchange their natural materials for financial benefits, advanced technology, or other valued goods and services.

The notion of interdependence has only recently been accepted in the United States as a legitimate view of international relations. This acceptance stems as much from the realization in academic circles that the state centric view is not appropriate to the complexities of contemporary world politics, as it does from an awareness in policy-making circles of the increasing difficulty of establishing and maintaining unilateral control over international events.

The academic view of interdependence has evolved in part from recent writings on transnational relations. These studies examine international transactions that are not controlled by the foreign policy organs of national governments but have a profound impact on the behavior of nation-states. The new perspective also comes from an increasing understanding of the constraints upon nations in their pursuit of economic gain. The policy view of interdependence can be traced most dramatically to a statement by the Secretary of State for the United States outlining American views on economic problems in the early 1970s.[3]

There is considerable disagreement in both academic and policy-making circles about the nature of particular interdependencies generated by the flow of energy across national boundaries. Even more profound disagreements exist as to whether interdependence is good or bad. Those who argue that interdependence is good do so on the grounds that shared recognition of joint problems could lead to shared definition of preferable solutions.[4] Those who argue that interdependence is bad do so on the grounds that any recognition of interdependence leads inevitably to compromises of national autonomy and reduces freedom of action in world politics. There are also those who argue that interdependence is merely a euphemism for domination and hegemony.[5] These disagreements persist as much in United States foreign policy circles as in those of other countries.

A related set of concerns pertains to the question of devising international procedures for managing evolving interdependencies. When the policies of one nation become the constraints of another, the issue of procedure is of more than simply academic significance.

Contemporary energy problems dramatize the close relationship between policies and constraints. Few would deny that a problem of ensuring continued access to energy resources exists in the West, yet there is little agreement regarding the definition of the issue, nor the extent to which it is viewed as problematical. By the same token, while almost everyone agrees that the energy issue has many ramifications in terms of its impact on the foreign policy of nations, precisely how national behavior has been or will be affected by the present situation remains far from clear. More important, however, is a growing realization both here and abroad of the increasing impact of resource questions on traditional foreign policy issues.

While many of the current energy concerns center around questions of shortages, ensured access to supplies has become an important concern for all nations. Equally important are the issues of cost and price—the cost of extracting domestic versus foreign energy sources, and the price to be paid in each case. Recent events have illustrated the extent to which prices can be manipulated with attendant consequences for everyone.

We are witnessing today a gradual recognition by all nations of a common predicament: how to meet the growing energy requirements without generating undue conflicts of an economic, political, ecological, or strategic nature. More specifically: how to accommodate the seemingly irreconcilable objectives of energy producers and energy consumers. The immediate energy-related issues revolve around petroleum. Over the long range the use of alternative sources of energy, where political and economic costs are acceptable, where safety is minimally ensured, and where technological solutions to production problems are feasible, will become of more central concern.

Much of what we know about the structure of energy transactions is based on our experience with petroleum. Despite uncertainties regarding contemporary political and economic problems related to petroleum trade, some established regularities emerge that can assist our understanding of a global energy system based on sources other than petroleum. Current interest in oil-related problems have focused primarily on the economic implications of dependence on external sources, and less on political issues or on their impact upon prevailing attempts to build viable international institutions for the management of energy flows. Yet, some of the most critical problems of a global system based on alternatives to petroleum center on the international arrangements to regulate the exploitation and flows of energy across national boundaries.

The World Petroleum Market

A dramatic rise in world petroleum consumption over the past decades provides the single most important fact underlying current global energy transactions. Figure 1-1 illustrates the magnitude of the increase. Our purpose here is less to explain this growth than to highlight some important changes that provide both background and context for present policies and postures. This section focuses on major structural changes in patterns of production, consumption, and trade

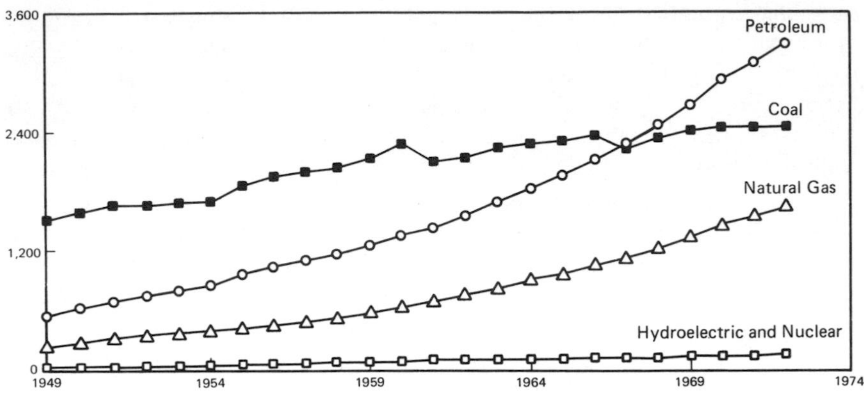

Source: United Nations, *World Energy Supplies*, Series J, Nos. 1-17 (New York: United Nations).

Figure 1-1. World Consumption of Major Energy Sources (In Million Metric Tons of Coal Equivalent)

from 1955 to 1973, and identifies new sources of petroleum that may lead to further changes. In subsequent chapters we argue that these developments were instrumental in the creation of an energy "problem" today, and that the structure of the world petroleum market itself harbored many of the sources of conflict between importers and exporters of crude petroleum.

Petroleum is presently the world's largest single source of energy and also a basic raw material for almost all the organic chemical products. For the most important uses there are as yet no commercially viable substitutes. Known world reserves are ample only until the turn of the century. These basic factors have generated heated debates concerning the extent to which the energy situation is one of crisis. Some argue that the crisis is real, in that petroleum is basically a depletable, nonrenewable resource and present rates of consumption cannot be sustained indefinitely given prevailing beliefs about known and projected reserves.[a] Others maintain that it is artificial, in that known reserves are extensive, and supply, if left to market mechanisms, would respond to price.[6] But these arguments are not mutually exclusive, and defining crisis in such dichotomous terms may confuse more than clarify it. Almost everyone recog-

[a]For a "limits" perspective on resource use, see Donella H. Meadows et al. *The Limits to Growth* (New York: Universe Books, 1972); Dennis L. Meadows and Donella H. Meadows, eds., *Toward Global Equilibrium* (Cambridge: Wright Allen Press, 1973); Allen V. Kneese and Blair T. Bower, eds., *Environmental Quality Analysis: Theory and Method in the Social Sciences* (Baltimore: The Johns Hopkins University Press, 1972); Harold W. Helfrich, Jr., ed., *The Environmental Crisis: Man's Struggle to Live with Himself* (New Haven: Yale University Press, 1970). For an explicit treatment of petroleum see, James E. Akins, "The Oil Crisis: This Time the Wolf is Here," *Foreign Affairs*, Vol. 51, No. 3 (April 1973), pp. 462-490.

nizes the existence of political factors that have successfully hindered the functioning of market mechanisms, making an otherwise geologically available resource one that is not readily accessible. We argue here that the present crisis is largely political, and that it has become so by virtue of the convergence of a peculiar set of circumstances.

Changing Structure and Evolving Crises

The world petroleum system—defined by patterns of production and consumption, imports and exports—has undergone a marked transformation over the past two decades, both in the magnitude of trade and in major actors and institutions. The situation has changed from one in which international oil companies dominated the petroleum industry to one in which national governments of the producing countries have become major actors, coordinating their policies and actions; where the governments of the consumer countries have become directly involved; and where the oil companies provide services to both. There have been changes in the patterns of alignments among producers and consumers, and a heightened awareness of the hazards of production and transport and the virtues of conservation. These developments have contributed to a situation in which the petroleum exporters are now able to manipulate prices to a considerable extent. The discovery of new reserves outside traditional areas of supply, such as those in the North Sea and the South China Sea, may change this situation in the years to come. But the effects, if any, will not be immediate.

Responsibility for the present crisis has been assigned by some observers to the exporting countries for raising petroleum prices in a seemingly arbitrary manner; by others, to the importing countries for placing extensive demands upon existing petroleum reserves; and by others still to the international oil corporations for allegedly encouraging the producers in their price escalation policies. The crisis is defined differently by different parties with different interests, goals, and objectives. What appears to be a problem when viewed from Washington may not be so regarded in Paris, London, Teheran, Moscow, or Peking.

There are at least four distinct issues at the core of current definitions of the energy crisis:

First is the issue of embargos of oil, specifically the ability of the producing nations to impede successfully the flow of petroleum to consuming nations. The political question is whether a nation can or should manipulate access to raw materials for political gains. Clearly, importers and exporters differ on this issue.

Second is the question of potential shortages of supplies at existing prices, apart from embargos, due largely to the rise in demand but also to the reluctance of some producers to increase production. So far oil-consuming nations have sought to meet their needs through imports rather than through the drastic reduction of internal demand or the adoption of other measures; and the producers have attempted to increase political and economic gains associated with their control of a nonrenewable resource. Some exporters have reduced their production schedules, others are accelerating.[b] Yet, all recognize the eventual depletion possibilities. This recognition has reinforced the exploitation of monopoly power based largely on the geographical concentration of petroleum reserves.

Third is the issue of price, around which the most salient differences between importers and exporters arise. Oil-consuming nations differ with respect to the criticality of petroleum to their individual economies, and to the extent they are in fact economically dependent upon imports. Yet, the objective of structuring a pricing system with markedly reduced prices from those prevailing in 1975 is shared by all. By contrast, the exporters, faced with a finite resource, are seeking to maximize political as well as economic gains—in some cases they even appear to forego economic benefits in anticipation of political gain.

The fourth issue is the availability of tanker capacity, refinery shortages, and pipeline capacities. These factors have been accorded only marginal importance in current debates. Yet, future decisions regarding infrastructure will inevitably be affected by embargos, production schedules, consumption patterns, import policies, and prices.

Institutional constraints in both importing and exporting countries add to the definition of crisis by making it difficult to adopt comprehensive energy policies. Oil-consuming nations have yet to develop national policies in which energy needs and requirements are evaluated and avenues for cooperation delineated. There sometimes are even contradictory energy-related policies within each country. In the United States, for example, oil import quotas in recent years may have reduced incentives for domestic exploration, and in the final analysis contributed to increased dependence upon imports.[c] Policies toward natural gas have made this alternative to petroleum largely nonviable on economic grounds.

By contrast, exporters appear to have more concerted national policies regarding petroleum. Nevertheless, there is little formal cooperation among producers on issues other than price, despite the apparent successes of the Organization of Petroleum Exporting Countries (OPEC). Common postures on such issues as production schedules and the allocation of market shares have yet to be worked out. Despite the apparent antagonisms in the world petroleum

[b]*New York Times*, March 4, 1975; see Chapter 5 for a treatment of the differing attitudes toward oil production within OPEC; see also U.S., General Accounting Office, *Issues Related to Foreign Sources of Oil for the United States*, Report B-179411, January 23, 1974, p. 20.

[c]For a detailed treatment of the Oil Import Program see, Edward H. Shaffer, *The Oil Import Program of the United States* (New York: Praeger, 1968); see also, U.S., Cabinet Task Force on Oil Import Control, *The Oil Import Question* (Washington, D.C.: U.S. Government Printing Office, 1970).

market, differences among exporters and among importers are extensive; with respect to some issues the differences are as great as those between producing and consuming nations.

The average growth rate of petroleum consumption in the immediate future is expected to be 1.3-3.8 percent.[d] This estimate is based on three assumptions: a static ratio of imports to domestic consumption at about the 1968 level; no production of liquid fuels from coals, oil shale, or tar sands; and continuation of the 1968 ratio of crude oil to liquified natural gas production. Of these, the first assumption is now clearly violated: imports have increased sharply since 1968. Consumption for the rest of the world is likely to increase at faster rates than in the United States, between 3.5 and 5.5 percent per year. These projections reflect the industrialization of large parts of the world where petroleum usage has so far been nominal, and assume continued population growth in developing areas.

The United States, Western Europe, and Japan consume about 80 percent of the world's production of petroleum. Although projections beyond 1980 are at best rough approximations, it is expected that in 1985 the same percentage is to be consumed out of a total base of over twice the present levels of production. Two thirds of projected petroleum demand in the United States may have to be imported, much of this coming from the Middle East. Furthermore, competition for Middle East oil is expected to increase among the advanced industrial states, including the USSR, because of considerations of quality, cost, availability, and perhaps adequacy of domestic oil reserves.[e] The major uncertainties are associated with prices.

National data on petroleum reserves signal geological differences. However, they must be assessed in the context of the quality of petroleum from each source, the domestic needs of the producing countries, their institutional capabilities, and the expected duration of known reserves given current rates of

[d] U.S., Congress, Senate, Committee on Interior and Insular Affairs, *Survey of Energy Consumption Projections*, 92nd Cong., 2nd sess., 1972, p. 20. For excellent studies of the world petroleum market see, M.A. Adelman, *The World Petroleum Market* (Baltimore: The Johns Hopkins University Press, 1972); Michael Tanzer, *The Political Economy of International Oil and the Underdeveloped Countries* (Boston: Beacon Press, 1969); Sam H. Schurr and Paul T. Homan, *Middle Eastern Oil and the Western World: Prospects and Problems* (New York: American Elsevier Publishing Company, Inc., 1971). For more historical studies of the international petroleum industry see, Joel Darmstadter, *Energy in the World Economy* (Baltimore: The Johns Hopkins University Press, 1971); Jack E. Hartshorn, *Oil Companies and Governments: An Account of the International Oil Industry in Its Political Environment* (London: Faber and Faber, 1962); George Stocking, *Middle East Oil: A Study in Political and Economic Controversy* (Nashville: Vanderbilt University Press, 1970).

[e] See, Schurr and Homan, *Middle Eastern Oil and the Western World*; John A. Berry, "Oil and Soviet Policy in the Middle East," *Foreign Affairs*, Vol. 26, No. 2 (Spring 1972), pp. 149-160; for an assessment of the impact of higher oil prices on the demand for Middle Eastern oil see, the Organisation for Economic Co-operation and Development, *Energy Prospects to 1985* (Paris: Organisation for Economic Co-operation and Development, 1974), pp. 7-17.

production. Nonetheless, estimates of reserves will serve as one standard against which patterns of production, consumption, flows, and dependencies may be evaluated. Table 1-1 presents the data upon which the discussion of the world petroleum market is based. These figures are for crude oil only, and do not include refined products.

Production

There are some marked changes in patterns of petroleum production over the past 20 years, only one of which is the exponential rise in output. In 1955 world production of crude petroleum was dominated by the United States, which produced 43 percent of the world total. The nearest competitor was Venezuela, which accounted for 15 percent of the total. By 1972 the situation had changed substantially; the centers of production were no longer in the Western Hemisphere. Although the United States was still the world leader in total production, it accounted for only 18 percent, followed by the USSR which contributed 15 percent of the world's total production. Saudi Arabia and Iran ranked third and fourth, respectively. Venezuela had dropped to fifth place. Thus, the single most critical factor in the production of petroleum since World War II has been the extensive development of Middle Eastern and North African fields. In 1972 these fields accounted for 41 percent of the total world production.[7] But the United States and Venezuelan decline is relative: Absolute levels of production are still extremely high. Nonetheless, by early 1974 it was apparent that the USSR and Saudi Arabia would replace the United States as the world's leading producers of petroleum. In 1972 members of the Organization of Petroleum Exporting Countries accounted for 52.5 percent of the world production of crude oil (other than those in the USSR). More recent figures are less reliable for comparative purposes. Furthermore, any data published after October 1973 must be viewed with great suspicion: no one is being completely candid about petroleum transactions. Figure 1-2 illustrates recent changes in the production of crude petroleum.

The general trend toward increased production, however, has been accompanied by periodic declines in the output of individual states, particularly in 1970-72. The largest declines were in Algeria and Libya, each reducing production by over 20 percent during this period. Venezuela, Iraq, Oman, and even the United States also experienced noticeable declines. These cuts may be attributed to a concern for environmental protection; to domestic political problems; to international conflicts that inhibit production increases; to the existence of unstable prices; to national security concerns; and/or to a concern for the exploitation of a critical nonrenewable resource.

For example, environmental concerns in the advanced industrial societies have placed a high premium on the low-sulphur crudes of Libya and Nigeria, depressing demands for high-sulphur crudes as produced in Venezuela. An example of internal political problems accounting for decreases in production is the Nigerian civil war. International conflicts centering on the Arab-Israeli dispute and the positions adopted by some Arab states have also accounted for declines. Petroleum prices in the United States may have resulted in lowering domestic production, if the oil industry's argument that the price of domestic oil was too low to warrant continued exploration and development of domestic fields is correct. The peak of production in the United States was in 1970. Considerations of national security in the United States, particularly the conservation of reserves, contributed further to the restriction of domestic production and the imposition of import quotas. Finally, many exporters, particularly in the Middle East, are limiting production in the belief that the value of revenues invested in international monetary markets would be lower than that of oil in the ground taking into account the amount of revenue they need or can profitably use at the present time. Increases in price and restrictions on production have common implications. Cutbacks in production raise prices for at least as long as cutbacks are in effect and, more important, preserve reserves over a longer period.

Despite cutbacks, the present world petroleum situation is one of potential surplus capacity. Yet, the critical issues of self-determination, national security and military strategy, and protection of nonrenewable resources have impeded the flow of petroleum across national boundaries. The influence of such factors makes the present crisis political rather than a reflection of real economics scarcity. But by the turn of the century, the scarcity of oil may well place economic limits on supply. More immediately, however, political constraints on the ready flow of petroleum have created problems of access, the reality of which cannot be denied.

Consumption

The growth in petroleum consumption is also impressive. Of the total energy consumed by the world in 1957, 30 percent was in the form of liquid fuel. By 1972 this figure increased to 43 percent and is still higher today. This growing reliance on oil reflects several important developments, most of which are related to comparative costs, and to environmental and technological factors. Middle Eastern and North African oil is relatively cheap in comparison with other fuels. In addition, petroleum consumption is much "cleaner" than coal, the technology is more developed than that of nuclear power, and hydroelectricity is not feasible in many areas. Together, these factors have made the advanced states rely increasingly upon petroleum as a primary source of energy.

With one exception all industrialized nations have increased their use of petroleum in relation to total energy consumed over the past 20 years. Only the

Table 1-1
World Petroleum Profile for 1972

(In 1,000 Barrels)

Country	Estimated Reserves 1/1/72	Percent World Reserves	Crude Production 1972	Percent World Production	Reserves Production Ratio	Demand Per Day	Production Demand Ratio	Imports[a]	Percent World Imports	Exports[a]	Percent World Exports
World	560,119,973	100.00	18,531,872	100.00	30.22	51,640	1.02	8,122,007	100.00	8,122,007	100.0
Algeria[b]	9,839,600	1.76	390,888	2.11	25.17	53	20.15	–	–	301,292	3.70
Canada	8,333,087	1.49	544,562	2.94	15.30	1,623	1.09	282,366	3.47	313,753	3.86
China[c]	12,500,000	2.23	186,660	1.01	66.97	484	1.05	n.a.	n.a.	n.a.	n.a.
Ecuador	6,070,545	1.08	34,262	0.18	177.18	n.a.	n.a.	n.a.	n.a.	n.a.	n.a.
France	98,890	0.02	10,720	0.06	9.22	2,189	0.01	739,084	9.09	–	–
Germany, W.	560,000	0.10	51,311	0.28	10.91	2,638	0.05	764,951	9.41	–	–
Indonesia	10,673,400	1.90	390,132	2.11	27.36	153	6.97	–	–	274,237	3.37
Iran	60,450,000	10.79	1,838,451	9.92	32.88	339	14.82	–	–	1,035,692	12.75
Iraq	33,100,000	5.91	529,236	2.86	62.54	81	17.85	–	–	716,368	8.82
Japan	24,880	0.00	5,348	0.00	4.65	4,540	0.00	1,707,355	21.02	–	–
Kuwait	66,023,000	11.79	1,099,792	5.93	60.03	156	19.26	–	–	927,582	11.42
Libya[b]	28,000,000	5.00	820,000	4.42	34.15	22	101.82	–	–	819,751	10.09
Nigeria	10,000,000	1.78	665,022	3.59	15.04	39	45.49	–	–	567,840	6.99
Oman	4,750,000	0.85	103,562	0.56	45.87	n.a.	n.a.	–	–	n.a.	n.a.
Qatar	4,800,000	0.86	176,412	0.95	27.21	n.a.	n.a.	–	–	168,743	2.07
Saudi Arabia	137,040,000	24.47	2,098,423	11.32	65.31	256	22.39	–	–	1,513,814	18.63
U.A.E.[d]	15,100,000	2.69	384,300	2.38	39.29	n.a.	n.a.	–	–	589,647	7.25

U.K.	3,000,000	0.53	625	0.00	0.00	2,157	0.00	983,803	12.11	–	–
USSR	60,000,000	10.71	2,884,080	15.56	20.80	5,977	1.32	–	–	141,359	1.74
U.S.	38,062,957	6.79	3,459,052	18.66	11.00	16,354	0.68	811,135	9.98	187	0.00
Venezuela	13,740,395	2.46	1,172,356	6.33	11.72	223	14.36	–	–	502,926	6.19

Note: n.a. = not available.

[a]The figures for imports and exports are estimates from the *International Petroleum Encyclopedia, 1973.* As of this writing, only estimates of petroleum trade are available. These figures are converted from metric ton quantities to barrels by a factor of 7.33 barrels per metric ton. This is an average conversion factor that does take into account the unique characteristics of each country's petroleum. For our purposes, the variation is not intolerable. This standard is based on Saudi Arabian light, 34° gravity.

[b]Voluntary conservation policies in Libya and Algeria have reduced the production levels from previous years.

[c]China's position has apparently increased significantly since 1972. In 1973 China doubled her production to 366,500,000 barrels with an attendant increase in exports. (See Yoshio Koide, "China Crude Oil Production," *Pacific Community*, Vol. 5, No. 3 (April 1974), p. 463).

[d]The figures for the United Arab Emirates (UAE) include only Abu Dhabi and are therefore understated. The UAE is a federation of seven Trucial Sheikdoms: Abu Dhabi, Dubai, Sharjah, Umm al-Qiwain, Ajman, Fujairah, Ras al-Khaimah.

Sources: Degolyer and MacNaughton, Twentieth Century Petroleum Statistics, 1973, (Dallas: Degolyer and Macnaughton, 1973); Petroleum Publishing Company, *International Petroleum Encyclopedia, 1973*, (Tulsa: Petroleum Publishing Company, 1973); United Nations, *World Energy Supplies*, Series J, No. 16, (New York: United Nations, 1971).

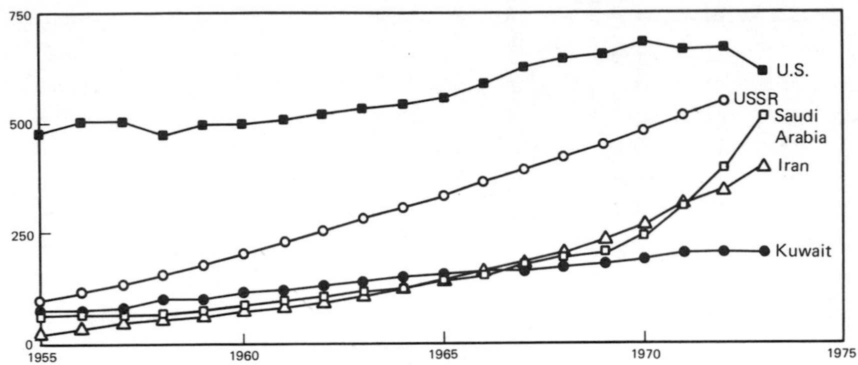

Source: United Nations, *World Energy Supplies*, Series J (New York: United Nations); Petroleum Publishing Company, *International Petroleum Encyclopedia 1974*, (Tulsa: Petroleum Publishing Company, 1974).

Figure 1-2. Production of Crude Petroleum (In Million Metric Tons of Coal Equivalent)

United States has maintained a relatively stable proportion of oil to total energy consumption, due to a relative abundance of coal, natural gas, and hydroelectric power. Over 50 percent of all petroleum consumed in the United States is in the transportation sector, where as yet no important alternative source of energy exists. This fact has accorded current imports of petroleum greater political importance than would be warranted on the basis of volume alone. In addition, the rate of growth in energy consumption in the United States will inevitably lead to continued reliance on imports at least until the turn of the century.

The projected growth of oil imports in Western Europe and the Far East is substantially greater than in North America. It is anticipated that Europe will remain the leading market for petroleum from the Middle East and North Africa. It is anticipated that imported oil will account for over 80 percent of European energy consumption by 1980, but this projection may not take sufficient cognizance of the North Sea discoveries and their pace of development.[f] It is expected, further, that Japan's petroleum needs will be supplied primarily by the Middle East, although new offshore discoveries in Indonesia and the South and East China Seas may modify this assessment. In any case, Japan's dependence on imported sources will remain.

[f]U.S., Congress, House, Committee on Foreign Affairs, Subcommittee on Foreign Economic Policy, *Foreign Policy Implications of the Energy Crisis*, 92nd Cong., 2nd sess., 1972, p. 233 (Statement by John G. Winger); the most optimistic assessment of the major consumers energy prospects, including the development of the North Sea fields, is the Organisation for Economic Co-operation and Development, *Energy Prospects to 1985*, pp. 88-116; see also, H.R. Warman, "The Oil Potential of the North Sea," paper delivered at the Financial Times Conference on the North Sea, Houston, 14th/15th November 1973.

These consumption patterns have interjected new tensions into the Western alliance. Japan and Western Europe have become concerned by the rate of increase in United States reliance on imports at a time when the availability of supplies to meet their own needs is in question. They are also apprehensive of American buying power and fear that the companies that dominate the international oil industry will give priority to United States needs at the expense of its allies.[8] Such perceptions are strong despite charges that the companies are more sensitive to European interests than to those of the United States.[g] Whatever the empirical foundations for such fears may be, they do point to potential sources of conflict between the United States and its allies and the way in which strategic and security issues may become dependent upon projected petroleum consumption.

Patterns of exports and imports, while closely related to production and consumption, reveal further problems of availability and access. For example, it was the entry of the United States, formerly the world's largest producer, into the export market that contributed to a situation of crisis for all consumers.

Exports

Between 1955 and 1970 total world exports of crude petroleum increased 361 percent. Today, trade in petroleum accounts for over 10 percent of total world trade in all commodities. There has been a transformation from the Western Hemisphere as the focal point of petroleum exports to other areas of the world, most notably the Middle East. In 1972 Saudi Arabia controlled 18.8 percent of the market; Iran, 16.4 percent; Kuwait, 11.6 percent; and Libya, 7.7 percent. Venezuela had only 8.1 percent of world exports in contrast to 35 percent in 1955.

By 1970 it was clear that no one state could dominate the export market for crude petroleum. The top five exporters were separated by a margin of only 3 percent; moreover, the market was characterized by surplus capacity. The conjunction of these factors, in addition to the United States' position as a major oil exporter, neutralized a selective Arab oil embargo against Western Europe in 1956 and again in 1967. At that time, United States ability to supply Western Europe with its own oil prevented the Arab producers from employing their petroleum exports for political gain.[9]

The declining preeminence of four major exporters—Saudi Arabia, Iran, Libya, and Venezuela—and the rise of minor exporters and their increasing

[g]See, for example, the charges of disloyalty that were leveled at the United States oil industry for their actions during the embargo of 1973-74, as reported in *The New York Times*, January 25, 1974; see also, U.S., Congress, Senate, Committee on Foreign Relations, Subcommittee on Multinational Corporations, "U.S. Oil Companies and the Arab Oil Embargo: The International Allocation of Constricted Supplies," a Report prepared by the Federal Energy Administration's Office of International Energy Affairs, 94th Cong., 1st sess., January 27, 1975.

importance in the world petroleum market are indicated in Figure 1-3. The critical point was 1970. Libya and, although to a much lesser extent, Algeria acquired a major export position in the oil market, at which point they systematically began to cut production. These events led to the 1970-71 pricing and participation agreement involving all major OPEC nations. Iran and Saudi Arabia then increased their exports. Despite differences in export policies, neither major nor minor producers could unilaterally control the market. On balance, the market share of the major exporters has been steadily declining since 1955, whereas the share of the smaller exporters has been increasing (see Figure 1-4). This trend, in combination with the shared gains accrued from the participation and pricing agreements, contributed to the eventual consolidation of OPEC.

Imports

Over the past 25 years there has been a dramatic increase in the total petroleum imports of Western Europe. The increase in Japan has been steady, and that of the United States most notable since 1970. (See Figure 1-5). OPEC controls an increasing share of the world export market, fluctuating around 85 percent of total world petroleum imports.

In 1955 the United States imported approximately 11 percent of its total crude oil consumption; 50 percent of this amount came from Venezuela. By mid-1973 the United States was importing 35 percent of its oil consumption,

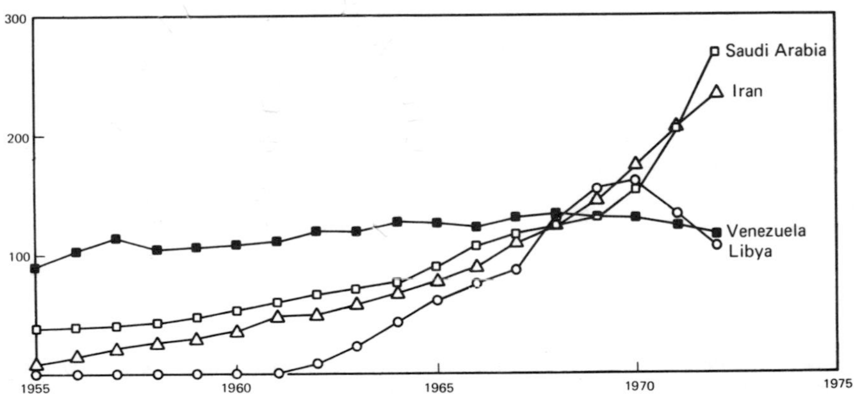

Source: United Nations, *World Energy Supplies*, Series J (New York: United Nations).

Figure 1-3. Four Major Petroleum Exporters (In Million Metric Tons of Coal Equivalent)

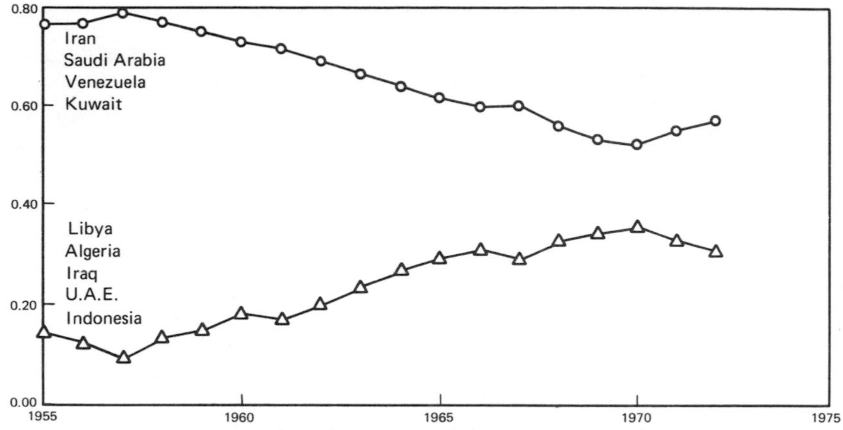

Note: Ecuador and Gabon are not included since they joined OPEC after 1972.

Source: United Nations, *World Energy Supplies*, Series J (New York: United Nations).

Figure 1-4. Percentage Exports of OPEC Producers

Arab oil contributed 5 percent of total United States consumption of crude oil and Eastern Hemisphere oil, 11 percent.[10] Some observers foresee United States oil imports increasing to 54 percent of the nation's consumption by 1980, with the Middle East and North Africa accounting for 70 percent of these imports.[11]

The near doubling of United States petroleum imports over the past three years can be explained by institutional factors: (a) stagnation in the domestic oil industry, (b) declines in the domestic production of natural gas, (c) delays in planned completion and operation of nuclear-powered plants for electric utilities, (d) technological problems encountered in the development of sulphur-control equipment for coal- and oil-burning equipment, and (e) environmental and safety concerns. The United States has traditionally attempted to maintain its imports of crude petroleum at a level between 10 and 20 percent of total consumption, a policy based on a preference for limiting dependence upon any one nation for a vital commodity, some concerns for maintaining some level of viability for domestic petroleum industry, and a desire to maintain a high degree of self-sufficiency in all areas that might effect the nation's economy or military security.[12] However, this policy appeared no longer viable after 1970 in the face of increased demands for petroleum and decreased domestic production.

Western Europe and Japan do not have the option of relying on domestic sources of petroleum, nor are alternative sources of energy commercially feasible. Europe has always imported over 90 percent of its total petroleum needs. Today the figure is close to 98 percent. In 1955 Western Europe

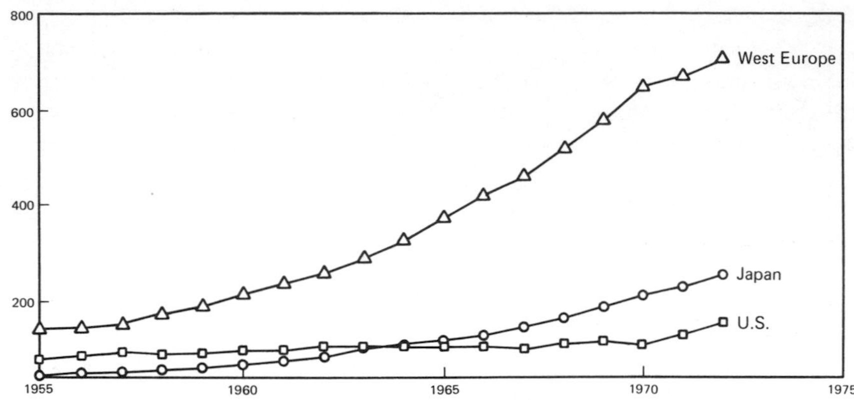

Source: United Nations, *World Energy Supplies*, Series J (New York: United Nations).

Figure 1-5. Imports of Crude Petroleum (In Million Metric Tons of Coal Equivalent)

commanded 51 percent of total exports. By 1972 Europe received 48 percent of total world exports; the difference is marginal, but it reflects the emergence of the United States as a significant importer of crude petroleum. More importantly, however, the Europeans also appeared to diversify their sources of imports.[h]

One logic behind diversification was that any state dependent upon imported oil ought not weaken its position further by becoming reliant upon any one exporter. By expanding its sources of imports, a state could reduce the risk of impeded access to this critical resource. This strategy emerged with the entry of new producers into the world petroleum market and was viable as long as an importing state was confronted with a large number of relatively autonomous, uncoordinated exporters.

For importing countries to reduce reliance successfully on any single supplier, one or more of the following conditions must hold: (1) There must be a large number of uncoordinated exporters; (2) they must have the capacity to meet a consumer policy of diversification; (3) consumers must be able to accommodate different petroleum grades; and (4) consumer demands must be sufficiently elastic to accommodate transportation costs.

For exporting countries, only major producers could selectively pursue a similar policy of diversification. The smaller exporters—Algeria, Libya, Indonesia, the United Arab Emirates, Nigeria, Qatar—tended to follow a pattern of export concentration. Such a policy is effectively precluded for the larger

[h]The data are from the United Nations, *World Energy Supplies, 1955-1971*, ST/STAT/SER.J/Nos. 1-16 (New York: United Nations, 1957-1973).

producers—Saudi Arabia, Kuwait, and Iran. The magnitudes of their exports are such that they readily, if not automatically, accommodate to diversification by the importers. The irony, however, is that consumer attempts to diversify, which may have been predicated on the desire to reduce dependence on single suppliers, have reinforced the bargaining position of all producers.

New Sources of Petroleum

Newly discovered oil reserves will in the future influence trade patterns substantially and might eventually provide the oil-consuming countries with new leverages and the producer countries with new problems. At the present time the following discoveries appear of some significance:

1. In the United States, the Alaskan North Slope Field, discovered in 1969, is considered to have about 10 billion barrels of oil as actual reserves, and 40 billion barrels in potential reserves. In addition, 26 trillion cubic feet of gas are presently classified as reserves, and 300 trillion cubic feet as potential reserves.[13] The major problems involve transporting petroleum from the northern parts of Alaska to the southern ports of the state. Environmental considerations have delayed the construction of an extensive pipeline.

2. The Canadian Arctic is estimated to have 72 billion barrels of oil as potential reserves and 300 trillion cubic feet of gas. The main obstacles to production are environmental. In addition, there is always the problem of raising sufficient capital to develop these fields.[14]

3. The area of the North Sea under British, German, Dutch, and Norwegian jurisdiction is estimated to have 30 billion barrels of potential petroleum reserves. An additional 21 billion barrels as well as 50 trillion cubic feet of gas are officially classified as reserves. The cost of bringing these fields into production has been estimated at 15 billion dollars. There are serious jurisdictional disputes over production and transportation. At the present time the United Kingdom insists that its government control 51 percent of any production venture.[15]

4. In the People's Republic of China inland reserves are estimated to be either 19 billion barrels of oil[16] or 3-10 billion barrels.[17] China may not possess sufficient technical expertise to develop these fields, nor the necessary infrastructure such as drilling rigs or pipelines. If these fields are developed in the immediate future, it is likely that production will be employed for export and not for domestic consumption. Indeed China is already beginning to export from existing fields, but in relatively small volume.

5. In the area of the Asian continental shelf claimed by China, Taiwan, Japan, Korea, North Vietnam, and South Vietnam, there are some highly speculative estimates of potential petroleum reserves. The United Nations Economic Commission for Asia and the Far East has labeled it as possibly one of the most

productive areas of the world.[18] It is believed that this area may hold the largest known deposits of petroleum. The trade journal *World Oil* estimated in 1970 that the Asian continental shelf would produce 400 million barrels of oil per day in five years, but in 1971 the journal admitted that its earlier estimate was an overstatement.[19] These estimates illustrate the highly speculative nature of prevailing assessments. In addition, there are significant jurisdictional difficulties. The People's Republic of China claims most of the continental shelf and has resorted to military action in the Paracel Islands in support of this claim. There is some exploratory activity in this area, aided by a recent agreement between China and the United States over the liability of exploration vessels.[20] Relatively little is known about the nature of the agreement or its potential effects upon relations between various claimants to the area.[21]

6. In 1974 new reserves were discovered near the state of Tabasco in Mexico. They are assessed at 20 billion barrels of oil, but this estimate is acknowledged to be high.[22]

7. Five billion barrels of oil are estimated as newly established reserves in Ecuador. The major difficulties are that the oil fields are located in inaccessible places. The completion of a new pipeline would assist considerably in resolving transportation problems.[23]

8. New reserves have been discovered off the Brazilian coast. They are estimated at 600 million barrels, an estimate that is likely to be too high.[24] Insufficient information is available to determine whether Brazil may, in fact, become a net petroleum exporter.

None of these sources can be considered as likely to allow for substantial export capacity in the immediate future. There are always time lags between exploration and development of any new oil field, difficulties in raising sufficient capital and obtaining adequate equipment, and obstacles in the development of the necessary pipelines and transportation facilities. In addition to uncertainties concerning the magnitude of potential reserves, there are also serious political and technological problems.

Everyone acknowledges the potential impact of these new finds upon the world petroleum market in the years to come, yet no one has yet offered a definite schedule, or a clear statement concerning the expected nature of these impacts. At least two possibilities emerge. On the one hand, these newly discovered deposits may eventually change the world petroleum market, and put pressures upon the existing oil exporters in a way that would reduce the cohesion of that group. On the other, the new producers may seek not to undercut the existing exporters but to accept prevailing prices. The magnitude of production in the new fields will influence the direction of these competing influences, as will the ability of present exporters to convince new entrants in the market to support the policies of established producers.

These newly discovered deposits of crude petroleum provide the basis for *potential* transactions and trade flows of oil and other commodities across international boundaries. Over the past decades, changes in flows have been accompanied by changes in the power relationships at the base of the world petroleum market. It thus seems likely that any potential trade flows will at least have the effect of setting in motion changes in the prevailing institutional arrangements for managing petroleum transactions.

Alternative Sources of Energy

The development of alternative sources of energy on a commercially viable basis may reduce the importance of petroleum and, by extension, the market strength of the oil-exporting states. New sources of energy will effectively change the structure of the world petroleum market and invariably interject new issues in international energy transactions.

The major alternatives to petroleum are coal, natural gas, nuclear fission, nuclear fusion, solar energy, geothermal energy, tar sands and oil shale, and other exotica. Different cost factors and time perspectives are attached to each, and different technological problems. So, too, the issues of national security are different, as are implications for political conflict among nations, and potentials for environmental degradation. Figure 1-6 presents the percentage of consumption for five sources of energy in relation to total world energy consumption. Four trends stand out:

First, the percentage of petroleum consumption to total energy consumed has increased from 25 to 40 percent between 1949 and 1974.

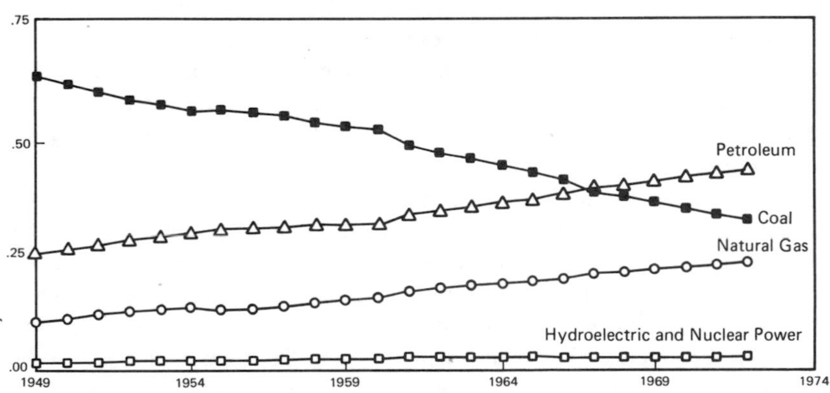

Source: United Nations, *World Energy Supplies*, Series J (New York: United Nations).

Figure 1-6. Alternative Sources as Percentage of Total Energy Consumption

Second, the total amount of coal consumed has remained fairly stable, but the share of coal in relation to other sources of energy has declined appreciably over the 25 years.

Third, the trends in natural gas appear similar to those in petroleum, although both volume and percentages in relation to total energy consumed differ considerably. The amount of natural gas consumed has increased markedly over the period, but its share as a percentage of total energy used has remained fairly stationary.

Fourth, since these figures do not disaggregate hydroelectric and nuclear power, it is difficult to specify differential trends over time. However, we know that the amount of hydroelectric power consumed has remained fairly stationary over time, whereas the percentage to total energy used has declined slightly. A different trend has taken place with respect to nuclear energy, such that both the amount used and the percentage to total energy consumed have increased over time dramatically.

These trends indicate that petroleum will remain the dominant energy source for many decades to come. However, its importance may recede in the economies of the major industrial states as other sources of energy become commercially viable. By the turn of the century we are likely to be confronted by a situation in which different countries use different mixes of energy sources.

Coal

An important characteristic of coal is that major consumers also produce the most and control the highest volume of known reserves.[25] The United States and the USSR together make the greatest use of coal, in about equal amounts. The USSR has the largest known reserves of coal, 56.5 percent of the world total in contrast to 19.5 percent for the United States. Together they control 74 percent of world reserves. The United States produced 30.9 percent of world coal in 1971 and the USSR 24.9 percent; they consumed 18.9 percent and 18.5 percent, respectively.

The other major producers and consumers are China, Poland, West Germany, and the United Kingdom. They have comparatively small potential in that their individual reserves are quite small, in no case greater than 5 percent of known world reserves. The People's Republic of China has been a fairly large producer in the past, providing 24.1 percent of the world's output in 1971. The other three countries produced less than 9 percent each. During the same year, China consumed 16.48 percent of recorded world consumption; the United Kingdom, 6.04 percent; Poland, 5.12 percent; and West Germany, 5.10 percent.

The major importers of coal are Japan (25% of world imports in 1972), Canada (9%), France (7%), and Italy (6%). Other West European countries also import coal but in relatively negligible amounts. The United States is the major exporter (about 27% of total world exports in 1972), followed by Poland (18%), the USSR (14%), Australia (12%), and West Germany (11%). Only Japan is clearly dependent on external sources for its coal consumption, but only to a fraction of the degree of its dependence on petroleum.

Natural Gas

The situation regarding natural gas is somewhat similar to that of coal in that the United States and the USSR are the major producers and consumers.[26] The USSR controls the largest reserves, accounting for 32.2 percent of the world's known deposits. The second largest deposits of natural gas reserves are in the Middle East, which contributed to 20.8 percent of the world total in 1974. The United States has only 12.6 percent, an estimate that is sometimes considered rather high. According to the *Wall Street Journal* (June 24, 1975), United States production of natural gas through conventional means could be 22 percent below present levels in 1985. Proven reserves have been steadily dropping for the last four years and reserves are at their lowest since 1956.

As with petroleum, the United States consumes slightly more than it produces domestically. In 1972 the country consumed 54.4 percent of world consumption, while producing 52.6 percent of world production. The reverse is generally true of the USSR, but the volume processed is considerably lower; in 1972 the USSR produced 10.01 percent of world production and consumed 18.8 percent.

Very little natural gas has been produced so far in the Middle East, although given the magnitude of known reserves in the area, this situation will change rapidly. Other major deposits of natural gas are found in Western Europe, Africa, China, and Latin America but in relatively small magnitudes—generally less than 10 percent of known world reserves. The producers are Canada (7.46% of total world production in 1972), the Netherlands (5.96%), Venezuela (4%), Iran (3.88%), and Rumania (2.99%). Consumption patterns for that year are somewhat different, in that all of Western Europe consumed 11.0 percent of world consumption; Canada, 4.5 percent; Latin America, 3.6 percent; and Eastern Europe, 3.5 percent.

Natural gas is becoming a more heavily traded source of energy, a consideration not entirely reflected in the figures cited above. In 1969 only 4 percent of world marketed natural gas production moved across national boundaries. In 1973 this figure increased to 7.6 percent, hardly a dramatic rise, but it may well signify an emerging trend.[27]

The United States is the major importer of natural gas (accounting for 37.9 percent of total world imports in 1972), followed by the USSR (19.5%), West Germany (13.7%), and France (11.2%). The large exporters are Canada (37.3 percent of total world exports in 1972), the Netherlands (32.4%), Iran (10.7%), and the USSR (6.6%). Algeria is also exporting natural gas, but the magnitude of its trade is still unclear.

OPEC members are rapidly moving in control of this source of energy, as reflected in flows of liquified natural gas (LNG). For example, 41 percent of LNG exports in 1973 were supplied by Libya and 27.1 percent by Algeria. Exports in liquified natural gas increased by 68 percent from 1972 to 1973, but it still remains a small fraction of world energy consumption.[28] It has recently been disclosed that the setting of natural gas prices was being discussed in the June 1975 meeting of OPEC. However, in contrast to its 65 percent control of world petroleum production, OPEC accounts for only 35 percent of world output of natural gas.[29]

Nuclear Fission

The world nuclear capacity has grown at rapid rates, from a capacity to generate 8,356 megawatts of nuclear-produced electricity in 1960 to 39,864 megawatts in 1972.[30] The United States had the largest capacity in that year, producing 41 percent of the world's total capacity. The United Kingdom ranked second (15%), followed by the USSR and France (7% each). During the same year, the United States had 32 operating nuclear generating units, the United Kingdom 29, the USSR 16, and West Germany 11. (See Figure 1-7.)

Reserves of uranium pose no immediate problem. The United States has by far the largest known reserves of less costly uranium and also the world's largest reserves even under assumptions of high prices. The growth of nuclear power in the United States is expected to double approximately every five years, a rate of growth accounted for largely by the initial low level of nuclear power for less than one percent of its energy needs. By 1985 this figure is projected to range from 15 to 30 percent of the country's total energy requirements.[31]

There are no reliable figures for consumption of uranium, although there are some indications of the availability of reasonably assured supplies at $10 per lb. The United States controls 29.9 percent of total OECD supplies; South Africa, 23.32 percent; Canada, 21.36 percent, and Australia, 8.19 percent. Niger is reputed to have about 4.61 percent.[32] Estimates on production of uranium indicate that the United States produced 50.35 percent of total non-Communist production of the world in 1972; Canada, 20.34 percent; South Africa, 15.64 percent; France, 7.01 percent; and Niger, 4.42 percent.[33]

At this writing there are also no reliable figures for flows of uranium.[34] However, it is estimated that France imports 94.72 percent (calculated in terms of total world imports by value in 1971), the United States, 2.69 percent; West Germany, 1.45 percent; and Japan, 0.82 percent. The major suppliers are Canada (66.5% of total world exports in 1971, again computed on the basis of value), Gabon (20.86%), Belgium-Luxembourg (4.9%), Australia and the United States

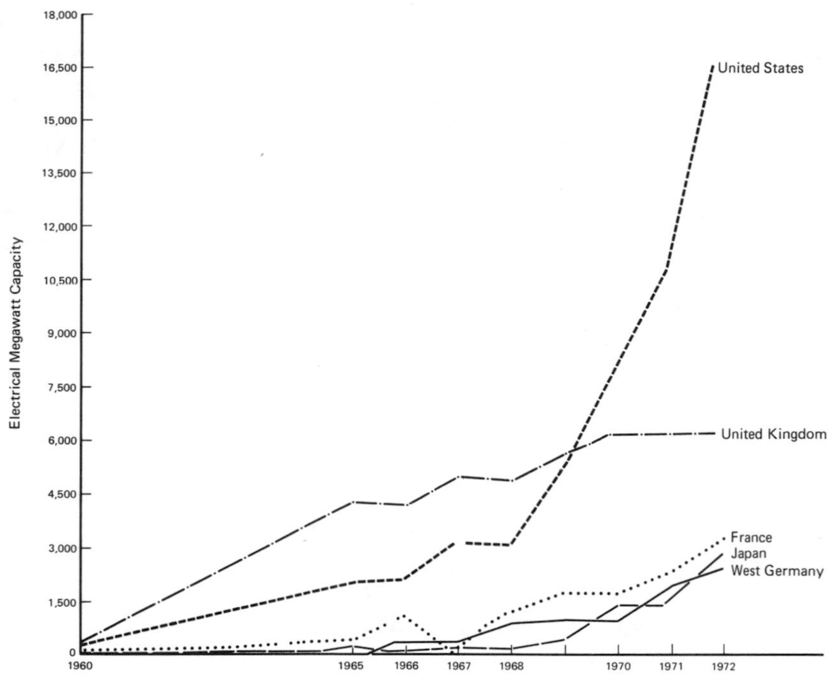

Note: The trend between 1960 and 1965 is a straight line extrapolation.

Source: Commissariat a l'Energie Atomique, *Rapport Annuel 1972.*

Figure 1-7. Nuclear Capacity to Generate Electricity, 1960-72

(2.85% each), and West Malaysia (1.32%). The U.S. Bureau of Mines estimated that the United States will continue to export uranium but that supplies will not be as extensive, given the growing worldwide demand for nuclear reactors. It is expected that after 1975 from 15 to 25 percent of United States uranium needs will be supplied from external sources.[35] This situation may well increase the country's concern for ensuring safe sources of supplies and possibly its autonomy in the nuclear area. As with petroleum, these projections may well be perceived as increasing United States dependence on external sources and thereby magnifying the implications of initial asymmetries in flows of uranium across national boundaries.

The breeder reactor is the next immediate phase in the development of energy technology. This will make the use of uranium more efficient by enabling an increase in the use of energy content of natural uranium from between 1 and 2 percent to about 60-70 percent, and the demand for uranium ore as a source of fuel among the industrialized nations will be reduced by as much as 60 percent. These estimates are speculative, yet appear increasingly plausible.[36] The Soviet nuclear program to develop large, economical, and fast breeder reactors is moving more rapidly than programs in the United States or Western Europe. The emphasis and the technological base are different, however—the Soviets preferring the use of graphite, not pressurized water reactors, as cheaper and safer than conventional reactors of similar size.[37] Fewer nuclear power plants are being installed in the USSR than in the United States, in part because the USSR has more untamed rivers and untapped reserves of fossil fuels. But, as in the United States, population concentrations are far from cheap fuel supplies.[38] Thus, the Soviet nuclear program is motivated also by anticipated large-scale domestic demands.[39]

Uranium must be enriched from the initial milling stages to a point where 2 to 5 percent of the uranium content is ^{235}U. At this time, the technology for enrichment (presently limited to gaseous diffusion) is expensive, complicated, and closely guarded. Three gaseous diffusion plants owned and operated by the United States government have to this point supplied most of the non-Communist world's requirements for enriched uranium.[40] There are also enrichment procésses that are being developed which use centrifuge and laser power. In addition, the United States clearly dominates international trade in the nuclear reactor industry. Most of the early licensing arrangements between the United States and other nations will terminate shortly and many foreign firms are anxious to enter the market. It is anticipated that by 1975 Western Europe and Japan will be able to manufacture the required components for their nuclear power facilities.[41] Canada alone, with its heavy water reactor (CANDU), has been able to break into the export market to a significant degree. This process has the decided advantage of being able to employ natural rather than enriched uranium.[42]

The major alternatives—coal, natural gas, and nuclear fission—will have only long term effects on the structure of the world petroleum market. The shift to these sources, or to a mix, will be tentative and slow. Solar energy, geothermal power, tar sands and shale oil have, at one point or another, been regarded as likely to become viable in the longer run. No one argues, however, that these sources will become economical before the turn of the century.

The price of petroleum has immediate effects on the extent to which industrial states will invest in the development of alternative sources of energy. Political factors inevitably yield important inputs into such investment decisions. The eventual development of commercially viable alternatives to petroleum will generate international impacts that may be fundamentally different from those associated with petroleum. For the time being, however, crude oil continues to dominate international energy transactions. Petroleum politics will remain of paramount concern to all nations, large and small, for many years to come.

Chapter 2 examines the changing power relations in the world petroleum market and changes in the relative strength of the international oil companies, the governments of oil-exporting states, and the governments of the oil-importing nations. We argue that changes in the power relationships of the major participants have been possible because of changes in patterns of production, consumption, imports, and exports of crude petroleum, and that these developments contributed to the formation and, so far, to the success of the Organization of Petroleum Exporting Countries.

Notes

1. Joseph L. Fisher and Neal Potter, "The Effects of Population Growth on Resource Adequacy and Quality," in *Rapid Population Growth*, Study Committee of the Office of the Foreign Secretary, National Academy of Sciences (Baltimore: The Johns Hopkins University Press, 1971), p. 237.

2. United Nations, *World Energy Supplies*, ST/STAT/SER.J/Nos. 1-16 (New York: United Nations, 1957-1973).

3. See Robert Keohane and Joseph Nye, *Transnational Relations and World Politics* (Cambridge: Harvard University Press, 1972); Richard N. Cooper, *The Economics of Interdependence* (New York: McGraw-Hill Book Company, 1968); see also, the statement of Henry Kissinger, U.S. Secretary of State, to the Washington Energy Conference, in the *U.S. Department of State Bulletin*, Vol. LXX, No. 1810 (March 4, 1974), pp. 201-206.

4. See Hayward R. Alker, Jr., Lincoln P. Bloomfield, and Nazli Choucri, *Analyzing Global Interdependence* (Cambridge: M.I.T. Center for International Studies, 1974), especially Lincoln P. Bloomfield and Hayward R. Alker, Jr., Volume I, *Analytical Perspectives and Policy Implications*, pp. 1-40.

5. David P. Calleo and Benjamin M. Rowland, *America and the World Political Economy* (Bloomington: Indiana University Press, 1973).

6. See Carl Kaysen, "The Computer That Printed Out W*O*L*F*," *Foreign Affairs*, Vol. 50, No. 4 (July 1972), pp. 660-669; see also, M.A. Adelman, "Is the Oil Shortage Real? Oil Companies as OPEC Tax Collectors," *Foreign Policy*, No. 9 (Winter 1972-73), pp. 69-106; see also, the critique of the Ford Foundation Energy Policy Project published by the Institute for Contemporary Studies, *No Time To Confuse* (San Francisco: Institute for Contemporary Studies, 1975).

7. DeGolyer and MacNaughton, *Twentieth Century Petroleum Statistics 1973* (Dallas: DeGolyer and MacNaughton, 1973), pp. 9-10.

8. U.S., Congress, House, Subcommittee on Foreign Affairs, *Foreign Policy Implications of the Energy Crisis*, 92nd Cong., 2nd sess., 1972, p. 156 (Statement by James E. Akins).

9. Sam H. Schurr and Paul T. Homan, *Middle Eastern Oil and the Western World: Prospects and Problems* (New York: American Elsevier Publishing Company, Inc., 1971), p. 35; U.S., Congress, House, Subcommittee on Foreign Affairs, *Foreign Policy Implications of the Energy Crisis*, 1972, p. 13 (Statement by Joel Darmstadter).

10. U.S., Department of the Interior Bureau of Mines, *Monthly Petroleum Statement*, March 1974, p. 2.

11. Robert Brougham, "An Oil Company View," in Oded Remba and Anne Sinai, eds., *Middle East Information Series*, No. 23 (May 1973), p. 58; see also, U.S., Congress, House, Subcommittee on Foreign Affairs, *Foreign Policy Implications of the Energy Crisis*, 1972, p. 4 (Statement by Joel Darmstadter).

12. U.S., Cabinet Task Force on Oil Import Control, *The Oil Import Question* (Washington, D.C.: U.S. Government Printing Office, 1970), p. 19.

13. The Petroleum Publishing Company, *International Petroleum Encyclopedia*, 1974 (Tulsa: The Petroleum Publishing Company, 1974), p. 242.

14. Ibid.

15. *The New York Times*, January 17, 1975.

16. Genevieve C. Dean, "Energy in the People's Republic of China," *Energy Policy*, Vol. 2, No. 1 (March 1974), p. 41; see also, *The New York Times*, November 11, 1973.

17. Yoshio Koide, "China's Crude Oil Production," *Pacific Community*, Vol. 5, No. 3 (April 1974), p. 464.

18. United Nations, Economic Commission for Asia and the Far East, *Asian Industrial Development News*, No. 6 (New York: United Nations, 1970), p. 24.

19. Facts on File, Inc., *Energy Crisis, Volume I, 1969-73* (New York: Facts on File, Inc., 1974), p. 75.

20. See, Dean, "Energy in the People's Republic of China," p. 54.

21. James Ridgeway, *The Last Play* (New York: Mentor, 1973), p. 93.

22. *The New York Times*, October 26, 1974; see also *Wall Street Journal*, June 16, 1975.

23. *The New York Times*, December 9, 1974.

24. *The New York Times*, December 23, 1974.

25. U.S. Bureau of Mines, *Mineral Facts and Problems*, 1970 (Washington, D.C.: U.S. Government Printing Office, 1971), pp. 46-60; United Nations, *World Energy Supplies, 1968-1971*, ST/STAT/SER.J/16.

26. The following data are from The Petroleum Publishing Company, *International Petroleum Encyclopedia*; DeGolyer and MacNaughton, *Twentieth Century Petroleum Statistics, 1973* (Dallas: DeGolyer and MacNaughton, 1973).

27. U.S. Bureau of Mines, *Mineral Industry Survey, World Natural Gas*, 1973.

28. Ibid.

29. *Wall Street Journal*, June 12, 1975.

30. Commissariat a l'Energie Atomique, *Rapport Annuel 1972* (Paris: Synelog, 1973).

31. U.S. Bureau of Mines, *Mineral Facts and Problems*, p. 235.

32. Organisation for Economic Co-operation and Development, *Uranium: Resources, Production and Demand.* A joint report by the OECD Nuclear Energy Agency and the International Atomic Energy Agency (Paris: Organisation for Economic Co-operation and Development, 1973).

33. Ibid.

34. See, Joseph A. Yager and Eleanor B. Steinberg, *Energy and U.S. Foreign Policy* (Cambridge, Mass.: Ballinger Publishing Company, 1974), Appendix A, Table A-11.

35. U.S. Bureau of Mines, *Mineral Facts and Problems*, p. 239.

36. See, Allen Hammond, "Breeder Reactors: Power for the Future," *Science*, Vol. 174 (November 19, 1974), p. 808; see also, Irvin C. Bupp and Jean-Claude Deriam, "The Breeder Reactor in the U.S.: A New Economic Analysis," *Technology Review*, July/August, 1974, p. 27.

37. Robert Gillette, "Nuclear Power in the U.S.S.R.: American Visitors Find Surprises," *Science*, Vol. 173 (September 10, 1971), p. 1003.

38. Ibid., p. 1006.

39. Ibid.

40. Yager and Steinberg, *Energy and U.S. Foreign Policy*, p. 350.

41. Ibid., p. 339.

42. *Wall Street Journal*, June 24, 1975.

2 Power Relations in Petroleum Politics: The Emergence of OPEC

Patterns of petroleum imports and exports reflect changing energy needs and preferences. These patterns have been supported by price, production, and marketing arrangements. In the past the international oil companies have controlled these arrangements; more recently exporting governments have assumed a more important role. The changing relationship between the oil companies and the Organization of Petroleum Exporting Countries reflects new power relations in the world petroleum market. This chapter examines briefly these changes and then focuses more extensively on the emergence of OPEC and the differences among its members.

The International Oil Companies

International oil concerns have controlled petroleum supplies since the time the earliest discoveries were made.[1] At the end of the 1930s petroleum imports to the United States and the West were managed by seven concerns: Standard Oil of New Jersey (now Exxon), Royal-Dutch Shell, Texaco, Socony (now Mobil), Gulf, Standard of California, and Anglo-Iranian (now British Petroleum). They were all vertically integrated, although to varying extents, and many of the transfers of products were undertaken as internal transfers within the same company or between affiliates.[2] The eighth major company, La Compagnie Française des Petroles, is of lesser size, but shares joint operating companies with the "Seven Sisters" in parts of the Middle East.[3] By 1971, United States oil concerns had either controlled or acquired rights associated with more than half the world's proven petroleum reserves. Far more striking is the fact that 70 percent of all oil-related investment outside the Communist bloc is now undertaken by American companies; 80 percent of all exploration investments for oil and gas are carried out by United States corporations.[4]

The international influence of the oil companies emerged from several factors. First, their monopoly of technology, knowledge, and skills gave them an unparalleled advantage for perpetuating their management and control of the petroleum market. Second, they supplied the necessary capital for exploration and development to a degree that could not, until very recently, be done by the oil-producing countries. And third, they have traditionally managed all transactions between exporters and importers of crude petroleum. Over the years, the oil companies have kept tight control of operations in the producing countries, thus effectively limiting the role of host governments in decisions affecting exploration of indigenous fields. In addition, the governments could increase prices only through the corporations.

The operating companies in the oil-exporting countries have generally produced and transferred oil at a little more than a fraction of the actual costs to the shareholder companies or affiliates. This oil, exchanged at posted prices to other affiliates, generated profit, an extensive portion of which was paid as tax to the host government. Increases in government revenues are not necessarily accompanied by a reduction of profit to the oil companies since the companies could pass these increases to the consumer.

In the past the oil companies have been charged with influencing national decisions in the exporter countries in favor of corporate profits; critics charged they were able to preserve their interests by presenting a united front and by preventing any attempts to change the status quo. More recently, they have been accused of becoming tax collectors for the oil-rich states to the detriment of the consumer countries.[5] The validity of this charge is perhaps less relevant than the fact that it signals a fundamental change in the institutional base of the world petroleum market. Three stories illustrate the changing power relationship of the oil companies and the exporter governments. The first is Iran, 1951-53; the second is Iraq, 1971; and the third, Libya, 1970.

From 1951 to 1953 Iran nationalized the oil concessions of the Anglo-Iranian Oil Company (now British Petroleum). The dispute over nationalization centered around the compensation to be paid to Anglo-Iranian. Iran argued that no compensation was to be made. Anglo-Iranian, then 51 percent owned by the British government, served notice to the world that any oil purchased from Iran would be served a lien to prevent delivery. This maneuver was successful due to support from the other international oil companies. Few countries sought to buy Iranian oil. Italy tried, but these purchases were immediately enjoined by the Italian courts in a suit brought by Anglo-Iranian.[6] In addition, all company personnel were withdrawn from the country, and Iranian production plummeted. In 1950 the country had produced 242.4 million barrels of oil; in 1953 production was officially registered at 9.4 million barrels. By 1955 Iran produced less than half the output five years earlier.[7] In addition, the investments of Anglo-Iranian were channeled to Kuwait, which rapidly became a substitute for Iranian oil. This development led to tensions between Iran and Kuwait. Ultimately, through a domestic political move generally known to have been directed by the Central Intelligence Agency of the United States, the prime minister of Iran was replaced and the oil companies reestablished their control over production operations.[8]

The story of Iraq is somewhat similar. Again, a strong posture by the international oil companies neutralized the government's efforts to shape production and transactions policies. In December 1961 Iraq nationalized 99 percent of the country's oil concessions. The holdings affected had been controlled by the Iraqi Petroleum Country (Shell, British Petroleum, Mobil, and Standard of New Jersey). The company quietly ordered its managers to reduce production. During the course of negotiations throughout the next three years Iraqi oil production grew only marginally. At a particularly difficult time in company-country negotiations, the company's production was reduced by 30 percent.[9] The companies did not suffer from this move since the other oil-producing states were willing to allow compensatory production increases. Iraq offered the confiscated areas to other corporations for immediate exploitation. No bids ensued. The international oil companies again presented a sustained posture of solidarity; these areas remained unexploited for the following seven years.[10] Investments originally intended for Iraq were diverted to developing the fields of Abu Dhabi. The diversion of investment funds created immediate competition for Iraqi oil.[11]

The first successful resistance to extensive control by the oil companies occurred in 1970, not in Iran or Iraq, but in Libya. In September of that year Libya nationalized the oil concessions of the Occidental Petroleum Company, whose only income came from Libyan fields. Occidental accepted a compromise that had the effect of raising oil prices by $0.30, and increased taxes to 58 percent of profit from the earlier level of 50 percent. Eventually, the other independent oil companies in Libya accepted the same terms.[a] Confronted with the prospects of losing the entire Libyan concession, all the major international petroleum companies agreed to these terms. The company-country relationship had clearly changed.

Several factors contributed to Libya's success. First, the timing was excellent for the initiative. Libya's low-sulphur oil was in great demand in Western Europe. In May 1970 Tapline (the Trans-Arabian Pipeline) in Syria was broken by a bulldozer; the regular flow of half a million barrels a day from Saudi Arabia was stopped. Repairs on the pipeline were delayed. To obtain Saudi oil, more tankers had to be employed. The increased demand on available tankers soon forced a dramatic increase in freight rates, which increased the advantage of the Libyan fields since these were closer to major consumers. Second, Libya was already cutting back production in line with the new conservation policies. The government had announced a reassessment of its needs for current revenues.

The success of the Libyan action is also attributable to the fact that the independents, whose only income came from Libyan oil, were of sufficient size in the world petroleum market as to threaten the interests of the major oil companies. The refusal (or inability) of the majors to sustain a united posture, as

[a]The term *independents* refers to oil corporations that (1) operate internationally and (2) are not subsidiaries of the eight major oil companies. The independents include Standard Oil of Indiana, Phillips, Occidental, Continental, Atlantic-Richfield, Union Oil, the Japanese Arabian Oil Company, and the Ente Nazionali Idrocarburi of Italy, among others. For an analysis of the independents in the United States energy industry see, Thomas D. Duchesneau, *Competition in the U.S. Energy Industry* (Cambridge, Mass.: Ballinger Publishing Company, 1975), and Neil H. Jacoby, *Multinational Oil* (New York: Macmillan Publishing Co., Inc., 1974).

they had done in Iran and Iraq, is critical in explaining Libya's success and had important ramifications for the eventual agreements of 1970 and 1971 with the other major petroleum exporters.[b] The Libyan experience signaled the emergence of exporting governments as prime determinants of the petroleum market. Indeed, the continuation of the Iraq story is further testimony to this change.

On June 1, 1972, Iraq nationalized the Iraq Petroleum Company. The government of Iraq maintained that its action was in response to the drastic loss of revenue occasioned by the cutbacks in the production of the Kirkuk oil field. It claimed that this cutback cost the country $86 million in tax and royalty revenues.[12] The companies argued that Kirkuk oil was no longer competitive due to lower European demand and increased tanker rates, so that the companies could not carry out the increase in production desired by the government. The Iraqi government accused the companies of deliberately seeking to punish the country for its independent national oil policy and charged that they had applied pressure to hinder the implementation of development programs for the petroleum industry in Iraq.[13] Both charges were denied by the companies. The dispute was settled on February 28, 1973, again with a victory for the government. The Iraq Petroleum Company accepted the nationalization of the northern field in the country in return for 15 million tons of oil and the rights in the Basrah fields, which the company plans to double in production.

There are differing views regarding what the multinational oil companies *should* have done, and whether a stronger posture may have forestalled the nationalization of the Iraq Petroleum Company. Similarly, it has been argued that when the first Libyan cutbacks in production were declared in 1970, a stronger posture by the companies and the consumer countries would have resulted in a reversal of the decision—as had been the case in Iran in 1953, and in Iraq in 1961.[c]

---

[b]One explanation for the refusal of the major oil companies to support Occidental lies in the personality of Occidental President, Armand Hammer. Hammer had himself violated one of the unwritten rules of the international oil industry by attempting to operate the La Brea y Parinas oil field in Peru, which was a nationalized Exxon field. Christopher Rand writes: "Yet Hammer, in 1970, made an honest appeal to his counter-part in Exxon, Chairman James Jamieson, for a guarantee of cut-rate crude oil, which would help him make a firm and honorable stand in Libya. . . . Since Hammer had also raided the far more powerful Exxon of one of its top Libyan negotiators and had offered the Peruvian government to operate the oilfield, which it had expropriated from an Exxon subsidiary, Jamieson turned the appeal down." See, Christopher Rand, *Making Democracy Safe for Oil* (Boston: Atlantic-Little, Brown and Company, 1975), pp. 8 and 279-80.

[c]U.S., Congress, Senate, *Hearings: Oil and Gas Imports Issues*, 93rd Cong., 1st sess., 1973, p. 1086 (Statement by M.A. Adelman). M.A. Adelman has called to our attention new evidence from Sir David Barren of Royal Dutch Shell and from the public testimony of Ambassador James E. Akins before the Senate Subcommittee on Multinational Corporations, October 11, 1973, which sheds some light on how the multinationals perceived the Libyan demands. See, U.S., Congress, Senate, Committee on Foreign Relations, Subcommittee on Multinational Corporations, *Multinational Corporations and United States Foreign Policy—Part 5*, 93rd Cong., 1st and 2nd sess., pp. 1-28 (Statement by James E. Akins).

Despite the frequency with which producing countries make demands upon the international corporations, they are also aware of their vulnerability. But there are some underlying conflicts of interest that cannot be ignored. For example, the oil companies seek significant profits before the expiration of their leases, while some exporter governments have voiced concern for spacing production and preserving known reserves for future exploitation. More recently, the exporters have argued that prices could be stabilized if the corporations would cut their allegedly exorbitant profit margins.

The changing role of the international oil companies has placed the exporters and the importers in direct confrontation for the first time in the history of the petroleum industry. Numerous cases of nationalization, expropriation, or negotiated sale of petroleum assets in the oil-exporting states led to conflict with the consumer countries. In many instances, official United States interests have been jeopardized. In response, the United States has threatened to prohibit all assistance to states that confiscate United States holdings.[14] This posture, combined with the United States' commitment to the protection of nationals resident overseas (and their property), clearly reflects concern for the protection of American petroleum investments abroad which stood close to $24 billion in 1974. Nonetheless, the companies have not given the United States any formal assurance of continued access to petroleum supplies, thereby compounding the country's uncertainties over its energy future.

This assurance has generally been an important factor in the military calculations of the consumer countries, most notably the United States. For example, in 1942 the Arabian-American Oil Company (a consortium of major United States companies) extended to the government of the United States an option to purchase at a discount extensive quantities of Saudi Arabian oil. The arrangement required that (a) the oil remain underground, (b) the company be responsible for ensuring sufficient reserves for any government requisition,[15] and (c) this guarantee be in exchange for United States government protection of the companies' interests. This offer suggested the importance the United States placed upon Saudi oil and the extent to which it viewed this source as part of its military reserves.[16] The United States appeared willing to tie its security needs to the strength of the corporations' control over reserves and production schedules. But this particular offer was withdrawn before formal completion largely because of corporate fears of government domination.

The entry of the USSR as a sizable petroleum producer has placed added pressure on both the oil corporations and the consuming nations. If current trends persist it might become an energy importer, placing added demands upon known reserves and emerging as a potential competitor for Middle East oil.[17] But some observers argue that there is no ecomomic or political reason for the USSR to become a major importer in the next ten years.[d] Others maintain that

[d]The assistance of Dennis Pirages in clarifying this point is noted with gratitude; see also, John A. Berry, "Oil and Soviet Policy," *The Middle East Journal*, 1972; see also, "Russian Fuel Crisis Looming?" *Petroleum Economist*, Vol. 42, No. 3 (March 1975), pp. 86-88.

past trends are the best predictors of future behavior. Nonetheless, the USSR's three-fold role, as supplier, consumer, and possible middleman, may be a source of additional friction in a system in which access to the basic commodity is impeded by the actions of individual nations, and may constrain further the behavior of the oil companies.

In the final analysis the oil companies are faced with certain imponderables. First, there are no viable alternatives to Middle East oil in the present decade. With projected increases in the petroleum needs of the United States and other importing countries, the pressures placed upon Middle East sources will increase. Second, by the early 1980s the revenues accrued to the oil-exporting countries will greatly increase their ability to manipulate the flow of oil, money, and industrial commodities. And third, as a result of the changing structure of the world petroleum market, the companies are finding themselves in a situation where their own maneuverability is reduced, where they are becoming the targets of both producer and consumer dissatisfaction, and where the benefits derived from their extraterritorial status may be lost.

With the growth of independent petroleum companies, the flexibility of the majors in pricing their goods and services within an integrated system was further constrained. Vertical integration had become a target for exporting as well as importing governments. The latter even required vertically integrated oil companies to base their transfers of goods and services upon open market prices.[18]

Now that importing countries are taking an active part in petroleum transactions, with their governments acting as direct agents, the companies may find themselves forced by both producers and consumers into institutional arrangements based largely on the needs of national governments and marginally—if at all—on their own needs. Much of this is speculation, of course. It assumes the development of shared values and expectations among exporters and importers, a contingency that at present seems dubious. Yet, there is some evidence of a search for alternative arrangements that may be mutually rewarding.

Assessing the implications of the foregoing for the international oil companies in the years to come is a hazardous enterprise. Their own policies, in conjunction with the changing import patterns of consuming states, have triggered critical changes in the structure of the world petroleum market and in the underlying power relations. These changes contributed to the emergence of OPEC as a challenger of established patterns of petroleum transactions and as an active critic of the existing structure of the world petroleum market.

The Organization of Petroleum Exporting Countries

The member countries of the Organization of Petroleum Exporting Countries are Abu Dhabi, Algeria, Ecuador, Indonesia, Iran, Iraq, Kuwait, Libya, Nigeria,

Qatar, Saudi Arabia, and Venezuela. Gabon was an associate member and has recently become a full member. Among them, they control over 70 percent of known world reserves.

The development of OPEC is conventionally traced to three factors: (1) the apprehension among the petroleum-exporting states regarding the ability of oil companies to cut prices without consulting host governments; (2) a realization among the more established exporters that the entry of new producers into the world petroleum market with lower prices might detract from established markets; (3) an increase in the technical knowledge and skills of the oil-producing countries, resulting in demands for changes in structure of prices and the taxing system. Such assessments overlook political factors and the convergence of circumstances that allowed for the development of the organization in 1960 and for its successful exercise of power 13 years later, in October 1973, when the first major price increases were announced.

It was the activities of *individual* states that set off a series of events leading first to formal organization in 1960, and subsequently, to the embargo of 1973. The formation of OPEC occurred through a set of trials and errors, through learning from past mistakes, and through the ability to adapt to changing conditions. The impetus for formal organization came from Venezuela. The critical events leading to embargo in 1973 occurred in Libya. In each case, the oil-exporting countries exhibited shrewd political judgment and excellent timing. In each case observers emphasized the economic implications of specific events, without rendering sufficient attention to their political causes and consequences.

The genesis of OPEC can be found in early attempts at cooperation between Venezuela and Iran, at the time of Iran's negotiations with its concessionaire, the Anglo-Iranian Oil Company, in 1949.[e] The information on its own tax arrangements given by Venezuela to Iran, Saudi Arabia, and other producing governments was in part responsible for changing the general method of payments from the oil companies. The first formal agreement among exporters was concluded in 1953, prescribing the exchange of information and frequent consultation regarding oil prices and policies between Iraq and Saudi Arabia.

Attempts by individual oil-exporting countries to improve their financial terms were at times successful, encouraging further attempts at international collaboration. The creation of the Arab League in 1945 provided the Arab producers with an organizational base upon which to develop further collaborative arrangements. Five years later a security pact, the Joint Defense and Economic Cooperation Treaty, gave oil an important position in the policies of the organization. The Department of Oil Affairs in the Arab League has been largely responsible for both the diffusion of information on the petroleum industry and the increase in technical skills of member nations. The initial decision of the Middle East producers to collaborate on oil policies had been

[e]For histories of the development of OPEC, see Zuhayr Mikdashi, *The Community of Oil Exporting Countries*, (Ithaca: Cornell University Press, 1972); see also, Fuad Rouhani, *A History of OPEC* (New York: Praeger, 1971).

primarily a political one.[f] Major producers elsewhere, most notably Venezuela, were motivated by other factors. The pricing policies of the oil companies provided an economic incentive for more effective cooperation and for a greater degree of coordination than could have been established on political grounds alone.

Venezuela had taken the lead in opposing price cuts announced by the oil companies in 1959. During that year posted prices in the Middle East were reduced by about 8 percent, amounting to $0.18 per barrel of oil.[g] The cut was initiated by British Petroleum. Venezuela protested to the British government, but the latter could not (or would not) intervene in company policies. During the same year Shell Oil Company of Venezuela reduced posted prices $0.05 to $0.15 per barrel, according to type of oil. These reductions were adjustments to the market situation in the United States and to the structure of the world market more generally, thus illustrating the importance of external factors in determining the revenues of exporting countries.

More drastic price reductions were announced in 1959 by the British Petroleum Company for their operations in Kuwait, Iran, and Qatar. Similar reductions were posted in Venezuela to meet the Middle East cuts in posted prices. The First Arab Oil Congress met during that same year, and although the participants voiced dissatisfaction and apprehension, no effective action was envisaged.

Venezuela took the lead in organizing the exporting countries in the form of an Oil Consultation Commission to establish international agreements to prevent waste of an important source of energy, to stabilize posted or reference prices in crude oil, and to increase the tax revenues of the producer countries. Disagreements among the oil-exporters contributed to the short life of this commission. But a clear precedent had been established and it remained for the producing countries to develop viable and institutional means of voicing their dissatisfaction with the policies and postures of the oil companies.

During the next year Venezuela tried again to organize the producers, this time with the collaboration of Saudi Arabia. In August 1960 the international oil companies reduced posted prices again by about 6 percent, amounting to

[f]For example, Iran's distrust over collaborating with Arab regimes was overcome by the manner in which the companies reduced the posted prices. Mikdashi quotes the Shah of Iran as saying that "even if the action was basically sound it could not be acceptable to us as long as it was taken without our consent." *Press Conferences of His Imperial Majesty Mohammad Reza Shah Pahlavi of Iran, 1960-1961*, Office of Information (Tehran, 1961), quoted in Mikdashi, *The Community of Oil Exporting Countries*, p. 33.

[g]Mikdashi, *The Community of Oil Exporting Countries*, p. 29. There is a slightly different interpretation of the events leading to the creation of OPEC. In 1959 Venezuela increased the taxes on the petroleum corporations working in Venezuela. These corporations, in an attempt to forestall further tax increases and to demonstrate to other oil producers their displeasure with such moves, reduced the prices of Venezuelan crude and increased production in the Middle East. Venezuela responded by meeting with other oil producers and, with the support of Sheik Tariki of Saudi Arabia. OPEC was created. See, Rouhani, *A History of OPEC*, pp. 76-77.

$0.10 a barrel. The cut meant a substantial loss of revenue to the exporting governments on the order of $300 million.[19] Following this price reduction, representatives from Iraq, Iran, Kuwait, Saudi Arabia, and Venezuela met in Baghdad. The Organization of Petroleum Exporting Countries was created in September 1960 to coordinate the policies of its members.

In short, the oil companies had initiated significant reductions in petroleum price in the late 1950s. These cuts were congruent with prevailing market conditions. OPEC was formed to prevent further reductions of posted price and, eventually, contributed to changing these conditions. The consumers' acceptance of these price reductions added further fuel to an already volatile situation. While collusion between the oil companies and consumer governments cannot be established, from the perspective of exporting countries this possibility was regarded as a fact. The political disputes between the exporting and the importing nations, many of which revolved around decolonization in the Middle East, contributed further to the grievances generated by reductions in posted prices.

Despite the creation of OPEC, however, the oil companies have continued to coordinate the market and facilitate the regulation of production schedules. Whatever the companies can sell at current prices, that much would be produced from their various sources. This function that the companies perform has relieved OPEC of the need to provide market coordination and has thus contributed to the strength of that organization. This situation has added further fuel to common charges in the West of collusion between the international petroleum concerns and the governments of oil-exporting states.

A series of country-company agreements have been negotiated since 1970. The most important agreements involved the provision for an exporter's participation or part ownership in the company's operations. For the first time the oil-producing governments were compensated for economic difficulties and currency devaluations in the consuming countries. The Teheran Agreement of February 1971 raised the basic posted price of oil $0.35 a barrel, an increase that followed a $0.09 per barrel raise in 1970.[20] Additional increases in response to inflation and to the rising demand for oil were also established. And, finally, it was agreed (1) to increase the producing countries' taxes from 50 to 55 percent of net taxable income, (2) to adopt a system for adjusting posted price with a premium for low-sulphur oil, and (3) to arrange means for additional temporary price increases to reflect high freight rates for oil tankers as long as the Suez Canal remained closed. The Geneva Agreements of January 1972, increased posted prices to restore to the producing countries the effective purchasing power that had been reduced by the 1971 devaluation of the United States dollar.[21]

In sum, OPEC emerged as an institutionalized response to a changing petroleum market and to the greater negotiating capabilities of exporting states. The highly concentrated structure of the industry, its vertical integration, and the nature of the concession system all proved ready targets for the dissatisfaction of the producer governments with their role in the petroleum market and their share of profits accorded to them by the oil companies.

Structural Divisions in OPEC

Contrary to popular views, there is no average oil-exporting state. To consider them all in the aggregate would overlook those differences upon which internal OPEC policies are predicated. Vast differences in political orientation, economic development, national objectives, size, and institutional capabilities, have provided considerable obstacles to the development of joint petroleum policies. To date, however, OPEC has been able to deter price competition among its members, increase profits, gain participation arrangements with the international oil companies, and conserve some oil reserves for future exploitation.[h]

Observers commonly characterize OPEC members in terms of population, known petroleum reserves, rates of production, and petroleum revenues, and on this basis draw some inferences regarding structural factors that may bear upon the cohesion of the group. Population size provides some rough indication of opportunities for spending petroleum revenues domestically. Population figures alone do not delineate investment possibilities but they indicate structural differences within OPEC. The ratio of known reserves to production yields the number of years such reserves are anticipated to last given current production rates. It can be employed as a rough indication of the extent to which production rates may deplete known reserves. The shorter this period is, the greater will be the pressures on an oil-exporting state to make some decision regarding production schedules in relation to anticipated use of revenues. Table 2-1 groups the members of OPEC according to these criteria. This division can be justified only in terms of the clues it might provide for interpreting the behavior of its members and identifying the dominant economic motivations.

The first group represents states with high petroleum reserves, with high needs for petroleum revenues, and with the institutional capacity required to employ these revenues for internal development. It includes Iran and Iraq, which together account for about one fourth of the organization's production, known reserves, and petroleum revenues, but only 14.2 percent of its population. Iran is a dominant member in OPEC, politically and militarily. We argue further along that its potential influence is enhanced to the extent that it can develop means of cooperating with Saudi Arabia and with other countries with higher known

[h]A summary of recent OPEC activities is found in Edward R. Fried, "World Market Trends and Bargaining Leverage," in Joseph A. Yager, and Eleanor B. Steinberg, eds., *Energy and U.S. Foreign Policy* (Cambridge, Mass.: Ballinger Publishing Company, 1974), p. 259; see also, Elizabeth Monroe and Robert Mabro, *Oil Producers and Consumers: Conflict or Cooperation*, A synthesis of an International Seminar, Center for Mediterranean Studies, Rome, June 24 to June 28, 1974 (New York: American Universities Field Staff, 1974).

Table 2-1
Structural Characteristics of OPEC Members
(Percentage of OPEC Total)

	Population 1972	Production 1972	Reserves 1972	Coverage in Years 1972	U.S. $ Revenues (Estimated 1973)
Iran	10.62	19.51	15.49	32.88	18.22
Iraq	3.53	5.61	8.48	62.54	6.66
Total	14.15	25.12	23.97	25.54%	24.88
Algeria	5.21	4.14	2.52	25.17	4.00
Indonesia	44.12	4.14	2.73	27.36	4.00
Venezuela	3.86	12.44	3.52	11.72	12.44
Nigeria	26.33	7.05	2.66	15.04	8.88
Ecuador	2.31	0.36	1.55	177.18	3.55
Total	81.88	28.15	12.90	21.22%	29.77
Saudi Arabia	2.83	22.26	35.13	65.31	22.66
U.A.E.	–	4.07	3.87	39.29	4.00
Total	2.90	26.34	39.00	28.00%	26.66
Kuwait	0.33	11.67	16.92	60.03	8.44
Libya	0.72	8.70	7.17	34.15	10.22
Total	1.05	20.39	24.10	25.21%	18.66
Total OPEC	100.00	100.00	100.00	41.39	100.00

Source: See Table 1-1, International Monetary Fund, *IMF Survey*, Vol. 4, No. 3 (February 3, 1975), p. 38.

reserves. It is also a major participant in the politics of the Middle East and the Gulf area, and it provides an important link to the interests of major consuming countries.

The second group, representing about 82 percent of OPEC's population, has the highest production rates, but the lowest known reserves, and includes Algeria, Indonesia, Venezuela, Nigeria, and Ecuador. These states will be under great pressure to increase production given reserves, needs, and relative capacities for domestic investment. They are a heterogenous group with no obvious cultural, political, or historical ties. None of these countries alone has the economic or political capability to shape OPEC policies. Their deviance from established directives may thus not severely compromise the common posture but it would generate important strains. At this writing, they do not gain from undercutting established OPEC prices; but this situation may well change.

The third group includes only Saudi Arabia and the United Arab Emirates, two states with small populations. Their combined population is 70 million, representing only 2.9 percent of OPEC population. They control 39 percent of the organization's proven reserves and possess the highest ratio of production to reserves. The distinguishing characteristic of these states is that they have relatively little domestic claims against petroleum revenues and their institutional base is such that these revenues cannot be profitably invested internally. In those terms, Saudi Arabia is clearly a pivotal state; it is also a key to inter-Arab politics, to Arab conciliation toward the United States, and to cooperation with Iran.

The fourth group includes Kuwait and Libya. They have smaller reserves, small populations, and lower production rates and, by extension, lower petroleum revenues. While there may be little justification in distinguishing them from Saudi Arabia and the United Arab Emirates, these differences provide the economic environment for other, more substantial, political distinctions such as influence in Arab politics, or position in the Cold War conflict, or ability to affect OPEC policies directly.

On structural grounds at least, Iran, Saudi Arabia, Algeria, and Kuwait constitute the four critical poles of OPEC. They also represent some important differences in strategies toward the disbursement of petroleum revenues, different pressures for price and production policies, and different orientations in regional and international politics.

In subsequent chapters, we will draw upon these structural differences to explain and predict the course of OPEC politics. We shall argue that the conjunction of structural differences and political objectives yields the evidence necessary to tell the story of the organization of oil-exporting countries and its impact upon the world petroleum market. Our hypothesis is that the cohesion of OPEC may be reinforced to the extent that cleavages develop in directions that cut across, rather than reinforce, structural and political divisions. Conversely, should shared structural differences coincide with, and reinforce, political ones, cohesion will not be maintained for long.

OPEC as a Cartel

A cartel is an agreement about price or price structure and output by firms in an industry. The success of a cartel depends upon the ability of small numbers of producers to dominate a market and regulate it on the basis of their oligopolistic power rather than on the basis of competitive supply and demand. Establishing policies on price, production schedules, and the allocation of market shares is essential for maintaining the cohesion of a cartel. Economists argue on both analytical and empirical grounds that the conditions most favorable for the success of cartels include:[22]

1. The existence of a few sellers.

2. The dominance of one seller.
3. An agreement about appropriate market shares.
4. A similarity of costs incurred in the production process.
5. A similarity in the sellers' predictions of the demand for their product.
6. The stability of that demand.
7. A similarity in ways and rates of discounting future profits.
8. The shared perception of risk.
9. Unorganized consumers for the product.
10. A compatible valuation framework by which sellers seek to maximize profits and buyers seek to minimize the cost of goods purchased.

Our purpose is to assess OPEC's performance according to these criteria and to identify sources of its strengths and weaknesses. We recognize that the actual sellers of petroleum are the international oil companies. However, in this context, one may regard the governments of the oil-exporting states as the sellers since they, in effect, view themselves as the producers of petroleum and as the ultimate sellers in the world petroleum market.

The conventional economic perspective on cartels assumes overriding importance to the goals of profit maximization and assigns equal valuation to that goal by individual sellers. Undoubtedly, maximization of a valued good is always a critical objective. But when the members of a cartel are national governments, this objective need not always be defined in terms of economic profit. The pursuit of economic *and* political goals is a feature of OPEC that distinguishes it from previous cartels. It is a feature that should not be obscured by an emphasis on profit maximization alone. In Chapter 7 we evaluate OPEC's performance as a cartel in economic terms and identify some political correctives for economic assumptions.

De Facto Members of OPEC

In Chapter 1 we noted eight countries where new sources of petroleum may have the potential for altering the world petroleum market. Of these, Norway, the People's Republic of China, and Canada are, at the time of this writing, de facto members of OPEC in that they have gained from OPEC policies and not deviated from that organization's price directives. Such behavior is inconsistent with conventional expectations regarding new entrants into a cartelized market, which argue that new entrants will invariably lead to price-cutting.

Norway has significant reserves of petroleum on the continental shelf. Since the country uses only 9 million tons of oil a year—in contrast with United States consumption of 829 million tons per year, or Canadian consumption of 87 million tons—oil discoveries in the magnitudes of 10 billion barrels make Norway a potential exporter of petroleum. Because of her geographical location, Norway is likely to become Western Europe's major source of oil. At the present time, this country is sending observers to OPEC meetings and has been accorded official observer status.

In a speech in February 1974 Foreign Minister Knut Frydenlund made reference to Norway's relations to OPEC, stressing that it was in Norway's interest to "enlarge contacts with OPEC as an organization. . . . Integrated as we are in the Western industrialized part of the world, we are interested in seeing that the supply of energy to the consumer countries is maintained at manageable prices. But our interests will also to some extent coincide with that of the producer countries, not least in connection with the question of control over resources and the pace of production."[23] The government of Norway is particularly concerned with its relationship to the oil companies and with the possibility of the rapid depletion of the country's reserves. Both of these concerns have contributed to a Norwegian proposal calling for a tax on oil companies' profits of 91 percent for all oil sold at a price above $3.73 per barrel.[24]

Norway has rejected an invitation to join the International Energy Coordinating Group proposed by U.S. Secretary of State Henry Kissinger in February 1974. As will be noted in Chapter 3, this group was originally intended to be a 12-nation coalition to share oil supplies in the event of another major embargo by the oil-producing states. Frydenlund stated: "But for Norway, which will not be an importer but an exporter of oil, the situation is different."[25] As a conciliatory gesture, Norway has requested the right to participate without being a full member of the group. This request was rejected. The United States indicated at one time that there would be no "middle ground" in the energy coordinating group and that Norwegian hopes of association with the Brussels groups were fruitless.[26] In addition, it has been noted that representatives of American oil corporations warned the Norwegians that the absence of cooperation in an eventual energy-sharing program would make it more difficult for Norway to acquire deep-sea retrieval equipment, an area in which the United States' technological leadership is well established.[27]

The Norwegians are under yet another set of political pressures. They need the support of NATO in their negotiations with the USSR over the Continental Shelf in the Barents Sea around the Spitsbergen Islands. But approximately 40 nations have concessionary rights to mineral resources in the area. The USSR would prefer either to control the area since it provides the only ice-free route to European waters, or to persuade the Norwegians to prevent other nations from exploiting these resources. At the time of this writing, talks between the USSR and Norway are still going on.[28]

The emergence of the People's Republic of China as a potentially large exporter is increasingly recognized by some consumer countries, notably Japan.

China's known reserves are increasing.[i] Its production is growing rapidly, with 54 million tons a year in 1973, an increase from 27 million tons one year earlier. Its exports to Japan are growing steadily,[29] and it has used its export capacity to further its strategic interests by countering Japanese-Russian energy agreements.[30] More important, China has raised its price of crude petroleum from $3.14 per barrel in 1973 to $8.60 in 1974, concommitant with OPEC increases.[31] Since October 1973, China has strongly supported the actions of OPEC. Chiao Kuan-hua, deputy foreign minister, speaking to the United Nations General Assembly on October 2, 1974, declared that the "historic pioneering action" taken by the Arabs could have enormous impact in the Third World's struggle against "imperialist plunder and exploitation," thus signalling China's support for the OPEC move.[32]

Canada's acceptance of OPEC prices may be due to limited export capacity. However, the government is also initiating significant cutbacks in oil exports. On November 23, 1974, Canada announced that exports of crude petroleum to the United States would be cut by 100,000 barrels per day, effective January 1, 1975. Presently the United States receives about 25 percent of its total imports of crude petroleum from Canada.[33] The Canadian action appears to be part of a comprehensive energy program initiated by the government to phase out all exports of crude petroleum to the United States by 1982. This policy is particularly dramatic in light of the fact that in 1972, all Canadian oil exports went to the United States. The new orientation is based on two considerations: First, the Canadian government is launching its own project independence, in an attempt to reduce the reliance of the eastern part of the country on imported oil. Second, this program is also designed to preserve Canadian reserves of crude petroleum, analogous to the efforts of many OPEC countries, most notably Libya and Algeria.[j]

In addition, Canada has followed the lead of practically all the oil-producing countries, including the United States, the USSR, and China, in increasing the price of its petroleum to a level comparable to that charged by OPEC. The present average price of Canadian oil in the United States is $12.10 per barrel. This price, which includes a high export tax, is similar to that set by OPEC (see Table 2-2). Canada has been engaged in talks with the Arab oil states concerning international development aid. Present discussions are for the organization of an international agency, with the Arabs providing the financial resources, and the

[i]See, Genevieve C. Dean, "Energy in the People's Republic of China," *Energy Policy*, Vol. 2, No. 1 (March 1974), p. 41; Yoshio Koide, "China's Crude Oil Production," *Pacific Community*, Vol. 5, No. 3 (April 1974), p. 464. For an overview of the oil industry in China see, H.C. Ling, *The Petroleum Industry of the People's Republic of China* (Stanford, California: Hoover Institution Press, 1975).

[j]*The New York Times*, November 22, 1974. For an account of the meeting between Canadian Prime Minister Elliot Trudeau and United States President Gerald Ford see, *The New York Times*, December 5, 1974.

Table 2-2
Representative Crude Oil Prices
(In U.S. Dollars per Barrel)

Country	Posted Price	Effective Date	Company Costs[a]		State Sales Price
			Equity[b] Oil	Buy Back Oil	
Abu Dhabi (Murban)	12.236	Nov. 74	10.81	n.a.	11.00
Arabian Light	11.251	Nov. 74	9.92	10.46	10.46
Iranian Light	11.475	Nov. 74	–10.488–		10.71
Iraq Basrah	11.272	Nov. 74	9.94	10.48	10.50
Kuwait	11.145	Nov. 74	–10.147–		10.365
Oman	11.898	Nov. 74	10.51	11.06	11.06
Qatar (Dukhan)	12.014	Nov. 74	10.60	11.17	11.17
Libyan	–	–	11.46	11.86	11.86
Algerian	–	–	–	–	12.00
Nigeria	14.691	Jan. 74	10.69	12.02	12.02
Indonesia	12.60	Jan. 74	–	–	–
Venezuela[c] (35°)	11.2156	Jan. 74	–	–	–
U.S. (old)[d]	5.25	Sept. 74	–	–	–
U.S. (new)	10.01	Sept. 74	–	–	–
Canada[e]	6.58[f]	Jan. 74	–	–	–

[a]Average company costs will vary according to the proportion of equity oil to participation in the liftings.

[b]Calculated by deducting 20 percent royalty *and* production costs (varying from 8 to 90 cents a barrel) from the posted price, applying 85 percent tax rate to the resulting taxable base, and finally adding back the royalty and production cost. For Nigeria the figure is based on the situation as of December 1974, when the Nigerian royalty rate was 16.67 percent and the tax rate 65.76 percent.

[c]Official tax-reference prices, excluding surcharge, freight premium, and sulphur premium.

[d]Domestic crude petroleum prices at the wellhead. The old petroleum prices are for price controlled oil, which accounted for 64 percent of all oil sold in July 1974. The new petroleum prices are for uncontrolled oil.

[e]In Canadian dollars.

[f]Canada applies an export tax on oil shipped to the United States, which is approximately $5.60 per barrel.

Sources: *The Petroleum Economist*, Vol. XLII, No. 3, March 1975, p. 118; U.S. Federal Energy Administration, *Monthly Energy Review*, November 1974, p. 41; *The New York Times*, January 30, 1975.

Canadians the technical expertise. Such an arrangement is viewed as an attempt to circumvent existing aid agencies which the Arab states consider to be dominated by the United States. Thus, the community of interests are crystallizing, leading to potential convergence between Canadian and OPEC policies.

The potential impact of other new sources of petroleum on the world market will not be apparent for some time. Even Mexico, which is expected to develop substantial export capacity in the future, appears committed to OPEC pricing polcies. Antonio Dovali Jaime, director general of Petroleos Mexicanos (PEMEX), recently stated that "Mexico will automatically boost its export price for crude if such an increase decision is taken as expected later this year by members of the Organization of Petroleum Exporting Countries, even though Mexico isn't an OPEC member."[34]

It may thus be a mistake to assume that the entry of these other new exporters will immediately lead to price reductions, disagreements over production schedules, or competition for market shares. None of these countries has as yet the export capacity to change the market dramatically, nor is any likely to develop that capacity within the next five years. For the time being OPEC domination of world petroleum exports continues to remain undisputed.

Summary

This chapter described changes in power relations in the world petroleum market and the evolving strength of the oil-exporting states. We compared the members of OPEC in terms of economic and demographic characteristics and pointed to major differences among them. Our observations on the position of the oil companies were, by necessity, sketchy and our hypotheses regarding the sources of OPEC demise inevitably tentative. The important question is not whether OPEC will disintegrate but *when* and *how*. If the cartel is a purely temporary phenomenon, consumer countries need develop only *ad hoc* means of responding to its pressures. Should OPEC persist over a longer period, then consumer nations will be confronted with the need to devise routinized means of responding to an adversary economic and political situation. The longer the cohesion of the cartel persists and its policies supported other oil-producing states, the more necessary it will be for the oil-importing countries to adjust their national policies to international constraints.

Notes

1. See Michael Tanzer, *The Political Economy of International Oil and the Underdeveloped Countries* (Boston: Beacon Press, 1969); Jack E. Hartshorn, *Oil*

Companies and Governments: An Account of the International Oil Industry and Its Political Environment (London: Faber and Faber, 1962); Leonard Mosley, *Power Play* (Baltimore: Penguin Books, Inc., 1974); Neil H. Jacoby, *Multinational Oil* (New York: Macmillan Publishing Co., Inc., 1974); Thomas D. Duchesneau, *Competition in the U.S. Energy Industry* (Cambridge, Mass.: Ballinger Publishing Company, 1975); Raymond F. Mikesell, ed., *Foreign Investment in the Petroleum and Mineral Industries* (Baltimore: The Johns Hopkins Press, 1971); James Ridgeway, *The Last Play* (New York: Mentor, 1973); Raymond Vernon, "Multinational Enterprises and International Price Formation," May 1975 (mimeographed); Edith J. Penrose, *The Large International Firm in Developing Countries: The International Petroleum Industry* (London: George Allen & Unwin, 1968); George Stocking, *Middle East Oil: A Study in Political and Economic Controversy* (Nashville: Vanderbilt University Press, 1970).

2. Hartshorn,, *Oil Companies and Governments*, p. 130.

3. Ibid., p. 107.

4. U.S., Congress, House, Committee on Foreign Affairs, Subcommittee on Foreign Economic Policy, *Foreign Policy Implications of the Energy Crisis*, 92nd Cong., 2nd sess., 1972, p. 232 (Statement by John G. Winger).

5. U.S., Congress, Senate, *Hearings, Oil and Gas Imports Issues*, 93rd Cong., 1st sess., 1973, p. 1067 (Statement by M.A. Adelman); see also M.A. Adelman, "Is the Oil Shortage Real? Oil Companies as OPEC Tax Collectors," *Foreign Policy*, No. 9 (Winter 1972-73), pp. 69-101.

6. Mosley, *Power Play*, p. 210.

7. DeGolyer and MacNaughton, *Twentieth Century Petroleum Statistics*, 1973 (Dallas: DeGolyer and MacNaughton, 1973), p. 9.

8. David Wise and Thomas B. Ross, *The Invisible Government* (New York: Random House, 1964), pp. 110-114.

9. Mosely, *Power Play*, p. 285.

10. Hartshorn, *Oil Companies and Governments*, p. 329.

11. Ibid.

12. Statement by Ahmed Hassan al Bakr, President of Iraq, quoted in Facts on File, *Energy Crisis, Volume I* (New York: Facts on File, Inc., 1974), p. 110.

13. *Middle East Monitor*, Vol. 2, No. 12 (June 15, 1972), pp. 1-2.

14. U.S., General Accounting Office, *Issues Related to Foreign Sources of Oil for the United States*, Report B-179411, January 23, 1974, p. 20.

15. Ibid., p. 27.

16. Ibid.

17. Oded Remba and Anne Sinai, "The Energy Problem and the Middle East," *Middle East Information Series*, No. 23 (May 1973), p. 6; see also, John A. Berry, "Oil and Soviet Policy in the Middle East," *The Middle East Journal*, Vol. 26, No. 2 (Spring 1972), pp. 149-160; see also, Arnold L. Horelick, "The Soviet Union, the Middle East and the Evolving World Energy Situation," *Policy Science*, Vol. 6, No. 1 (March 1975), pp. 41-48.

18. Zuhayr Mikdashi, *The Community of Oil Exporting Countries* (Ithaca: Cornell University Press, 1972), p. 42.

19. Mikdashi, *The Community of Oil Exporting Countries*, p. 33.

20. U.S., General Accounting Office, *Issues Related to Foreign Sources of Oil for the United States*, p. 31.

21. Ibid.

22. See, Davis B. Bobrow and Robert T. Kudrle, "Theory, Policy and Resource Cartels," an expanded version of a paper presented to the American Political Science Association, Chicago, Illinois, August 29-September 2. 1974; see also, William Fellner, *Competition Among the Few: Oligopoly and Similar Market Structures* (New York: Alfred A. Knopf, 1949); Roger Sherman, *Oligopoly: An Empirical Approach* (Lexington, Mass.: Lexington Books, D.C. Heath and Co., 1972); Martin Shubik, *Strategy and Market Structure: Competition, Oligopoly, and the Theory of Games* (New York: John Wiley & Sons, Inc., 1959); Mancur Olson, *The Logic of Collective Action* (Cambridge: Harvard University Press, 1965); Mikdashi, *The Community of Oil Exporting Countries.*

23. The Royal Norwegian Ministry of Foreign Affairs, Oslo, February 1974, as cited in the Organization of Petroleum Exporting Countries, *Weekly Bulletin: Review of the Press*, Vol. V, No. 14 (April 5, 1974), pp. 2-7.

24. *The New York Times*, December 10, 1974.

25. *The New York Times*, November 13, 1974.

26. Ibid.

27. Ibid.

28. *The New York Times*, November 26, 1974.

29. *Far East Trade and Development*, No. 10/12, China Issue, 1973, p. 277; Organization of Petroleum Exporting Countries, *Weekly Bulletin: Review of the Press*, "China Surges Towards Major Oil Power Status," Vol. 6, No. 13 (April 1, 1974), pp. 3-8; *Petroleum Economist*, "Chou En-lai's Million B/D," Vol. 41, No. 2 (February 1974), pp. 49-50.

30. *The New York Times*, December 4, 1974.

31. *Petroleum Economist*, "Chou En-lai's Million B/D," February 1974, p. 50.

32. *The New York Times*, October 13, 1974.

33. U.S., Department of the Interior, Bureau of Mines *Monthly Petroleum Statement*, December 1974, p. 16.

34. *Wall Street Journal*, June 16, 1975; see also, the *Middle East Economic Survey*, Vol. XVIII, No. 40 (25 July 1975), p. 6 and No. 42 (8 August 1975), p. 8.

Part II: The Structure of Energy Interdependence

3 Economic Effects of the Petroleum Cartel: Prices, Payments, and Proposals

Increasing trade in petroleum and higher prices have given rise to complex economic transactions, providing every state with new opportunities for influencing other states, while making each more sensitive to the actions of others.[a] This chapter traces the economic reverberations of rising prices and examines the reactions of the oil-importing countries and the policies of the exporting nations. We shall begin with the petroleum price increases of October 1973 and identify their multiple consequences. Clearly, the actual financial consequences of higher prices for any particular importer or exporter cannot be stated with any certainty. Wherever possible we have reported the range of various estimates and the assumptions upon which they are based.

Increases in Petroleum Prices

The first price increases by the oil-exporting states in 1973 precipitated a series of impending "crises" hitherto latent in the patterns of petroleum flows. These crises were latent in the sense that the accelerated increase of petroleum imports in the West, and the shift of import sources from the Western Hemisphere to the Middle East, created significant changes in the world petroleum market that could be exploited by the oil-rich states. The transfer of funds from the consuming to the producing countries has given rise to a situation characterized by a wide range of economic linkages between them *and* by a high degree of mutual penetration of each other's economies. The interaction of these factors has had an extensive impact upon the international economic system, perhaps even calling into question the viability of several major currencies.

This rise in prices is a clear consequence of the changing power relations in the world petroleum market. During the last three months of 1973 the posted (or tax reference) price for Middle East crude petroleum was raised by the oil-producers from about $3.01 to about $11.65 per barrel, thereby expanding their government revenues from $1.76 to over $8.00 per barrel.[1] (See Table 3-1.) The effect on actual prices (taking into account costs, taxes, royalties, oil company profits, and return to the host government) has also been extensive.[2] As of January 1974, posted prices have remained stable, but the government share through equity crude—that crude petroleum at least 51 percent owned by OPEC governments—has increased dramatically. Most of the crude sold in the

[a]This chapter is written with the research assistance of Richard Samuels.

Table 3-1
Evolution of Government Take on Equity Oil for Selected Gulf Crudes, 1971-74

	Dollars/Barrel										
	1971		1972	1973					1974		
Country/Oil	Pre-15 Feb.	15 Feb.	20 Jan.	1 Jan.	1 June	1 Aug.	1 Oct.	1 Dec.	1 Jan.	1 July	1 Oct.
Saudi Arabia											
Arabian light	0.989	1.261	1.448	1.516	1.702	1.804	1.770	2.998	7.008	7.113	8.260
Iran											
Iranian light	0.983	1.250	1.430	1.497	1.683	1.783	1.750	3.119	7.133	7.240	8.407
Kuwait											
Kuwait	0.958	1.231	1.406	1.472	1.659	1.747	1.716	2.890	6.966	7.070	8.211
Abu Dhabi											
Murban	1.005	1.272	1.458	1.527	1.717	1.821	1.787	3.521	7.578	7.692	8.981
Iraq											
Basrah	0.933	1.240	1.419	1.487	1.675	1.772	1.739	2.952	7.010	7.116	8.262

Source: Parra, Ramos & Parra, *International Crude Oil and Product Prices, 15 October 1974* (Beirut: Middle East Petroleum and Economic Publications, 1974), p. 79.

Gulf since 1974 has been equity crude. The return to the oil-exporting states under posted prices was based upon taxes and royalties. Now, however, the governments own the oil and sell it to the companies at a percentage (higher than 93%) of the posted price. Table 3-1 yields an indication of government shares per barrel of oil. Posted prices are becoming a less relevant referent for total government revenues as the trend toward participation increases.

In 1973 revenues accrued to the petroleum-exporting countries amounted to $25 billion. The October move increased this amount almost four-fold, bringing total revenues to about $100 billion annually.[3] At that time it was estimated that at least $65 billion would have to be processed through international financial markets in 1974 alone—about $55 billion from the major oil consuming nations and about $10 billion from the poorer states—and that the oil-exporting countries could control more than half the world's monetary reserves in the next decade.[4]

Analysts and policy makers alike differ in their assessments of these developments, and their assignment of responsibility for an apparently tenuous international situation.[5] It is often noted that the cost of petroleum production in the Middle East lies far below price, even before the October increases, and that even then supply and demand did not govern world prices. Almost everyone agrees that there is, as yet, a wide margin for further possible price increases.[6] In the long run, an upper price threshold will be set by the commercial availability of alternative sources of energy; in the shorter term, by the degree of cohesion among the oil-exporting states.

Balance of Payments Problems

The size of the import bill for petroleum is a clear indicator of the monetary impact of the present energy situation. It is estimated that if petroleum consumption does not decline appreciably due to the increased prices cumulative payments for petroleum may well reach at least $500 billion by 1985. While the precise magnitudes are subject to debate, they are large enough to strain the capacities of the world monetary system.[7] Indeed, the question of financial instability might be the most severe problem resulting from current energy transactions.

Even before the unprecedented price increases of 1974, knowledgeable observers were expressing concern over trends in energy flows.[8] World energy trade was expected to double by 1985 amounting to 20 percent of all international trade.[b] In the absence of any drastic changes in consumption

[b]The total (f.o.b.) value of world exports increased from $518 billion in 1973 to $768 billion in 1974. The oil-exporting countries accounted for $43.4 billion of the total for 1973 and $133 billion for 1974. The total value (c.i.f.) of world imports increased from $529 billion to $764 billion. The oil-exporting countries increased their imports more rapidly than any other group of countries, from $21.3 billion in 1973 to $36 billion in 1974. See International Monetary Fund, *IMF Survey*, Vol. 4, No. 5 (March 10, 1975), p. 79.

patterns, the United States alone was expected to account for about one third of the world's energy market supplies. One half of that amount would have to be obtained from abroad. This fraction could have resulted in an additional United States balance of payments deficit estimated at $20 billion or more by 1980.[9] Even before 1973 it was also likely that by 1985 the United States would be importing a large amount of refined products with a higher value than crude petroleum. In such an eventuality, the balance of payments deficit would have been about $15 billion larger, perhaps even approaching a total of $40 billion.[10] The Chase Manhattan Bank gave still higher estimates.[11] Even under the most optimistic conditions, it was extremely unlikely that United States exports of goods and services could offset outflows of such magnitude. These figures were all speculative before 1973 but they turned out to be glaring underestimates. In 1974 the United States increased its exports to OPEC nations by 80 percent to $8.1 billion, which counterbalanced only a third of the United States oil import costs of $24.6 billion.[12] Table 3-2 illustrates the impact of increased petroleum prices upon the balance of payments.

The implications of the oil import bill for Western Europe and Japan cannot be estimated with any precision. Despite uncertainties in prevailing assessments, it is argued that countries with large deficits could reach the limits of their credit in international markets.[13] Such arguments are presented primarily with reference to Italy and, to a lesser extent, France, with no specification as to when this would occur. In the absence of compensatory inflows, it is possible that the international reserves of the oil-importing countries ($173 billion including gold holdings in 1973)[14] would be exhausted in several years if their entire foreign exchange holdings were spent on petroleum payments.

Table 3-2
Balance of Payments Impact of Increased Oil Prices
(Billions of U.S. $)

Country	Balance of Payments for 1974	Oil Payments 1974
U.S.	−10.58	24.6
France[a]	−5.50	n.a.
Germany	10.40	8.50
Japan	−6.80	15.90
U.K.	−9.00	8.30

Note: n.a. = not available.

[a]The French Government set a $10.1 billion ceiling on oil imports in 1974. As of this writing there are no hard figures to indicate the success of the policy.

Sources: *The New York Times*, September 25, 1974, January 30, 1975, March 5, 17, 30, 1975; *Financial Times* (London), March 3, 6, 15, 30, 1975; *The Japan Economic Journal*, January 28, 1975.

Assessments such as these do not specify the conditions under which those developments would occur. The analysis is simple: Oil bills could be \$80-100 billion per year for the consumer countries and their total reserves are \$173 billion. Therefore, two years of oil payments could deplete all financial reserves. This is an extremely simplistic view since it ignores growth in reserves, any notion of credit, and the multitude of factors influencing both oil bills and monetary reserves. Nonetheless, it is conventionally believed that if compensatory policies are not agreed upon long before this point is attained, the development of large-scale monetary dislocations, of which the loss of purchasing power of major currencies may only be a minor feature, would develop. The magnitude of the large transfers of wealth after 1973 has begun to distort the existing exchange relationship among currencies.[15]

Acceptance by the oil-exporting states of a particular currency serves to strengthen it in relation to others, and accumulation of their stocks of that currency may distort financial markets far in excess of any perturbation yet experienced by the industrial economies. For example, reports in December of 1974 that Saudi Arabia was no longer willing to accept payments in sterling effectively devalued the British pound, forcing the Bank of England to allocate an estimated \$250 million in support of its currency.[16]

Two distinct, but related, financial problems arise as a consequence of the rise of petroleum prices. The first pertains to the inability of OPEC countries to absorb enough imports from the oil-consuming nations to ensure sufficient global liquidity. This problem is commonly referred to as primary recycling. The second pertains to the differential reentry of petroleum revenues in the economies of the oil-consuming nations because high-risk countries, such as Italy, do not attract the investment of surplus revenues. This problem is referred to as secondary recycling. The first problem may well be a question of time. The second is a question of unevenness. Secondary recycling is problematic only if primary recycling is not well handled.

It is generally agreed that the technical handling of primary recycling has to date been done rather well. Both William Simon, Secretary of the Treasury, and Gerald Parksy, Assistant Secretary of the Treasury, have argued that international financial institutions were effective in recycling of petroleum revenues.[17] Nonetheless, official concerns persist regarding impending pressures upon the international banking system. Simon attributed the difficulties that did occur to internal management problems associated with inflation, restrictive monetary policies, and rising rates of interest, rather than to the massive inflows of petroleum revenues.

Secondary recycling problems arose largely because some OPEC nations announced their refusal to hold assets in Italian or British currencies. In the last months of 1974, the British deficit was as much as \$1 billion per month. The situation for Italy was not much better. In addition, observers in the West fear that uneven inflows in the consumer countries might accentuate competition among them to increase their exports to the oil-producing countries in order to protect their own currencies. Such competition would place obstacles in any consumer efforts to devise institutionalized means of accommodating to the requisites of secondary recycling.

It is not at all clear where effective control over financial transactions lies: Both oil-exporters and oil-importers appear vulnerable to the actions of the other. The consequences of the transfers of funds lie beyond the direct influence of any single nation and reflect interrelated predicaments. The oil-consuming countries' trade deficits become the oil-producing countries' financial surpluses. This dual problem is aggravated by any OPEC decision to produce more petroleum than is required to pay for imports of goods and services. (This decision is discussed in Chapter 5.) As long as the oil-exporting states continue to meet the petroleum requirements of the consumer countries at present or higher prices, recycling problems will persist.

Surplus Petroleum Revenues

Despite uncertainties about the size of the surpluses to be accumulated by oil-exporting states in the near future, one estimate is that OPEC monetary reserves will increase from under $10 billion in 1972 to over $567 billion in 1985.[18] The Middle East monetary holdings have increased by more than 50 percent during 1974. Saudi Arabia alone has tripled its reserves since 1971. It is also estimated that cumulative OPEC surpluses, including returns on investment, would increase to about $450 billion by 1980.[19] However, there are differing estimates.[c] For example, one projection of OPEC surpluses averages $40 billion per year to 1980. This figure is based on the assumptions that petroleum prices will decline, that petroleum demand will also decline (from an increase of 11% to 12% per year to about 4%), and that total OPEC imports will grow about 15 percent per year. Accumulated interest and dividends, in addition to existing balances of $15 billion, would raise this total to some $300 billion.[20] Regardless of the precise figures involved, it appears certain that the monetary flows reflect

[c]Experts disagree about the expected size of the surplus revenues for OPEC over the next five to ten years. Initial estimates range from an accumulation of $300 billion in 1980 (Thomas R. Stauffer, "Oil Money and World Money: Conflict or Confluence?" *Science*, Vol. 184, No. 4134 (April 19, 1974), p. 323) to $500 billion (Gerald A. Pollack, "The Economic Consequences of the Energy Crisis," *Foreign Affairs*, Vol. 52, No. 3 (April 1974), p. 453). More recent studies by the First National City Bank, Irving Trust Company, the Morgan Guaranty Trust Company, and the *Financial Times* (London) indicate that surplus revenues will disappear by 1980 due to (1) increased OPEC expenditures on imports, and (2) the decline of oil prices due to a drop in petroleum. However, Walter J. Levy, an oil economist, predicts a cumulative surplus of $449 billion in 1980. Different assessments of the rate of OPEC expenditures on imports account for these discrepancies. See *The New York Times*, June 4, 12, and 16, 1975, and the Morgan Guaranty Trust Company of New York, World *Financial Markets*, June 1975. For a summary of conflicting estimates, see *The New York Times*, February 13, 1975.

qualitative and not merely quantitative changes in existing patterns of international economic transactions.

If we project such trends into the future, it is not improbable for the financial assets of the oil-exporting countries to reach 2 to 3 percent of Western financial markets by 1980.[21] Today, the Arab oil-exporters alone control 4.4 percent of the world's monetary reserves; they have 1 percent of the world's population, and their per capita monetary reserves range from 1 to 20 times those of the United States.[22] The Middle East is becoming the world's most rapidly growing store of capital.

No one disputes the fact that, in the absence of petroleum exports, the trade balance of oil-producing countries would be in deficit. Less clear, however, is the precise magnitude of surplus revenues anticipated for individual oil-exporting states. States with small populations like Abu Dhabi, Saudi Arabia, or Libya will have extensive surplus revenues. Countries like Iran, Venezuela, Indonesia, Nigeria, or Ecuador, on the other hand, are not likely to have financial surpluses in relation to their development plans (see Chapter 4) or from their international financial commitments (see Chapter 5).

Table 3-3 presents the value of petroleum exports to the oil-producing states as a percentage of the value of their total commodity exports. Fluctuations in exchange rates and accounting differences make it difficult to identify the precise contribution of oil to the total revenues for each government. Dependency upon petroleum ranges from 100 percent in the case of Abu Dhabi and Qatar to 44.6 percent in the case of Indonesia. It appears that in 1971-72 Kuwait received 98.5 percent of its total government revenues from the sale of oil; Libya, 93.9 percent; and Venezuela, 65.5 percent. While reliable estimates

Table 3-3
Petroleum Exports as a Percentage of Total Exports, 1970
(In Millions of U.S. Dollars)

Country	Total Exports	Oil Exports	Percentage of Oil to Total Commodity Exports	Trade Balance
Algeria	1,009	639	63.3	–248
Indonesia	1,009	450	44.6	126
Iran	2,355	2,089	88.7	697
Iraq	1,100	1,031	93.7	591
Kuwait	1,654	1,580	95.5	1,029
Libya	2,357	2,355	99.9	1,803
Nigeria	1,240	713	57.5	183
Saudi Arabia	2,334	2,259	96.8	1,624
Venezuela	2,655	2,398	90.3	1,015

Source: OPEC, *Annual Statistical Bulletin: 1971* (Vienna: OPEC, 1972).

for the other states are difficult to obtain, it is unlikely that petroleum revenues account for less than 50 percent of all government revenues in any oil-exporting state.

This nearly total dependence of the oil-exporting countries upon petroleum revenues is often compared to the importance of petroleum in the economies of the industrial countries. However, the problem of adjusting to a potential absence of a critical resource is quite different for oil-exporters and for oil-importers. For the exporters, population size and rate of change, level of economic development, alternative sources of revenues, and priorities in economic policy together determine their dependence on petroleum. For some importers, this dependence will persist as long as alternative sources of energy are not commercially viable.

Emergence of a Fourth World

Increases in petroleum prices have added over $10 billion to the import bill of the nonoil-exporting countries of the developing world. Attendant increases in food and fertilizer prices add another $24 billion.[23] The net impact has been to double their balance of payments deficits from $10 billion in 1973 to $20 billion in 1974, offsetting the flows of concessionary loans and grants from the developed nations.[24] The following figures illustrate the percentage increase of total commodity imports represented by higher oil costs from 1973 to 1974, for select Third World countries: Uruguay, 39 percent; Thailand and Senegal, 26 percent; India, 24 percent; the Philippines, 23 percent; and Korea and Ethiopia, 20 percent. These figures are only superficially indicative of the consequences of increased petroleum prices.[25]

The less-developed countries are unevenly affected by the price increases. The richer members will suffer the same problems facing the advanced industrial societies; the effect may be temporary. Countries like Taiwan, Korea, Brazil, and Turkey will not be incapacitated by the present "crisis." Those states of Asia and Africa whose terms of trade have worsened by 20 percent over the past two years and whose development prospects are most severely affected may well have suffered permanent setbacks. It is those countries that are labelled the "Fourth World."

Increases in petroleum prices accentuate economic problems in poorer states and have strong multiplier effects upon their development difficulties. The food crisis, for example, does not reflect actual shortage, except in some areas. Many developing countries rely on foreign imports to meet their food and fertilizer needs cheaply, and some governments have overestimated the productive capacity of the "green revolution."

The emergence of the Fourth World—another still poorer group of nations—creates further cleavages in the international system and new hierarchies of poverty and inequalities. The Fourth World is dependent upon decisions made elsewhere. It cannot exert a direct influence on the direction or nature of evolving policies, nor does it have any substantial power to shape the priorities of the oil-exporters or the major consumers. Neither the threat of cartelizing major primary commodities, such as tin, bauxite, and copper, among others,[d] nor recourse to moral arguments are likely to be effective. Analysts maintain that the conditions for the cartelization of other primary raw materials are absent and that any such efforts will inevitably fail.[e] Morality is of marginal relevance in a world of power politics.

So far, both producers and consumers of crude petroleum have attempted to provide some assistance to the Fourth World. The figures for official development assistance as recorded by the International Monetary Fund are as follows: $11.3 billion from the Development Assistance Committee (DAC) of the Organisation for Economic Co-operation and Development (OECD), and $1.1 billion from countries with centrally planned economies.[26] There is some confusion about OPEC commitments to the Fourth World. The IMF reports $2.54 billion in Official Development Assistance, but also reports total disbursements of the oil-exporting countries in 1974 as totalling $5.6 billion.[27] It appears certain, however, that the fate of the Fourth World will be decided as an outcome of any arrangement between major producers and consumers of crude petroleum.

Consumer Options for Reducing Economic Vulnerability

Several options in response to evolving economic interdependencies are available to both oil-importers and oil-exporters. Each option is accompanied by gains and losses and each involves a different set of policy instruments and different time horizons. For example, oil-importing nations may seek to (1) reduce their consumption of petroleum; (2) promote their exports to the oil-producers in order to offset financial deficits; (3) reduce capital outflows to non-OPEC nations and encourage compensating capital inflows from OPEC; (4) devaluate national currencies; (5) invest in the economies of the oil-exporting states; and (6) develop collaborative financial policies among oil-importing nations.

[d]See, *The New York Times*, March 24, 1974; April 7, 10, 14 and 30, 1974; May 3, 8, and 14; and June 6, 1974, on the actions of the Third World toward cartelization of other commodities. See also, C. Fred Bergsten, "The Threat is Real," *Foreign Policy*, No. 14 (Spring 1974), pp. 84-90; Zuhayr Mikdashi, "Collusion Could Work," *Foreign Policy*, No. 14 (Spring 1974), pp. 57-67.

[e]For assessments of the difficulties involved in the cartelization of other commodities see, Benson Varon, "What are the Opportunities for Raising LDC's Earnings from Exports of Non-Fuel Minerals through OPEC-Type Cooperation–A Brief Answer," Trade Policies and Export Protections Division, Economics Department, International Bank for Reconstruction and Development, February 11, 1972 (mimeographed); see also, Stephen D. Krasner, "Oil is the Exception," *Foreign Policy*, No. 14 (Spring 1974), pp. 68-83.

Five of these six alternatives largely involve the management of capital flows. They have all been reflected at one time or another in the proposed policies of the consumers. There is yet another option available to consumer countries that does entail neither a change in consumption patterns nor the development of financial instrumentalities or appropriate recycling mechanisms, namely, the use of force. That option is examined in Chapter 6. Here we consider the other six possibilities for consumer countries.

Reducing Petroleum Consumption

The reduction of petroleum consumption by the importing nations is largely a long-term policy. New habit patterns need to be developed, new policies for restricting consumption adopted, and new methods for enforcing such policies established. There are strong institutional constraints. Policy instruments for reducing consumption are not well developed, nor are the goals clearly articulated. Nonetheless, United States government assessments hold that there have been marked declines in petroleum consumption in some sectors over the past year and that the United States could reduce its rate of energy growth significantly without damaging the economy.[28] It has been estimated that energy use could grow at a rate as low as 1.5 percent per year from 1973 to 1985 without damaging the economy. This growth rate would be less than half the annual rate of increase between 1947 and 1973 which stood at 3.1 percent per year.[29] In support of these assessments, analysts cite the recent decline in world energy consumption of 3 percent in 1974 from 1973 levels. World consumption of crude petroleum dropped by 3.2 percent to 2.66 billion tons in 1974.[30]

Promoting Exports

The promotion of exports as a means of offsetting the balance of payments deficits is a policy of limited economic impact in the short term, although potentially extensive in the long run. In 1972 the United States exported about $2.6 billion of goods and services to the major oil exporters;[31] United States exports accounted for 18 percent of the total imports of oil-rich states.[32] Recent figures from the Department of Commerce indicate that although United States exports to OPEC countries increased in 1974 the net oil deficit was about $10 billion.[33]

Aside from Germany, whose trade balance is strongly in surplus, all the consuming countries will have difficulties paying their oil bills. In the cases of Italy and the United Kingdom, the currency drains occasioned by rising prices exacerbate net dollar outflows.[34] Thus, despite anticipations of substantial

Table 3-4
Increases in Consumer Exports to the Oil-Exporting Countries
(Millions of U.S. Dollars)

	Jan.-Dec. 1973	Jan.-Dec. 1974	Change (%)
U.S.	3,807.0	7,034.0	+84.76%
U.K.	1,962.8	2,832.1	+44.28
France	1,868.3	3,050.6	+63.28
Germany	2,308.4	4,117.0	+78.34
Japan	2,821.4	5,610.4	+98.85

Note: The International Monetary Fund defines the "oil-exporting countries" as including Algeria, Bahrain, Brunei, Ecuador, Gabon, Indonesia, Iran, Iraq, Kuwait, Libya, Nigeria, Oman, Qatar, Saudi Arabia, Trinidad and Tobago, the United Arab Emirates, and Venezuela.

Source: International Monetary Fund and the International Bank for Reconstruction and Development, *Direction of Trade*, February-May 1975, (Washington, D.C.: International Monetary Fund, 1975).

growth in trade over the next few years—at 10 percent per year for Western Europe compounded over the decade, and 17 percent for Japan—these countries will find it difficult to employ trade as a means of countering the consequences of increased petroleum prices.[35] It is expected that the expansion of trade in Western Europe and Japan will be primarily directed toward the United States, not toward OPEC. Nonetheless, exports to OPEC countries have increased faster than initially expected. Table 3-4 illustrates the change between 1973 and 1974.

Reducing Capital Outflows

The option of reducing capital outflows of consumer countries to non-OPEC nations and encouraging compensatory inflows from OPEC is considered by some exporters as particularly promising. Observers argue that encouraging large-scale investments in the West by the oil-exporting countries would increase their stake in the continued economic well-being of the consumers. There has been much talk in the past months, but comparatively little in the nature of conclusive arrangements.

Businessmen and government officials of the major importing countries have attempted to secure markets for their exports and attract OPEC investments. Brokerage houses have been established in the Middle East, and substantial sales of government bonds have been made.[f] However, the emphasis of oil-rich

[f]For a complete breakdown of the disposition of surplus oil revenues in 1974 see, International Monetary Fund, *IMF Survey*, Vol. 4, No. 6 (March 24, 1975); p. 81; see also, Morgan Guaranty Trust Company of New York, *World Financial Markets* (January 21, 1975), pp. 2-4.

investors is on short-term, highly liquid accounts. This strategy makes long-term bank lending a tenuous proposition at best.[36] Table 3-5 illustrates the relative success of efforts to attract surplus oil revenues by consumer countries.

At the same time, however, there is a marked reluctance by the consumer countries to allow uncontrolled investments of oil funds in some industrial sectors, most notably in defense-related industries. In some countries there are legal prohibitions against investments by foreign governments. Observers also note that ownership of major enterprises may disturb equity markets or raise antitrust motions in the United States.

Encouraging the repatriation of profits accrued from the foreign investments of American oil companies is a related option for consuming nations. In 1972 such capital outflows amounted to between $1.5 and $2.0 billion a year. Any

Table 3-5
Estimated Quarterly Use of Surplus Oil Revenues in 1974
(In Billions of U.S. Dollars)

	I	II	III	IV	Year
United Kingdom	3.3	6.7	6.0	5.0	21.0
British government stocks	0.4	0.1	0.2	0.2	0.9
Treasury bills	0.4	0.7	0.7	0.9	2.7
Sterling deposits	–0.1	0.7	1.1	–	1.7
Other sterling investments	0.1	0.2	0.3	0.1	0.7
Foreign currency deposits	2.5	4.5	3.4	3.4	13.8
Other foreign currency borrowing	–	0.5	0.3	0.4	1.2
United States	1.1	2.3	5.0	2.6	11.0
Government and agency securities	0.5	1.4	2.3	1.8	6.0
Bank deposits	0.6	0.8	2.3	0.3	4.0
Other	–	0.1	0.4	0.5	1.0
Other Countries	2.6	6.0	4.5	7.5	20.6
Foreign currency deposits	1.5	3.5	1.5	2.5	9.0
Special bilateral facilities and other investments	1.1	2.5	3.0	5.0	11.6
International Organizations	–	0.5	0.8	2.3	3.6
Total	7.0	15.5	16.3	17.4	56.2

Source: International Monetary Fund, *IMF Survey* Vol. 4, No. 7 (April 14, 1975), p. 110.

increase in the repatriation of profits would increase the net contribution to the balance of payments.[37] Policies for encouraging repatriation remain to be developed.

Devaluating Currency

Currency devaluation is a discrete financial adjustment not a long-term policy. In theory, any individual country could undertake monetary adjustments equal to the overall trade deficit, taking into account long-term capital inflows, private as well as public. By this standard Japan should devalue about 10 percent to 20 percent, and the United States about 13 percent.[38]

The possibility of devaluations of such magnitude may increase incentives for collaborative arrangements among oil-importing nations and for the development of joint monetary policies at least within the OECD. OPEC is concerned with the value of petroleum and not intrinsically with currency arrangements among Western countries. Devaluation would enable OPEC to buy more goods and services from the West, but the oil-exporting countries are likely to oppose such a move, since it would reduce the value of their own monetary reserves. In addition, if OPEC reacts to devaluation by initiating further price increases greater than the devaluation itself, this reaction will increase the real cost of oil imports and accelerate Western investments in alternative sources of energy.

Other Consumer Options

Investing in the economies of the oil-exporting states may be an attractive policy. However, this option is not viable in the short run, largely because of the constraints of absorptive capacity in the oil-exporting states (see Chapter 4), although it is viewed with favor by some states, most notably Libya (see Chapter 5).

Another policy option for consumer countries is to develop collaborative financial arrangements between importers of crude petroleum. Several such plans have been put forth by the oil-importing countries to date, with varying degrees of official collaboration. The oil-exporting states have reacted, sometimes by criticizing individual proposals, sometimes by presenting their preferred alternatives.

Recycling Proposals by Consumer Countries

In the past two years, the oil-consuming nations have put forth a series of proposals for recycling petroleum revenues, reducing their dependence on petroleum imports, and sharing oil supplies. There have been at least six major proposals for regulating energy transactions and import payments. Each proposal implicitly addresses itself to evolving changes in the world petroleum market, and consequently, to international politics at large. But they differ in terms of projected costs, control over decision making, definition of goals and objectives, and identification of allies and adversaries. Four of the six regard the worldwide impact of higher oil prices as temporary aberrations, to be remedied through joint action by the consuming nations.

The six plans are:

1. The United States "safety net" of "financial solidarity" put forth by Secretary of State Henry Kissinger and Treasury Secretary William Simon in November 1974.
2. The U.S. Trust Fund Plan proposed during the same year.
3. An International Monetary Fund Oil Facility, presented in January 1974 by Johannes Witteveen then Managing Director of the IMF.
4. A plan proposed initially by Emile Van Lennep, the Secretary General of OECD, in November 1974.
5. The Kleinman Plan, a privately initiated proposal, originally presented in February 1974 by David T. Kleinman, professor of finance at Fordham University, to the Central Bank of Venuzuela.
6. Another privately initiated recycling proposal published in *Foreign Affairs*, January 1975, co-authored by Khodadad Farmanfarmaian of Iran, Armin Gutowski of West Germany, Saburo Okita of Japan, and Robert V. Roosa and Carroll L. Wilson of the United States.

Each plan puts forth a particular institutional arrangement in response to the economic predicament of the oil-importing countries, and a strategy for the reinvestment of surplus revenues and for solutions to the problem of meeting import payments. A seventh plan has been accepted by the OECD countries in April 1975 as a compromise among the four governmental proposals.

United States Safety Net

The United States "safety net" of "financial solidarity" was the first formal response of consumer countries to higher oil payments. It was designed to "reduce the vulnerability" of the industrialized nations by creating a loan and guarantee facility to aid those OECD nations with payment difficulties. It was regarded as an effort to supplement rather than replace the role of the private financial markets.[39] This plan presupposed cooperation on energy as well as monetary policies. Its purpose was to distribute, at commercial rates of interest, funds flowing back to the OECD nations from the oil-exporting countries. The

United States argued for an oil floor price to stimulate the development of non-OPEC energy sources, and had hoped for approval by other OECD countries by March 1, 1975.

The proposed "safety net" relied on a $25 billion fund, an amount covering about 60 percent of the $40 billion deficit, which was expected for the industrial nations in 1974. The fund would be raised by the OECD countries. The United States would contribute nearly $8 billion, about 30 percent of the total, to be raised through the sale of securities or through governmental borrowing. It was proposed that West Germany also bear major financial responsibility, and that the fund be administered by the governments of Western Europe, North America and Japan.[40]

The *official* goals of the plan were to:

> Protect financial institutions from excessive risks posed by an enormous volume of funds beyond their control or capacity;
>
> Insure that no one nation is forced to pursue disruptive and restrictive policies for lack of adequate financing;
>
> Assure that no consuming country will be compelled to accept financing on intolerable political and economic terms;
>
> Enable each participating country to demonstrate to people that efforts and sacrifices are being shared equitably—that national survival is buttressed by consumer solidarity.[41]

Implicit in these official goals are some operational or *actual* objectives. These include: (1) correcting balance of payments imbalances among oil-consuming nations; (2) protecting the oil-consumers against the threat of sudden withdrawals of funds by the oil-exporters; (3) maximizing freedom of investment for the consumers by channelling OPEC surplus revenues accordingly; (4) protecting private financial institutions from carrying too great a risk; and, most importantly, (5) reducing the possibility of bilateral agreements between the OECD countries and the oil-exporters.

It was stipulated that a common loan and guarantee facility be created to redistribute $25 billion in 1975, and as much again in 1976. These funds would be allocated to the recipients by a new organization to be developed specifically for this purpose. The plan stipulated that no country "should expect financial assistance that is not moving effectively to lessen its dependence on imported oil."[42]

The authors of the United States "safety net" of "financial solidarity" plan did not envisage any opposition to their proposal. However, West Germany voiced disagreement largely on the grounds that the plan was inflationary.[43] On balance, this proposal appears to be an attempt of the United States to retain political influence within the OECD and to reestablish Western influence over petroleum-related transactions. OPEC resistance to this plan derives largely from their opposition to a U.S. domination of the petroleum market and to any proposal that does not give them an active role in determining international economic arrangements.

U.S. Trust Fund

The U.S. Trust Fund Plan, proposed by Secretary of State Kissinger in conjunction with the "safety net" plan, calls for the creation of a "trust fund" for channelling funds at concessional rates to the poorest states. A $1-2 billion fund is proposed for a collective yearly deficit of $20 billion. The sources of the fund would be national contributions from interested states including the oil-exporting countries. The IMF would contribute the profits from gold sales specified for this purpose. Control of the proposed Trust Fund would be in the hands of an Interim Committee of the IMF and the joint IMF-IBRD (International Bank for Reconstruction and Development) Development Committee.[44]

The *official* goal of this second United States proposal is to meet the unfinanced balance of payments deficits of the poor states associated with their oil payments. The *actual* goal is to enlist the support of the Fourth World in any political confrontation between OPEC and the oil-consuming nations. The proposed means for achieving both objectives is the creation of a trust fund managed by the IMF to lend at interest rates recipient countries could afford.

This proposal is likely to be supported by the Fourth World even though it is of no great financial magnitude. Its value is largely symbolic for the United States, although possibly extensive for the poor states. The consumer countries of the West are not likely to oppose this plan; however, OPEC will. The organization is in principle opposed to recycling proposals that do not involve the oil-exporting countries in the management of the financial arrangements. This proposal seems to have been supplanted by the IMF oil facility.

IMF Oil Facility

The third major recycling plan is an International Monetary Fund Oil Facility, first put forth in January 1974 by the managing director of the IMF.[45] This Oil Facility is presently implemented. It was the first international recycling response to the oil payments dislocations of 1973-74. The precedent for this arrangement was a 1960 IMF agreement that "the provision of foreign exchange to Fund members to assist in the compensation of short-term fluctuations in the balance of payments constitutes a legitimate use of Fund resources."[46] This agreement became the basis for the arrangement implemented 14 years later.

The amount of the 1975 Oil Facility funding was set at Special Drawing

Rights (SDR)[g] of 5 billion ($6.2 billion), almost twice the amount of the 1974 facility which actually disbursed SDR 2.5 billion. It was proposed that the IMF borrow from surplus countries, including the oil-exporting states. Thus far, the IMF has borrowed 2.86 billion SDR from the 11 lenders, but it controls the fund and to make the decisions regarding eligibility and allocations. Table 3-6 identifies the lenders for 1975.

Table 3-6
Lenders to the 1975 Oil Facility
(In SDRs)

Lender	Amount	Percent of Total
Non-OPEC		
Austrian National Bank	50,000,000	1.74
National Bank of Belgium	100,000,000	3.49
Deutsche Bundesbank	300,000,000	10.48
Kingdom of the Netherlands	200,000,000	6.99
Bank of Norway	50,000,000	1.74
Swiss National Bank	150,000,000	5.24
Total Non-OPEC	850,000,000	29.72
OPEC		
Central Bank of Iran	410,000,000	14.33
Central Bank of Kuwait	200,000,000	6.99
Government of Nigeria	200,000,000	6.99
Saudi Arabia Monetary Agency	1,000,000,000	34.96
Central Bank of Venezuela	200,000,000	6.99
Total OPEC	2,010,000,000	70.27
Total	2,860,000,000	100.00

Source: International Monetary Fund, *IMF Survey*, Vol. 4, No. 12 (June 23, 1975), p. 177.

[g]The term *Special Drawing Rights (SDRs)* refers to a unit of financial exchange based upon the value of 16 major world currencies. Currencies selected are those for countries whose share of world exports of goods and services exceeded an average of 1 percent over the five year period 1968-72. SDRs are insulated from monetary fluctuations in individual countries and are administered by the International Monetary Fund (IMF). In the June meeting of OPEC in 1975, the members decided to calculate the value of oil in SDRs, effective October 1, 1975, in order to protect the value of oil from inflation. Iran initially opposed this procedure, arguing that the strengthening of the dollar would yield substantial benefits to the OPEC countries, which would be diluted under a system in which the value of oil was pegged to SDRs. At that time, Iran continued to favor a system under which the value of oil would be tied to a basket of commodities rather than currencies. See *The New York Times*, June 20, 1975. Subsequently, Iran shifted its support to the use of SDRs as the unit of account for oil prices. See the *Middle East Economic Survey*, Vol. XVIII, No. 36 (27 June 1975), p. 1.

The *official* objectives of the Oil Facility are to assist members with balance of payments needs in helping to meet the calculated impact of their balance of payments in 1975.[47] An *actual* added goal is to ensure global liquidity. These objectives are to be undertaken through the IMF distribution of loans; by this borrowing from surplus nations at an interest rate of 7 1/4 percent and extending them for seven years at an interest rate of 7 3/4 percent.

The IMF anticipates political support from all its members since the facility mitigates against massive financial dislocations associated with oil payments. The actual sources of political support is likely to come largely from the poorer countries of Asia, Africa, and Latin America. Some opposition may come from OPEC in line with the organization's general reactions to recycling proposals. Table 3-7 illustrates the actual uses of the Oil Facility for 1974.

OECD Financial Support Fund

The Van Lennep Plan, which subsequently became the OECD Financial Support Fund, was designed less as a recycling plan than a response to fears that the United States "safety net" would deplete the exchange reserves of the richest industrial nations. Van Lennep first proposed a fund of $25 billion designed to ensure an equitable burden upon each of the OECD nations in the creation of a common fund, and to ensure shared distribution of power in the extension of distributional discretion to all OECD members. In turn, the OECD as a whole would guarantee the fund. This arrangement differs from the Kissinger-Simon plan in that it would be funded only by the countries with surplus balance of payments. The OECD would also control allocations to applicants.

The *official* objective of the Van Lennep proposal was to "enable the very large amounts of capital that will henceforth be flowing out of the oil-producing countries to be made available in the geographical locations–and in forms–that will most facilitate the continued expansion of world trade and employment."[48] The *actual* goal was to facilitate the "balancing" of flows of surplus petroleum revenues to the economies of the West by extending loans to those OECD nations with significant balance of payment deficits.

The Kissinger-Simon "safety net," the Van Lennep Plan, and an earlier plan proposed by the European Economic Community merged in 1975. A $25 billion facility was agreed upon in Paris on April 9, 1975, labelled the OECD Financial Support Fund. It was also agreed that the IMF Oil Facility would presently remain a separate mechanism. This arrangement stipulated that risks on loans would be shared in proportion to the quotas of each of the member nations. The distribution of quotas is based on a formula that gives about equal weight to each member's GNP and its foreign trade. The United States has 27.8 percent of the total quota; West Germany, 12.5 percent; Japan, 11.7 percent; and France, 8.5 percent. It has been agreed that the fund will develop its own administrative

Table 3-7
Use of Oil Facility for 1974

	Number of Purchases	Amount Purchased (Million SDRs)
Industrial countries		675.000
Italy	2	675.000
Other developed countries		802.700
Cyprus	2	8.100
Greece	3	103.500
Iceland	2	17.200
New Zealand	2	109.300
Spain	1	296.200
Turkey	1	113.200
Yugoslavia	3	155.200
Developing countries		1,021.551
Bangladesh	3	51.500
Burundi	1	1.200
Cameroon	1	4.620
Central African Republic	3	3.300
Chad	2	2.205
Chile	2	118.500
Costa Rica	2	18.837
El Salvador	2	17.890
Fiji	1	0.340
Guinea	1	3.510
Haiti	3	4.800
Honduras	1	16.785
India	1	200.000
Israel	1	62.000
Ivory Coast	1	11.170
Kenya	3	36.000
Korea	4	100.000
Malagasy Republic	3	14.300
Mali	2	5.000
Nicaragua	2	15.500
Pakistan	3	125.000
Panama	1	7.370
Senegal	1	15.525
Sierra Leone	2	4.914
Sri Lanka	3	43.500

Table 3-7 (cont.)

	Number of Purchases	Amount Purchased (Million SDRs)
Sudan	2	28.710
Tanzania	3	31.500
Uganda	2	19.200
Uruguay	2	46.575
Yemen, People's Democratic Republic	2	11.800
Total		2,499.251

Source: International Monetary Fund, *IMF Survey*, Vol. 4, No. 7 (April 14, 1975), p. 107.

infrastructure, and that decisions be taken by a Governing Committee composed of representatives from member states.[49]

The *official* goals of the fund are to "avoid unilateral measures which would restrict international trade or artificially stimulate exports" and to develop and coordinate national energy policies.[50] The *actual* goal is to collectively subsidize the balance of payments deficits of member countries so that international trade and finance would not be disrupted. An attendant objective, therefore, is to reduce incentives for bilateral arrangements between consumer countries and oil-exporting states.

The means of carrying out these arrangements is through the development of guarantees so that deficit countries could obtain loans to subsidize deficits. The United States proposed that participating countries provide either direct financing through the transfer of funds or an individual guarantee for borrowing by the fund in financial markets. West Germany proposed that the Financial Support Fund borrow in financial markets against collective guarantees by the participating members.[51] Both procedures were accepted. All the OECD countries now support the fund.

Kleinman Plan

The Kleinman Plan was the earliest private initiative for the resolution of the recycling issue. The proposal appeared first in the July 1974 issue of *Petroleum Economist.*[h] Professor Kleinman suggested that although the poorer states have been hardest hit by the increased oil prices, they now have a unique opportunity

[h]David Kleinman, "Oil Money and the Third World," *The Banker*, Vol. 124, No. 583 (September 1974), pp. 1061-1064. This plan was originally proposed in 1967 to the Brazilian Government. See U.S., Congress, House, Committee on Foreign Affairs, Subcommittee on Inter-American Affairs, *Hearings, Capital Markets and Economic Development: The Kleinman Plan*, 92nd Cong., 2nd sess., July 1972.

for economic development. Kleinman called for the investment of OPEC directly in the economies of the poorer states. In turn, these funds would be recycled back into the industrial nations through orders for manufactured goods, services, and massive development projects. The OPEC nations, Kleinman argued, would benefit from such an arrangement and the industrial nations will find a stable recycling process. In addition, the expected demand of the poorer countries for the manufactures of the advanced states would provide for the sustained growth of the major oil consumers.[52]

The financial size of the proposal is unspecified; however, the major source of support is expected to come from OPEC. OPEC would also control the allocation and disbursement of investment funds in the poor states by relying largely on established market mechanisms. The *official* goal of the plan is to assist the Fourth World in its economic development. The *actual* objective is to facilitate the recycling of surplus petroleum revenues through assistance to marginal countries. Political support would be expected to come largely from the poorer countries and from OPEC. Kleinman expects support from the OECD as well. However, OPEC may oppose it on the same grounds as the other four proposals.

Foreign Affairs Proposal

The second privately initiated recycling plan appeared in the January 1975 issue of *Foreign Affairs* by an international group of individuals.[53] The proposal is for the establishment of a large OPEC mutual securities fund that would provide a supply of petrodollars available for investment in central bank bonds. Envisioning a recycling effort in which the OPEC nations would share the risks of large-scale global lending, this plan calls for the creation of an OPEC Fund for Government Securities to purchase securities issued by consumer nations, and an OPEC Mutual Investment Trust to coordinate OPEC investments in the West. The participation of Robert V. Roosa, former U.S. Undersecretary of the Treasury for Monetary Affairs and creator of the Roosa Bonds for the Eurocurrency market may explain a similarity in spirit between past proposals of this sort and the *Foreign Affairs* plan.

This proposal is based on yet unspecific short-term notes with OPEC as their primary guarantors and distributional power vested equally in OPEC and OECD nations. It recognizes the interdependencies among producers and consumers more explicitly than do the government plans and proposes a larger role for OPEC. The authors argue that a transnational technocracy with broad experience could provide general directives for the allocation of funds largely through market mechanisms. The avoidance of any reliance on the IMF and the IBRD reflects the authors' awareness and concern for OPEC fears that, as presently constituted, these international institutions are dominated by the oil-consuming countries of the West.

The *official* goals of the proposal in *Foreign Affairs* is to supplement a bewildering array of individual arrangements with an effective outlet for the investment of national funds. The *actual* goals are to ensure global liquidity by directing safe investments of OPEC surplus revenues, and to engage OPEC in an institutional framework for recycling these surpluses.

The authors argue that the oil-exporting states would support this proposal because OPEC investments would be coordinated and risks would be minimized; and that the OECD would support it because effective recycling of surplus petroleum revenues would be ensured. Despite the role accorded to OPEC it is unlikely that the organization would lend its support, on the grounds that this proposal does not give oil-exporting countries sufficient discretion over allocation or management of the funds.

A Comparison

Of the four initial governmental proposals and the two private ones, the Kissinger-Simon position was least willing to acknowledge the changing nature of the world petroleum market and looked upon the consuming countries as the major actors in this system. The United States refused to negotiate directly with OPEC prior to a consumer agreement for fear of legitimizing it as an international organization. This plan also assumed that by joint action the consuming nations can control petroleum transactions and reduce the maneuverability of OPEC; and further, that the leverages available to the oil-exporting countries could be effectively neutralized if the OECD nations would adopt a floor price set at $7-8 per barrel in order to make investments in alternatives to petroleum economically viable. In its original form the Kissinger-Simon plan would have affected the members of OECD unevenly.

The U.S. "Trust Fund" plan and the IMF Oil Facility both looked beyond the interests of the oil-importing nations and took account of the concerns of the larger international community and specifically of less developed countries. This was also true of the Kleinman plan. All three proposals sought broader guarantors and a wider distributional power base. The Van Lennep plan emerged to counter the Kissinger plan by proposing a more equal distribution of responsibility among the OECD countries. Neither proposal sought to enlist the participation of the oil-exporting countries or take account of the Fourth World. Only the plan presented in *Foreign Affairs* took specific cognizance of the transnational linkages triggered by rising petroleum prices and viewed the OPEC nations as prospective financial guarantors for the underlying requisite funds, while seeking participation of both OPEC and OECD nations to execute distributional functions. It was conceived as an international regime to develop regularized means of interaction between exporters and importers, and drew upon both for political support.

Table 3-8 compares the four initial governmental proposals and the two private ones in terms of financial size, anticipated guarantor, distribution of power, stated objectives, operational goals, and projected supporters. On the basis of this assessment we have then made some estimate of potential sources of opposition to each plan. This comparison provides a brief sketch of the recycling suggestions and the political preferences of the oil-importing nations.

Although individual government-to-government agreements for oil supplies persist, notably in terms of barter arrangements, there has been a gradual evolution of postures, plans, and preferences, and a coalescing of perspectives. The development of the OECD Financial Support Fund as an elaboration and extension of the governmental plans proposed earlier illustrates bargaining and compromise among oil-consuming countries. Concessions were made by the United States insofar as it agreed to meet with the producer countries. Concessions were made by the Europeans insofar as they agreed to initial United States stipulations for consumer cooperation. What can effectively be implemented over the long term depends very largely on the reactions and responses of the oil-exporting countries.

Producer Responses to Consumer Proposals

In addition to *what* is decided, the question of *who* decides is also central to the current controversies. The oil-exporting states maintain that they have acquired control over pricing and production policies after a long struggle with the multinational oil companies and that they have neither the desire nor the intention of relinquishing this control to the consuming countries or to international agencies. This sentiment explains much of the exporters' resistance to any recycling plans that deny them discretionary power over the allocation of funds or influence over prevailing energy transactions. Therein lies the core of the political problem between exporters and importers.

Two reinforcing themes are reflected in the official statements of the oil-exporting states: One is a jealous protection of their newly acquired control over petroleum production, pricing, and distribution, and a desire to extend this control over the disbursement of surplus revenues; the other is a fear that the United States is seeking to deny them influence in what they consider to be an emerging international economic order with a more diffuse distribution of power. These two concerns are shared by all the oil-exporting states, regardless of political persuasion, level of development, or disbursement strategy.

A brief selection illustrating such expressed political perceptions indicates their pervasiveness; first, from Boumediene of Algeria:

> The real policy of the U.S. is not to lower prices but to control the courses of energy and thus ensure its political power.[54]

Table 3-8
Alternative Recycling Proposals: Comparisons and Summary

Recycling Proposal	Size	Sources of Monetary Resources	Location of Formal Control	Official Objectives	Actual Goals
Kissinger-Simon "Safety Net"	$25 billion	United States and West Germany	Major oil consumers	1. To create a financial "safety net" for consumers 2. To reduce dependence on "unreliable" oil	Break up the cartel
U.S. "Trust Fund"	$1.5-$2.0 billion	IMF OPEC	IMF	1. To assist Fourth World in financial need	Elicit Fourth World support
IMF 1975 Oil Facility	$6 billion	IMF	IMF	1. To ensure global liquidity	Ensure global liquidity
Van Lennep	$25 billion	OECD	OECD	1. To equalize distribution of recycled petrodollars	Direct petrodollar investment
Kleinman	Unspecified	OPEC	OPEC, Fourth World	1. To assist Fourth World in financial need	Assist Fourth World
Farmanfarmaian, Gutowski, Okita Roosa, & Wilson	Unspecified short term funds	OPEC	Transnational technocracy	1. To ensure global liquidity	Ensure global liquidity

A high-ranking official in the Organization of Arab Petroleum Exporting Countries (OAPEC), Ali Attiga, elaborates as follows:

> The most fundamental change in the government-company relationship in our area took place last October when basic decisions regarding pricing and production became the responsibility of the oil exporting countries . . . the significance lies not so much in the sharp increases in oil prices . . . but really in the emergence of oil exporting governments as decisionmakers with regard to the exploitation and management of their most valuable natural resource.[55]

Saudi Arabia, the most conservative of the oil-exporting states, also takes strong opposition to any form of international control over petroleum-related decisions. Sheik Yamani, usually conciliatory in his statements, declared:

> The major industrial countries and some of their supporters from the rank of the developing countries are . . . attempting to establish a sort of guardianship over the pricing policies of the producers. . . . We do not foresee the possibility of solving our problems and therefore of increasing the volume of our oil production on the basis of global agreements or arrangements.[56]

Proposed Means	Proposed Instrumentalities	Proposed Sources of Support	Expected Sources of Support	Proposed Sources of Opposition	Expected Sources of Opposition
1. Create a floor price for energy 2. Reduce consumption 3. Reinforce consumer cohesion	1. Creation of the International Energy Agency & Program 2. Market rate loans to needy & cooperative through IEA	OECD	OECD minus recalcitrants (France, Italy)	OPEC	OPEC and recalcitrant consuming nations
1. Subsidize the oil related deficits of the Fourth World	1. Loans to Fourth World on lower than market rates 2. Loans through IMF-IBRD mechanism	Fourth World OPEC	Fourth World	–	OPEC
1. Institutionalize recycling	1. Market rate loans to countries with balance of payments deficits	OPEC, IMF members	Deficit IMF members	–	Surplus IMF members, OPEC
1. Coordinate OECD investment policies	1. Loans to financially weakened OECD members	OECD	OECD	–	OPEC
1. Recycle through Fourth World	1. National and regional capital markets 2. Creation and sale of securities 3. Funds lent to banks accumulated in selling securities	OPEC, Fourth World OECD	Fourth World	–	OPEC, OECD
1. Institutionalize recycling	1. Creation of mutual fund for OPEC investors 2. Creation of OPEC fund for government securities	OPEC, Fourth World OECD	OECD	–	OPEC

In the past, even the illusion of control was an impossibility; at present, control is regarded as an operational goal, one that shapes more critical objectives. But there are other reasons for the exporting countries' apprehension of consumer plans. They see in the United States posture veiled threats intended to communicate the possible use of force. In his speech to the United Nations General Assembly Special Session in April, 1974, Secretary of State Kissinger had stated:

The transfer of resources from the developed to the developing nations essential to all hopes for progress—can only take place with the support of the technologically advanced countries. The politics of pressure and threats will undermine the domestic base of this support.[57]

This threat constitutes an essential feature of petroleum politics for both exporters and importers. The oil-exporting countries recognize their dependence upon the West but impute to it subservience and subordination. This reaction is most clearly demonstrated in a response to the *Foreign Affairs* recycling proposal, described above, published in the Iranian *Kayhan International*, entitled the "$600 Billion Hold-Up Plan"

A careful study of the blueprint [Wilson-Roosa Plan] shows that the authors have assumed OPEC governments to be rather insipid children incapable of handling their just income from irreplaceable natural resources. Thus the $600 billion sum at stake would be OPEC's in little more than a bookkeeping sense. OPEC nations would be like the prodigal son who sold his father's heritage and lived a rich man's life for a few years. . . .[58]

Furthermore

All these [recycling plans] however are varieties on the same theme: Let us look after your money because you cannot do it yourself.[59]

Colonial history and memories of a dominated past cause them to place considerable emphasis on the issue of control. Beyond the question of material gains and losses, they are also concerned with their position in international politics. Never again do they want to be protectorates, governed by international guardians. This fear of losing control over petroleum-related decisions and over the allocation of surplus revenues is expressed also in an anti-imperialist posture:

Handing over a large part of the decision-making process to people and institutions beyond our national control would only gain us a reputation of insanity . . . those who speak of launching an invasion of OPEC countries and those who furnish a blueprint for what they hope would be the biggest hold-up in history share the same imperialistic frame of mind.[60]

The two perspectives–recognition of dependence on the West, yet fear of domination–have provided OPEC with the basis for a joint response through a strategy of disaggregated interdependence. Recognition of *mutual* sensitivities and vulnerabilities has increased, simply because formally dependent nations have now acquired new leverages. As Boumediene of Algeria put it: "Relations between the two are no longer those between an elephant and a mouse but between two elephants."[61] But there is also an acute awareness that persisting dependencies cannot be eradicated simply by an accumulation of financial reserves. The basic question therefore is: Would OPEC continue to accept major power hegemony in the present international economic order or would it seek to restructure that order? The oil-exporting states do not yet have a common response but they have begun to reach some agreement regarding their preferred strategies for recycling surplus petroleum revenues.

In January 1975 the oil-exporters convened in Algiers to consider granting credits to industrial countries, including specific credits for the purchase of oil.[62] It was stipulated that such arrangements should not interfere with the right of OPEC to allocate petroleum revenues and that credit transactions be carried out either directly between the states concerned or through international multilateral financial institutions, but in either case without the intervention of "intermediate powers." Observers noted "the determination of OPEC countries to be masters of their own destiny and to hang on to their newly acquired financial elbow room."[63] This meeting was the first official attempt to develop some guidelines for capital transactions that would be broad enough to allow for national discretion, yet specific enough to enable coordinated action. Throughout the deliberations it became apparent that they all shared a common concern for more effective participation in the international monetary system.

The tone at the Algiers conference was not ideological. Much of the discussion centered around the Western recycling proposals and the worldwide economic effects of inflation in the industrialized states. The declining credit worthiness of some oil-consuming countries was regarded with alarm particularly in terms of impact on the value of OPEC oil revenues.[64]

Several specific suggestions were put forth as correctives to Western recycling proposals. These included: (1) prohibiting floating exchange rates for major currencies; (2) according developing countries an effective voice in decisions about currency valuation; and (3) increasing the voting rights of these countries in the International Monetary Fund and the World Bank to a 50 percent basis. These measures were then incorporated in an official OPEC statement issued in March 1975 outlining the organization's position on these issues and on its desired role in the world financial community.[65]

In sum, the oil-exporting countries were rejecting their traditional role of recipients in international exchanges. They were demanding greater participation in economic decisions and the financial power commensurate with their control of a critical resource.

Producer Options for Managing Surplus Revenues

Against this background, it is worth considering the options available to the oil-exporting states for managing their surplus oil revenues. These include (1) restricting production of petroleum, thus placing bounds on surplus revenues; (2) absorbing these revenues by increasing imports from the consuming countries; (3) investing in the industrial and financial sectors of Western economies; (4) seeking downstream investments in the consumer countries, and (5) investing in each other's economies. These options are not mutually exclusive, of course, and some oil-exporting countries have chosen a combination.

Restricting Petroleum Production

Cutbacks in oil production have already been adopted by almost all the members of OPEC. For some states cutbacks have been motivated by a concern for

Table 3-9
OPEC's Oil Production
(In Average Number of Barrels per Day)

	1973	1974	January 1975	March 1975
Abu Dhabi	1,300,000	1,414,000	819,000	1,154,380
Iran	5,800,000	6,021,000	5,543,000	5,547,380
Iraq	1,954,000	1,850,000	2.072,000	2,100,700
Kuwait	3,022,000	2,547,000	2,078,000	2,069,510
Libya	2,188,000	1,490,000	969,000	945,000
Nigeria	2,056,000	2,250,000	2,056,000	1,712,610
Qatar	570,000	518,000	514,000	429,220
Saudi Arabia	7,600,000	8,479,000	7,890,000	6,297,700
Venezuela	3,366,000	2,976,000	2,680,000	2,535,290

Sources: *The New York Times*, March 4, 1975, March 9, 1975, March 11, 1975, April 7, 1975; *The Petroleum Economist*, Vol. XVII, No. 6 (June 1975), p. 240.

preserving a scarce resource; for others by a concern for stabilizing petroleum prices; and for still others by a desire to conform to general OPEC directives. Table 3-9 illustrates OPEC oil cutbacks from 1973 to mid 1975. Clearly, actual output is only a fraction of production capacity.

Importing from the West

All of the oil exporting states have attempted to absorb some of their revenues by increasing their imports from the oil-consuming countries of the West. For example, Iran has signed an economic agreement with the United States committing itself to the purchase of $15 billion worth of American goods and services over the next five years.[66] Included were such items as nuclear plants, housing units, electronics, fertilizer plants, and the building of superhighways. According to Kissinger, "this is the largest agreement of this kind that has been signed by any two countries."[67]

A study prepared for the OECD in July 1975 presents an optimistic assessment of the anticipated development of OPEC balance of payments and expenditures on goods and services purchased from the West. Projections for the high absorbers (Algeria, Ecuador, Indonesia, Iran, Iraq, Nigeria, and Venezuela) and the low absorbers (the Gulf States, Kuwait, Libya, and Saudi Arabia) are noted in Table 3-10. These figures must be viewed as upper bounds and may well overestimate the import potential of OPEC countries.[68]

Investing in Western Economies

OPEC members have tended to concentrate largely on the European currency market, rather than on distinct national money markets, a policy guided by the desire to obtain high returns on short-term deposits and to protect their anonymity in foreign markets. The fact that consumer countries are clearly not prepared to accept mass foreign ownership of major enterprises reinforces the producing countries' concern for maintaining anonymity in their investments.[69] There are already signs of political problems ahead. For example, in September 1972 Saudi Arabia suggested to the United States that its exports to the United States be free of the oil import quota, in return for which the Saudis would make extensive investments in the United States.[70] This request was rejected. The encouragement given to OPEC investments in the United States has been cautious, limited largely to the purchase of United States government bonds.

Investing Downstream

Seeking downstream investments in consumer economics is a variant on the two foregoing options. So far, OPEC participation in downstream investments are of two kinds. In one case, the objective is involvement in downstream operations at home, while seeking to export refined products (Iran has followed this pattern). In the other, participation is in downstream investments abroad, directed primarily to the export of crude oil (Saudi Arabia has preferred this option). In principle, the latter approach could lead to substantial investments in the consumer countries, including investments in refining activities in the United States. In practice, however, such investments would hardly absorb Saudi Arabia's excess earnings, particularly if future returns on these investments are taken into account.[71]

Investing in Oil-rich Economies

The option of investing in each other's economies has been adopted by the major oil-exporters. In some cases, most notably Kuwait, this policy had been pursued well before the increases in oil prices of October 1973. As early as 1971, Kuwait is estimated to have provided at least $1 billion in grants, loans, and gifts to the other Arab countries.[i]

In the long run, domestic investments by the oil-exporting states in their own economies and in those of neighboring countries may conceivably have some

[i]See, Ragaei el-Mallakh, *Economic Development and Regional Cooperation: Kuwait* (Chicago: The University of Chicago Press, 1968), for a background on Kuwaiti disbursements.

Table 3-10
Possible Evolution of OPEC Current Balances
(Billion U.S. Dollars at 1974 Prices)

	1974	1975	1976	1977	1978	1979	1980
High absorbers							
Oil exports (f.o.b.)	56	52	53½	55	56½	58	59½
Other exports (f.o.b.)	4	4	4	4½	4½	5½	6
Imports (f.o.b.)	23½	34½	42	48	52½	56	59½
Trade balance	36½	21½	15½	11½	9	7½	6
Services and private transfers	–8½	–8	–7½	–8	–8½	–9½	–11
Official transfers	–½	–½	–½	0	0	0	0
Current balance	27½	13	7½	3½	½	–2	–5
Low absorbers							
Oil exports (f.o.b.)	53½	46½	48½	50	49½	48½	48
Other exports (f.o.b.)	1½	1½	2	2	2	2	2½
Imports (f.o.b.)	9½	13	14½	16	17	18	19
Trade balance	45½	35	36	36½	34½	32½	31½
Services and private transfers	–5	–1½	–½	½	2	2½	3½
Official transfers	–1	–1½	–2½	–3	–3½	–4	–4½
Current balance	39½	32	33	34	33	31	30½
Total OPEC current balance	67	45	40½	37½	33½	29	25½
Memorandum items:							
Additional investment income[a]							
High absorbers	1	4	4	3½	3½	3	2
Low absorbers	2	8	8½	10	12	12½	14

Growth of import volumes (percent)							
High absorbers	38	46	22	15	10	7	6½
Low absorbers	42	36	12	10	9	6	7
Cumulative OPEC current balance (from 1974)[b]	67	104½	137	165	186	204	215

Note: Detail may not add, due to rounding.

[a]Increase in investment income from the 1973 level.

[b]This is not the sum of OPEC current balances.

Source: International Monetary Fund, *IMF Survey*, Vol. 4, No. 15 (August 11, 1975), p. 231.

impact on the balance of payments of the consuming countries by generating goods produced locally that could compete with foreign imports or even be exported to foreign markets. In oil-rich countries with small populations, industrialization will give rise to an expanded export market that is not necessarily accompanied by an expansion of imports. Such a situation, while eventually ameliorating the recycling problem, could also provide the oil-exporting states with still other leverages in their interactions with the oil-importing countries of the West.[72]

So far, the members of OPEC have not yet developed concerted strategies for managing their surplus petroleum revenues. They differ on the extent to which they have opted for each of these five strategies and the extent to which their choices represent integrated policies rather than idiosyncratic responses to the management of their new riches.

Neither producers nor consumers have as yet developed coherent responses to the challenge of OPEC or to the new economic interdependencies generated by increases in oil prices. Both parties to the petroleum dispute are searching for ways of resolving their respective predicaments. There is an atmosphere of great uncertainty. Oil-exporters and oil-importers are both seeking to increase their control over petroleum-related transactions; yet, neither fully recognizes the constraints on national behavior posed by the structure of energy interdependence.

Notes

1. Parra, Ramos and Parra, *International Crude Oil and Product Prices, 15 October 1974* (Beirut: Middle East Petroleum and Economic Publications, 1974), p. 79.

2. Thomas R. Stauffer, "Oil Money and World Money: Conflict or Confluence?," *Science*, Vol. 184, No. 4134 (April 19, 1974), p. 321.

3. Ibid., p. 322.

4. Ibid.

5. See, M.A. Adelman, "Is the Oil Shortage Real?" *Middle East Information Series*, Vol. 24 (May 1973), and James Akins, "The Oil Crisis: This Time the Wolf is Here," *Foreign Affairs*, Vol. 51 (April 1973), pp. 462-490, for the polar views.

6. U.S., Congress, House, Committee on Foreign Affairs, Subcommittee on Foreign Economic Policy, *Hearings, Foreign Policy Implications of the Energy Crisis*, 92nd Cong., 2nd sess., 1972, pp. 414-415 (Statement by M.A. Adelman).

7. Gerald A. Pollack, "The Economic Consequences of the Energy Crisis," *Foreign Affairs*, Vol. 52, No. 3 (April 1974), p. 453.

8. See, Sam H. Schurr and Paul T. Homan, *Middle Eastern Oil and the Western World: Prospects and Problems* (New York: American Elsevier Publishing Company, Inc., 1971).

9. U.S., Congress, House, Subcommittee on Foreign Economic Policy, *Hearings, Foreign Policy Implications of the Energy Crisis*, p. 215 (Statement by Representative Lester Wolff).

10. U.S., Congress, House Subcommittee on Foreign Economic Policy, *Hearings, Foreign Policy Implications of the Energy Crisis*, p. 234 (Statement by John A. Winger).

11. U.S., Congress, House, Subcommittee on Foreign Economic Policy, *Hearings, Foreign Policy Implications of the Energy Crisis* p. 5 (Statement by Joel Darmstadter).

12. *The New York Times*, January 28, 31, 1975.

13. M.S. Mendelsohn, "World Money—What is Not Happening, and Why," *Euromoney* (May 1974), p. 32; see also, Stauffer, "Oil Money and World Money," p. 323; see also, Table 3-2.

14. Pedro-Pablo Kuczynski, "The Effects of the Rise in Oil Prices on the Third World," *Euromoney* (May 1974), p. 37.

15. Richard N. Cooper, "The Invasion of the Petrodollar," *Saturday Review* (January 25, 1975), pp. 10-13; see also, Jack E. Hartshorn, "A Diplomatic Price for Oil," *Pacific Community*, Vol. 5, No. 3 (April 1974), pp. 363-379; Walter J. Levy, "World Oil Cooperation or International Chaos," *Foreign Affairs*, Vol. 52, No. 4 (July 1974), pp. 690-713.

16. *The New York Times*, December 11, 1974.

17. Statement of the Honorable William E. Simon, Secretary of the Treasury, before the Subcommittee on Financial Markets of the Senate Finance Committee, Washington, D.C., January 30, 1975, Department of the Treasury, *News*, January 30, 1975; Remarks of the Honorable Gerald L. Parsky, Assistant Secretary of the Treasury, before the Investment Association of New York, at the Bankers Club, New York, New York, January 14, 1975, "Recycling of Oil Revenues and the Role of U.S. Capital Markets," Department of the Treasury, *News*, January 14, 1975.

18. International Monetary Fund, *IMF Survey*, Vol. 4, No. 2 (January 20, 1975), p. 30.

19. Pollack, "Economic Consequences of the Energy Crisis," p. 461.

20. Stauffer, "Oil Money and World Money," p. 323.

21. Ibid., p. 324.

22. U.S., General Accounting Office, *Issues Related to Foreign Sources of Oil for the United States*, Report B-179411, January 23, 1974, p. 55.

23. G.V. Subba Rao, "The Predicament of Developing Countries," *Saturday Review* (January 25, 1975), p. 18.

24. International Monetary Fund, *IMF Survey*, "Higher Oil Import Bills Cut Back Real Income and Terms of Trade of Poorer Nations," Vol. 4, No. 3 (February 3, 1975), p. 39.

25. Ibid.

26. International Monetary Fund, *IMF Survey*, Vol. 4, No. 9 (May 12, 1975), p. 141.

27. International Monetary Fund, "Financial Assistance from Oil Exporting Countries to Developing Countries," May 8, 1975 (mimeographed).

28. *The New York Times*, January 5, 1975.

29. *The New York Times*, February 3, 1975.

30. International Monetary Fund, *IMF Survey*, Vol. 4, No. 10 (May 26, 1975), p. 160.

31. International Monetary Fund, *International Financial Statistics* December 1973); U.S. Department of Commerce, *U.S. Exports*, FT455/1972 (1972).

32. Ibid.

33. *The New York Times*, January 31, 1975; International Monetary Fund, *IMF Survey*, Vol. 4, No. 5 (March 10, 1975), p. 80.

34. Stauffer, "Oil Money and World Money," p. 323.

35. U.S., Congress, Senate, Committee on Interior and Insular Affairs, *Hearings, Oil and Gas Imports Issues*, 93rd Cong., 1st sess., 1973, p. 524 (Statement by William Letson).

36. Minos Zombanakis, "Arab Funds and the Markets," *The Banker*, Vol. 124, No. 581 (July 1974), p. 751; *The New York Times*, November 14, 1974.

37. U.S., Congress, House, Subcommittee on Foreign Economic Policy, *Hearings, Foreign Policy Implications of the Energy Crisis*, p. 162 (Statement by Robert Hunter).

38. Stauffer, "Oil Money and World Money," p. 323.

39. See the speech by U.S. Secretary of State Henry Kissinger, in Chicago, November 14, 1974, in *The Department of State Bulletin*, Vol. 71, No. 1849 (December 2, 1974), pp. 749-755.

40. Ibid., p. 753.

41. Ibid.., p. 754.

42. Ibid.

43. *The New York Times*, October 21, 1974.

44. Kissinger, *The Department of State Bulletin*, p. 755.

45. See, the text of the speech of Johannes Witteveen, Managing Director of the IMF in the *Middle Eastern Economic Survey*, Vol. XVII, No. 14 (January 25, 1974), pp. 1-7.

46. "Fund Policies and Procedures in Relation to the Compensatory Financing of Commodity Fluctuations," *IMF Staff Papers*, Volume 18, 1960, pp. 3-4.

47. International Monetary Fund, *IMF Survey*, Vol. 4, No. 7 (April 14, 1975), p. 108.

48. Highlights from the speech of OECD's Secretary General, Emile van Lennep, to the Consultative Assembly of the Council of Europe, 23rd January 1974, "Consequences of the Oil Price Rise: The Need for International Action," *OECD Observer*, No. 68 (February 1974).

49. *OECD Observer*, No. 74 (March/April 1975), pp. 9-13.

50. Ibid., p. 9.

51. Ibid., p. 10.

52. Kleinman, "Oil Money and the Third World," p. 1064.

53. Khodadad Farmanfarmaian, Armin Gutowski, Saburo Okita, Robert V. Roosa, and Carroll L. Wilson, "How Can the World Afford OPEC Oil?" *Foreign Affairs*, Vol. 53, No. 2 (January 1975), pp. 201-222.

54. President Boumediene of Algeria in an interview with *Le Monde* on 5 February 1974, in *Middle East Economic Survey*, Vol. 17, No. 16 (8 February 1974), p. ix.

55. Dr. Ali A. Attiga, "The Role of OAPEC in Promoting Cooperation Between its Members and Oil Importing Countries," *Middle East Economic Survey*, Vol. 17, No. 30 (17 May 1974), p. 6.

56. Shaikh Zaki Yamani, "Producer-Consumer Relationships in the Oil Industry: A New Era," *Middle East Economic Survey*, Vol. 17. No. 30 (17 May 1974), pp. 4-5.

57. Henry Kissinger, Speech to the Sixth Special Session of the United Nations General Assembly devoted to Problems of Raw Materials and Development, *Middle East Economic Survey*, Vol. 17, No. 26 (19 April 1974), p. 10.

58. Mahmoud Hasseni, "$600 Billion Hold-up Plan," *Kayhan International*, January 18, 1975.

59. Ibid.

60. Ibid.

61. President Boumediene of Algeria in an interview with the Beirut daily *al-Nahar* on 19 October 1974, in the *Middle East Economic Survey*, Vol. 18, No. 1 (25 October 1974), p. 5.

62. *Middle East Economic Survey*, Vol. 18, No. 15 (31 January 1975), p. 1.

63. Omar Kassem, "The Attitude of the Oil States to Recycling and the U.S.," *Euromoney* (March 1975), p. 14.

64. Fereidun Fesharaki, "The Petrodollar Myth," *Kayhan International*, January 18, 1975.

65. *The New York Times*, April 1, 1975.

66. *The New York Times*, March 5, 1975.

67. *The New York Times*, March 5, 1975.

68. International Monetary Fund, *IMF Survey*, Vol. 4, No. 15 (August 11, 1975), p. 230.

69. Pollack, "Economic Consequences of the Energy Crisis," pp. 458-459.

70. U.S., Congress, Senate, Committee on Interior and Insular Affairs, *Hearings, Oil and Gas Imports Issues*, p. 1073 (Statement by M.A. Adelman).

71. See, Yusuf J. Ahmad, *Oil Revenues in the Gulf: A Preliminary Estimate of Absorptive Capacity* (Paris: OECD, 1974), pp. 122-150; see also, Joseph A. Yager and Eleanor B. Steinberg, *Energy and U.S. Foreign Policy* (Cambridge: Ballinger Publishing Company, 1974), pp. 277-310.

72. Pollack, "Economic Consequences of the Energy Crisis," p. 456.

4 Politics in the Middle East: Conflict and Convergence

Current debates on recycling proposals ignore the political implications of various arrangements.[a] Insufficient recognition is given to the political pressures upon the oil-exporting countries themselves. This chapter examines recent political changes in the Middle East and the implications of these changes for petroleum politics. The primary emphasis is upon the Arab states and Iran. However, the policies of the oil-rich countries cannot be divorced from Middle East politics in general, and their economic policies are both shaped and constrained by political objectives.

Political Conflicts

Ninety percent of OPEC's petroleum reserves are located in the Middle East, where three sets of political conflicts converge and provide important influences on the development of petroleum policies. These are (1) the superpower competition between the United States and the USSR; (2) the conflict between the Arab states and Israel; (3) and inter-Arab conflicts. Each conflict influences the postures of the oil-exporting states in their disputes with the consumers and their responses to various plans for recycling surplus oil revenues. In the last analysis, economic influences may well be overshadowed by political calculations.

Although the cold war has now lost much of its earlier momentum, the United States and USSR presence in the Middle East serve as grim reminders of the continuing political conflict between the superpowers. Memories of the Dulles diplomacy die hard. From the perspective of the oil-producing countries, their dispute with the oil-consumers cannot be wholly divorced from the now relatively subdued cold war.

The conflict between Israel and the Arab states is only one step removed from the cold war. Indeed, the Arabs frequently attribute the extension of the superpower politics in their region as a consequence of the creation of the new state. Israel's immediate adversaries—Egypt, Jordan, and Syria—are not oil-exporters, but they have always been instrumental in shaping inter-Arab policies and will influence the policies of their neighbors, particularly in light of the revenues needed to support any future war effort.

But it is the conflicts emerging from inter-Arab politics that will bear most

[a]This chapter is written with the collaboration of Ijaz Gilani.

directly on producer-consumer relations: First, the greater the political cohesion among the Arab states, the more likely it is that a united policy on oil price and production will persist. Second, the greater the cohesion among the Arab states, the more likely it is that investments of oil revenues will be directed toward the Middle East, thereby possibly reinforcing this cohesion. Clearly, the Organization of Arab Petroleum Exporting Countries (OAPEC) cannot unilaterally dictate the policies of OPEC, but its cohesion is essential to the survival of the larger organization. The Arab countries have traditionally found it difficult to reconcile their divergent perspectives and priorities in any collaborative effort. The more radical states have opposed the United States presence in the Middle East and its support for Israel. The more conservative states have opposed Israel, but have been more accommodating to the United States presence. All oppose a permanent Soviet presence, yet some, like Syria and Iraq, acknowledge it as an important element in their attempt to cope with the complexities of modernization and with their military inferiority vis-à-vis Israel.

There is still another source of volatility in Middle East politics, namely, the relationship between Iran and the Arab states. The more tense this relationship, the more difficult it will be for the oil-exporting countries to develop viable pricing and production policies. Indeed, Iran is closely tied to the cold war, hosting United States bases and making extensive weapon purchases from the United States and Western Europe. It will influence inter-Arab politics to the extent that it is perceived as posing a military threat to Saudi Arabia or to other states in the Gulf.

Iran's strength in the Gulf area is being viewed with increasing apprehension by the Saudis who possess neither the manpower nor the military skills to engage in any confrontation. United States weapons sales to Saudi Arabia interject yet another cold war dimension in regional politics by alienating Syria and Iraq, both of whom are supplied militarily by the USSR. These sales also link disputes over military power in the Gulf to United States calculations for forestalling the development of Soviet naval power in the Indian Ocean and ensuring Israel's military security. Some analysts even argue that Iran is emerging as the guarantor of these objectives.[b] Its increasing military strength will present the Soviets with a credible strategic deterrent; and its traditional support for Israel will provide the United States with assurances that, in the last analysis, Iran's capabilities could be used to guarantee Israel's security. These two objectives become increasingly viable as Iran emerges as the dominant military power in the area, and by some calculations, surpassing even Israel in military hardware. Given the manpower base of the country and its level of technological sophistication, such assessments are not implausible.

---

[b]Rouhollah K. Ramazani, "Emerging Patterns of Regional Relations in Iranian Foreign Policy," 1974 (mimeographed); see also, Shahram Chubin, "Iran Between the Arab West and the Asian East," *Survival*, Vol. 16, No. 4 (July/August 1974), pp. 172-182; see also, *The New York Times*, January 5, 8, 9, 10, 12, 13, 1975, for accounts of the Shah's visit to Egypt.

So far, both Saudi Arabia and Iran have tried to protect the cohesion of OPEC. And so far, at least, power politics in the Gulf has not shaken their new collaboration. Further, Iran's relations with the other Arab states have improved considerably over the past year, as reflected in Iran's growing investments in the region. Iran's role in OPEC is unquestionably great, but the key to cohesion among the oil-exporting states is to be found in the nature of politics among the Arabs.

New Directions in Arab Politics

It is difficult to separate the history of the Arabs from that of the Turks. The Ottoman Empire's control for four centuries over people who considered themselves Arab tended to blur the distinction between the two. The Arab revolt of 1916 against Ottoman rule marks the first overt act of Arab nationalism in the twentieth century. The leaders of the revolt had expected British support for an Arab political entity, but it did not materialize. During the interwar period, several abortive plans for unity were put forth, many of which were conceived in terms of political unification.

The League of Arab States was formed in March 1945 and constituted an initial, limited, but institutionalized means of cooperation among the newly independent Arab states. The league's headquarters are in Cairo and Egypt's influence on all league activities has always been pervasive. The league has no formal power over its members—they are bound only by those resolutions for which they have voted—and serves mainly as a formal means of communication to present a united front toward the outside world. The league has drafted many plans for Arab cooperation in economic, technical, and military issues with some limited success, but none of its ambitious schemes for formal unification have gained any ground nor has it been able to prevent frequent inter-Arab conflicts. Numerous complaints have been raised against the political power of Egypt by the other Arab states, yet Cairo's influence has remained strong. Nonetheless, the member states have tended to value the importance of the league in providing a common political front for working toward regional cooperation.

The formation of United Arab Republic (U.A.R.) in 1958 represented the first official attempt toward unification. Its short life illustrated again the inappropriateness of political integration as a base for community building in the Middle East. The initiative for union came from Syria. Egypt sought political coordination with a dominating influence. Fear of a Communist take-over in Syria precipitated a Syrian acceptance of Egypt's conditions for unifications. The U.A.R. was patterned according to the polity in Cairo with representative institutions possessing very limited powers. Political parties in Syria were disbanded and the country's long tradition of competitive politics was suppressed by an Egyptian style of administration. The experience aroused bitterness and opposition in Syria. The army officers who had supported unity with Egypt in 1958 began strong opposition and, three years later, a movement for secession took place. Egypt opposed the move. The conflict led to a serious crisis in the Arab League. Relations between the two countries improved from 1962 onward, but official diplomatic ties were not resumed until 1966. A new defense treaty was also signed, marking the end of an episode that everyone eventually came to recognize as having been unfortunate. But inter-Arab conflicts did not cease.

The years following the breakup of the first Arab Republic often witnessed bitter diplomatic and in some cases military confrontation between competing Arab states. The frequent summit meetings during this period illustrate the nature of these conflicts and the persistence of disagreement.

The first important summit meeting was held in Cairo in 1964 when the U.A.R. and Jordan resumed diplomatic ties following a bitter dispute. The Arab states agreed to set up a joint military command in the event of war with Israel. Some progress was made on joint Arab use of the Jordan River. Despite an air of harmony, disagreements persisted. The next meeting was also held in Cairo during the same year, convened largely to deal with the Saudi-Egyptian conflict over Yemen. No resolution ensued. During the following year, the Arab leaders met in Casablanca. It was boycotted by Tunisia in protest against Egypt's domination of the Arab League. Three years later, the Arab leaders met in Khartoum. Two issues were considered: First, Iraq proposed to halt oil production for three months (September to November) as a means of applying pressure on the West in protest against Israel's occupation of Arab territory in June of that year. This move was supported by Algeria, and opposed by Saudi Arabia, Kuwait, and Libya. Second, the prospects for a cease-fire in Yemen were discussed. Saudi Arabia and Egypt could not agree. This conference ended, as did the others, on a note of discontent and persistent conflict.

In 1969 a summit meeting of the 14 Arab states was held in Rabat, Morocco, in the effort to achieve some minimal agreement over attendant differences. The conference ended in a dispute over the refusal by Saudi Arabia and Kuwait to increase their financial contributions for strengthening Arab forces in their conflict with Israel. President Nasser walked out of the meeting after rebuking Saudi Arabia's King Faisal and Kuwaiti ruler Sheikh Sabah al-Salem al Sabah for rejecting demands for financial assistance. Syria, Iraq, and Southern Yemen boycotted the ceremony closing the meeting in protest against the Saudi and Kuwait decisions. The conference was hastily adjourned; no communique was issued.[1]

The summit meeting of September 1973 between Egypt's President Sadat, Jordan's King Hussein, and Syria's President Assad revealed new political directives in regional politics. Egypt announced resumption of diplomatic relations with Jordan. Syria also mended its dispute with Jordan and with Egypt. The conference terminated on a rare note of cooperation.[2] In October of that year, Tunisia and Algeria also resumed diplomatic relations with Jordan and endorsed Hussein's decision to send military support to Syria.[3]

In retrospect, it appears that Sadat's strategy of reassessing Egypt's regional role involved first, improving the country's relations with each of the other Arab states; second, persuading them of the new constraints on Egypt's policies and of the country's concern for concentrating on domestic problems once the conflict with Israel had been reduced to some acceptable level; and third, establishing a basis of cooperation among the Arab states that would allow for concerted action in the event of another war with Israel. Sadat sought to convince the other Arab leaders that Egypt's objectives in this conflict were limited, that they revolved around regaining control over lost territory, and that it was not regarded as a vehicle for extending Egyptian domination over the other Arab states. For the first time in their history, the Arab states presented Israel with a relatively united front.

Wars with Israel

The war with Israel in 1967 was an important landmark in the development of regional community in the Middle East. The devastating defeat was a humiliation shared by all the Arabs. Its most dramatic consequence was a reassessment of the basis of inter-Arab politics and the development of a more realistic view of the possibilities for, and types of, cooperation in the area. This new sense of pragmatism provided much of the background for present attempts to develop viable policies toward petroleum prices and production. Increasingly, the Arab oil-exporters realized that such policies cannot be made on economic grounds alone, but that the political objectives and aspirations of all Arab countries—resource-rich as well as resource-poor—must also be taken into account. It is this realization that makes the petroleum issue assume political significance in the Middle East that transcends its purely economic implications.

The 1967 war proved to be an enormous burden on the Egyptian economy, severely shook Egypt's traditional role as leader of the Arab states, and destroyed the belief in Nasser's Arab revolution. Egypt had now become financially dependent upon the resources of the oil-rich and politically conservative Arab states. The country's economic plight necessitated extensive financial assistance. The deterioration of diplomatic relations with the West made it difficult to turn to either the United States or Western Europe. Increasing military dependence upon the USSR and its allies had resulted in an extensive financial debt. The oil-rich Arab states were in a position to assist Egypt—but at a price. The price was a political one. Concessions on the part of Egypt and a willingness to reassess its dominating political posture in the region were rendered in exchange for economic support. Most of this support came from Saudi Arabia. In addition, underlying differentials between the two countries—in population and technology—provided some added rationale for Saudi Arabia's willingness to replace the loss of revenues from the Suez Canal, which now lay under Israeli occupation. Egypt could supply the oil-rich states with skilled manpower and its superior technology could be employed to compensate for their lack of skilled labor. The Egyptians, in effect, agreed to reevaluate their regional as well as international policies in return for specific economic benefits. The acquisition of these benefits entailed economic dependence on others. But this time the dependence was upon other Arab states.

One notable outcome of the 1967 war and of the Egyptian concessions was the relative depoliticization of community-building efforts in the Arab world. The old symbolisms of political unity now appeared singularly incongruous with the events of the recent years. Nasser had insisted on symbolic politics and reinforced the Arab tradition of rhetoric in public discourse. Both the rhetoric and the accompanying politics were resented, and in some cases actively opposed, by the more conservative Arab states. The death of Nasser effectively removed the most serious impediment to such depoliticization and the common defeat at the hands of the Israelis left none of the Arab leaders any traditional prestige to protect or fight for. The old ideological conflicts had lost their meaning, and certainly their salience. Israel had defeated Nasserite Egypt, Ba'athist Syria, and Hashimite Jordan—all with equal ease. Differences among them regarding preferred postures toward the Israeli threat now seemed singularly irrelevant. They all suffered loss of territory. The Israeli presence had acquired a reality that far transcended any one's expectations during the first days of June 1967 when Nasser threatened to mine the Straits of Elat and close the passage to Israeli shipping. The bluff proved to be costly.

A new basis of concensus that developed following the 1967 war was by no means complete. The war of October 1973 was a military success for the Arab states. Political gains had also occurred. They had shaken the belief in Israel's military invincibility and questioned the stereotype of the backward, incompetent, tent-dwelling, ignorant Arab. These attainments provided the basis for greater cohesion and reaffirmed the need for a more pragmatic posture on the issue of Israel. It is revealing to note, for example, that none of the official communiques issued from Cairo during the October war included any reference to the "destruction" of Israel. The emphasis was on regaining Egyptian territory.

The collaboration in October had become functionally specific. Different Arab countries made contributions toward a unified strategy in some areas but withheld their cooperation in others. For example, Iraq collaborated in the military sphere by sending troops to the Syrian front but refused to participate in the oil embargo, a somewhat uncharacteristic decision for an avowedly radical state. Libya assisted the Egyptians financially but withheld support of Egypt's policy of moderation toward Israel. Saudi Arabia and Kuwait assumed leadership of the oil embargo but made no contribution to the military confrontation. Algeria, Morocco, and Tunisia gave complete political support to the states bordering Israel but only symbolic military assistance.

Such selected and functionally specific cooperation reflects the evolving pragmatic approach to Arab politics. It also reflects different political interpretations of national interest. Although this procedure prevented a complete coherence of policies, it reaffirmed the new distribution of power in the area and the development of substantial, yet selective, cooperation.

Israel and Petroleum Politics

No one can dispute the centrality of Israel in Arab politics. Less well understood, however, is the relationship of the conflict with Israel to the cohesion of OPEC. Israel undoubtedly serves as a unifying focus for inter-Arab conflicts. However, the Arab-Israeli dispute by itself cannot explain the price increases of October 1973 nor the ability of the oil-exporting states—Arab as well as non-Arab—to maintain a unified posture on petroleum prices.

The 1973 war was obviously a catalyst, triggering a set of events in the Middle East and elsewhere that have transformed the world petroleum market. But the background conditions for this catalyst to be effective had been developing over time. Two different developments converged in 1973, leading to the embargo and the attendant increases in petroleum prices.

The first set of developments relate to changing power relations between the international oil companies and the oil-exporting states, described briefly in Chapter 2. We noted how the early success of the oil companies in controlling the policies of the national governments, as they pertained to price and production schedules, gave way to a situation in which the governments were able to make demands upon the oil companies and to withstand the pressures brought to bear by the international oil industry. The stories of Iran in 1953, Iraq in 1961, and Libya in 1970 represent the changing power relations in petroleum politics. The success of the Libyan move in 1970 persuaded OPEC of the companies' weakening position, and the changes in the world petroleum market reinforced their ability to pressure the companies for substantial economic concessions.

The second set of developments pertained exclusively to inter-Arab politics. The series of military defeats by the Israelis reinforced the Arabs' sense of grievances against the West as well. At the same time, they gradually realized that some pragmatic moves were necessary if the stalemate following the latest defeat of 1967 were to be shaken. To the Arab states, it seemed plausible to believe that stalemate favored Israel, and that the longer the occupation of Arab territories persisted, the more likely it would be that these territories would be annexed by the Jewish state. The settlements on the Golan Heights and on the West banks accentuated these fears. Coordinated action was deemed as necessary. Yet, previous efforts at coordination had been singularly unsuccessful.

Cooperation was necessary, so the Arabs realized. But also important was the need to find some ways of persuading the West to pressure Israel into adopting a more conciliatory posture vis-à-vis the occupation of territories acquired in 1967. So far neither the United States nor the European countries appeared disposed to use their influence with Israel for resolving what the Arabs considered to be a central predicament.

Petroleum was the logical weapon to use. But the Arabs had tried to wield it in 1967, with no success. What assurances did they have that this time the use of a political instrument could be at all effective?

Changes in the power relationships between the international oil companies and the oil-exporting states, increases in the oil consumption of the Western countries over the past five years, increasing Western reliance on Middle East petroleum, and the success of the Libyans in gaining the initial concessions that transformed company-country relationships—all contributed to the general assessment on the part of the Arab oil-exporting countries that the use of petroleum as a political instrument could be effective if it were integrated in a broader strategy for shaking the stalemate of 1967.

Little is known about the development of this rationale or the policy debates that eventually led to the Egyptian crossing of the canal on October 6, 1973. The record of the periodic summit conferences since 1967 indicated a change in political orientation and in established patterns of political interactions among the Arab states. But few clear indications of impending developments were apparent.

The convergence of the two sets of developments noted above, with the integration of petroleum as a political instrument within a broader strategy involving military action, constitutes the essence of the story of October 1973. In this context, the conflict with Israel can be viewed as a multiplier effect upon an already changing situation. It was the catalyst, a sufficient condition for embargo and for the subsequent political and diplomatic moves. It may even have been a necessary condition for the initial increases in petroleum prices. But it was only one, albeit a major, factor in the sequence of events that eventually led to both embargo and a rise in the price of crude oil.

In short, it is important to distinguish between the role of Israel in Middle East politics and in petroleum politics more generally. The issue of Israel is, of course, central in inter-Arab politics. It is important, but not primary, in determining the course of events that led to fundamental changes in the power relationships between the oil-exporting nations and the oil-importing nations. The interconnections between the cold war on the one hand, and the Arab-Israel conflict on the other, tend to reaffirm the role of Israel in petroleum politics, but Israel can be accorded neither sole credit nor central responsibility for the cohesion of the oil-exporting states.

The use of petroleum as a political instrument represents most dramatically the development of pragmatic politics in the Arab states. The oil-rich countries had long been aware of the importance of their key resource, but they had not been able to make use of it for political purposes. The 1973 war and the events surrounding the oil embargo represented most clearly their use of economic instruments for attaining political objectives.

Policy Changes and the Division of Power

The development of pragmatic politics in the Arab world must also be placed within the context of changing political orientations. Arab states still differ substantially on the definition of the central goals of the broader community as they do with regard to their own individual objectives. Countries like Saudi Arabia, and other countries in the Gulf area, are concerned mainly with preserving traditional values in an era of accelerated social change. Egypt, Algeria, Tunisia, and Lebanon have placed economic development at the forefront of their national priorities. Still others, Syria, Iraq, and Jordan, despite impressive economic advances, are motivated primarily by security considerations. Libya and the Palestine Liberation Organization (PLO) have as their primary goal the establishment of the Palestinian identity separate from, and independent of, that of the other Arab states.

Nowhere is the transformation in political orientation more apparent than in the case of Saudi Arabia. When King Faisal came to power the country's finances were in poor condition. By the late 1960s the Saudi economy was reorganized and its resources managed more securely. The war in Yemen had placed a drain upon the country's finances. However, as the price of petroleum was raised, revenues rose dramatically. Saudi Arabia controlled resources of such magnitude that it could readily subsidize the war effort in Jordan and Egypt. By 1973 it had assumed a pivotal role in petroleum policies and the country was now wielding the political power that was congruent with its economic role, and certainly with its traditional role as the spiritual leader of the Arab world. On all three counts, it was encouraged by the other Arab states. Saudi Arabia's close relations with the United States may have been instrumental in enabling it to obtain the support of other Arabs for a posture of moderation in regional politics. As a result of these developments, the Saudis were no longer viewed by the other Arab states as peripheral to regional politics. Saudi Arabia emerged by means of its subsidies and by common consensus as the new economic power of the region. Its dominant role in the formation of the Organization of Arab Petroleum Exporting Countries in 1968 reinforced its new position of economic leadership.

Unlike the tribal desert society of Saudi Arabia, Egypt had entered the post-1945 era with the heritage of sophisticated, old civilization and an effective modernization experience under British rule. Its bureaucratic and institutional capabilities were far more developed than the other Arab countries, and for a long time it had the only university in the region. Its population and relatively advanced technology had contributed to its position of leadership in the Arab world. But the 1960s witnessed a steady decline in Egypt's regional power. The breakdown of the United Arab Republic, the apparent ineffectiveness of its socialist policies, and the war in Yemen had all contributed to the weakening of its position. The 1967 war simply reaffirmed the loss of power and prestige. The change of name, from the U.A.R. to the Arab Republic of Egypt, signalled a change in policy and symbolized the limited scope of the country's regional objectives. The new leadership recognized its dependence on other Arab leaders. Sadat systematically sought to reconcile Egypt's relations with both the radical and the conservative states in the area. By the end of September 1973 Egypt had improved its relations with all the Arab countries. As a result of Sadat's actions the Arab community now presented a posture of loose consensus and collaboration. In changing its role of a hegemonial power to an interdependent one, Egypt explicitly recognized the importance of the differences in attributes and capabilities that characterized the Arab regimes and sought to draw upon these variations in developing a unified posture toward Israel. The war of 1973 showed the results of coordinated action not by dependence or domination but by cooperation among interdependent polities. Egypt essentially abandoned its revolutionary policies and relinquished its pivotal position in the politics of the Arab world, partly because of its dependence on subsidies from the oil-exporting countries, but largely because of the new pragmatic orientation of the Sadat government.

In Algeria political changes over the past five years have also been dramatic. The country's long war of independence against French colonial rule had given rise to a revolutionary regime, seeking leadership of the Arab world. But the men who had overthrown Ben Bella in 1964 redirected the country's goals and objectives from revolution toward development and growth. They increased their level of technical knowledge and skills and improved their management of the nation's oil industry. Throughout, they were remarkably successful in maintaining close ties with France. Equally remarkable was their ability to develop ways of exporting unskilled labor to France, thereby increasing their interdependence with the former colonial regime. During the 1973 oil embargo it was the oil minister of Algeria who accompanied the Saudi oil minister on his tour to the consumer capitals. The Algerian oil minister symbolized the Arab countries' capabilities of increasing their own technical expertise without total reliance upon the West. Belad of Algeria and Yamani of Saudi Arabia were poles apart on political orientations and preferences. But they represented the new Arab technocrats; political differences became less important as recognition of the need for coordinated policies increased. Under the leadership of President Boumediene, Algeria became the new technocratic leader of the Middle East, rejecting the old revolutionary posture of the early days of independence.

Kuwait also assumed a technological role and took the position of the new research and development center of the area. The country supported major research enterprises both domestically and in other parts of the Middle East, and drew upon the skilled manpower of the more populated, but resource-poor, states to staff an emerging industrial and scientific center in the Middle East.

Libya had traditionally remained on the periphery of inter-Arab politics, and the conservative monarchy espoused politically reactionary values. The revolution of 1970 changed this situation. The radicalism of Colonel Khaddafi's regime had been accompanied by economic gains for Libya. Indeed, it was Libya that had precipitated the increases in petroleum prices by unilateral action in 1970. But rather than concentrating on economic development, Khadaffi focused on political symbolism. Large oil revenues were employed to subsidize a variety of radical causes. Thus, while Egypt moved away from the politics of symbolic appeal, Libya assumed a position of leadership on that issue. The new government in Libya was religiously fundamental with a staunch opposition to communism. Opposition to the traditional order of King Idris extended to a notable suspicion of Saudi Arabia and the other conservative states. Libya espoused the Palestinian cause at about the time Egypt began to adopt a more pragmatic perspective on a dispute that had now become one over miles of national territory.

In Syria, too, a policy change was taking place. The country's marked concern for national security emerged directly from its colonial heritage. Historically Syria had consisted of the entire Fertile Crescent, with Damascus and Baghdad as key metropolitical centers. Syria was at the forefront of the rebellion against Ottoman rule. At the close of World War I the Arabs of the Fertile Crescent had found themselves divided into three separate protectorates: Iraq and Transjordan went to the British; Syria was given to the French. Of all the Arab lands, the Fertile Crescent had not retained a political entity congruent with its geographical bounds. The other countries had been more fortunate. Despite these developments, Syria had maintained the intellectual leadership of the Arab nationalist movement attained since the rise of Ba'ath party, a radical, Pan-Arab organization with well formulated doctrines of socialism, focusing on anti-capitalism, anti-imperialism, and anti-Zionism.

The Ba'ath concept of unity was considerably more sophisticated than Nasser's populism. The Syrians have always found it difficult to adjust to the Egyptian definition of Arab unity and opposed Nasser's insistence on the dissolution of political parties in Syria during the brief union with Egypt. The defeat of 1967 further accentuated the country's concern for security and accounts for the relatively intransigent stance on the issue of Israel. But the procedure for the disengagement of Syrian and Israeli troops following the 1973 war was an important landmark and indicates a major change in Syria's foreign policy. There, too, a distinctly pragmatic approach to Arab problems was emerging.

The Palestinians, also, have assumed a new role in the Middle East. Their political successes derive from the failure of the Arab states in the conflict with

Israel. They had been relatively effective on their own in the 1930's when they opposed British plans for Palestine. After World War II the Arab states took over the cause of the Palestinians. Following the defeat of 1967, the Palestinian leadership espoused a national cause distinct from the broader issue of Arab unity. The Arab governments accepted Yasir Arafat as the legitimate leader of the entire Palestinian movement. The observer status accorded the PLO at the United Nations extends the legitimacy of this organization far beyond the confines of regional politics.[4] The PLO espoused a dramatic cause whose reality needed no confirmation in the Arab world. Ideological fervor, moral outrage, and belief in a just cause fueled the Palestinian movement, which even the military strength of Israel could not dampen.

In sum, fundamental changes in domestic and regional politics in the Middle East contributed to the dispersion of power in the area. The political realities of the mid-1970's were fundamentally different from those one decade earlier. Dramatic transformations were in the process of taking place and old cleavages were being reassessed. New lines of political discourse were emerging. Opposition to Israel was no longer the major political concern of each state. Regional preoccupations centered increasingly around Arab development, and not around hostility toward the Jewish state.

Critical Differentials in the Middle East

Recent efforts by the Arab states to use their differences in population, resources, and technology for political purposes contributed further to political changes in the region. The political implications of differentials among the Arabs have not been sufficiently appreciated in the West. These differences are now defining major policy imperatives in the Middle East.

The differences in population are indeed formidable. The populations of the Middle East states range from about 37 million in Egypt to one million in Kuwait, and even lower in the neighboring principalities. Iran and Turkey are the second most populous states, followed by the Sudan and the Maghreb countries. The highest rates of population growth are found in the Arabian Peninsula where the annual rate of increase is about 8 percent per year in Kuwait (much of which is accounted for by immigration); in Qatar, 7.3 percent; and in Trucial Oman, 5.3 percent. In North Africa the highest rates of growth are reported in Libya (with a population of about 4 million) and the lowest in Egypt and Tunisia, both averaging around 2 to 2.3 percent per year. The smallest states are growing more rapidly; the largest states have a lower rate of growth (see Table 4-1).

Marked differences in resources reinforce the differences in population. Generally, the oil-rich countries are those with the smallest populations and, accordingly, those with the least need for earning revenues from petroleum sales.

Differentials in knowledge and skills are even more striking. The most populated and resource-poor countries are also the most technologically advanced; the resource-rich countries are those with the lowest population and the greatest demand for skilled manpower. Egypt is by far the most developed; it has the largest population in the region, yet the greatest needs for resources; its petroleum production barely covers domestic consumption. Lebanon and Jordan are also comparatively skilled, but neither produces any oil. Kuwait, Saudi Arabia, and the Emirates are the most resource-rich, have the lowest populations and are the most in need of technical skills. These imbalances have contributed to large-scale movements of skilled manpower—from the countries with high populations but low resources to those with high resources and low populations. Over half the population of Kuwait is drawn from neighboring states and well over 70 percent of the labor force are noncitizens. Similarly, educated Egyptians, Lebanese, Jordanians, and Palestinians find employment in the oil states. Such population movements may be contributing to the redistribution of knowledge and skills in the area. So, too, the flow of funds from the resource-rich to the resource-poor countries—in the form of government-to-government grants or subsidies, or remittances from migrant workers—reflect new interdependencies.

Another important difference among the countries of the Middle East pertains to their respective use for petroleum revenues. The requirements of Iran and Algeria are more immediate, more pressing, and more extensive than those of Kuwait or Saudi Arabia. Algeria and Iran have developed the administrative bases to draw upon petroleum revenues and channel them into productive investment projects. Kuwait, Saudi Arabia, and Libya do not have the capacity required to use all their potential revenues immediately, nor do they have a large population base. These structural factors define national priorities and the thrust of major development programs.

Development Plans and National Priorities

Development plans indicate the extent to which the economic interests of the individual Arab states are consistent with the new directions in regional politics. In addition, they reflect the anticipated economic interdependencies among these states, the projected investments of the oil-rich countries in the economies of their poorer neighbors, and the possible uses of economic power for political gain.

Of central concern to analysts in the West and elsewhere is the extent to which the development plans of the oil-exporting states represent a realistic assessment of planned expenditures both at home and abroad. Economists in the West question the validity of these plans and the accuracy of the assumptions

Table 4-1
Select Structural Indexes for Seven Middle Eastern Countries

Country	Population (in Millions) Mid-1974 Estimate	Population Growth Rate, 1974	Density (in Square Kilometers) 1973	Percent Urban, 1973 (Estimated)	Percent Literate Male, Different Years and Age Groups
Algeria	15.9	3.4	7	50.3	42 1971 15+
Egypt	38.0	2.8	36	43.2	48 1966 10+
Iran	32.2	2.8	19	42.6	33 1966 15+
Iraq	10.7	3.3	24	61.4	37 1965 15+
Kuwait	1.0	9.8[a]	50	22.1[b]	55 1970 15+
Morocco[c]	16.8	3.3	37	36.8	21 1971 15+
Saudi Arabia	8.6	2.7	4	n.a.	n.a.

Note: n.a. = not available.

[a]Adjusted for net migration.

[b]The definition of "urban" used by the United Nations for Kuwait includes Kuwait City (Dasman, Sarq/1, Sharq/2, Murgab, Salihia and Qibla) and Labourers City.

[c]Morocco is included here only for comparative purposes. As a nonoil exporting state, it has remained relatively peripheral to petroleum politics.

Sources: The Environmental Fund, "World Population Estimates, 1974," (Washington, D.C.: The Environmental Fund, 1974); United Nations, *Yearbook of National Accounts Statistics, 1973*, ST/ESA/STAT/SER.0/3/Add.2 (New York: United Nations, 1975); United Nations, *Demographic Yearbook, 1973*, ST/STAT/SER.R/2 (New York: United Nations, 1975); Atef M. Khalife, *The Population of Egypt* (Cairo: Institute of Statistical Studies and Research, 1973); United Nations, *World Energy Supplies*, ST/STAT/SER.J (New York: United Nations, 1973).

upon which they are based. Their criticisms are based on the fact that economies of the oil-exporting states cannot at the present time accommodate large scale domestic investments and that the constraints of absorptive capacity are difficult to transcend on short order.

Absorptive capacity is the ability to use new capital productivity, once initial costs are covered, to yield an acceptable rate of return. This ability is constrained by social, managerial, institutional, and educational factors that reduce the productivity of new investment projects as the level of these investments increase over time. No one fully understands the nature of these constraints or how they may be reduced, but everyone agrees that time is required to expand skills, educate management, and develop institutional

Gross Domestic Product, 1970 (in Millions U.S. Dollars)	Percent GDP Derived from Agriculture, 1970	GDP Per Capita, 1970 (in U.S. Dollars)	Energy Consumption, 1971 (Million Metric Tons of Coal Equivalent)	Per Capita Energy Consumption, 1971 (Kilograms/ Capita)
4,640	n.a.	324	7.365	499
7,211	25	216	9.699	285
11,671	18	407	30.560	1,026
3,637	17	385	6.216	638
3,036	–	3,995	8.479	10,203
3,352	31	229	3.092	203
5,094	4	658	7.669	963

infrastructure.[c] The specific nature and manifestation of these factors may differ

[c]For a survey of the meanings assigned to the notion of absorptive capacity and an interpretation of this concept as a learning and adaptation phenomenon, see R.S. Eckaus, "Absorptive Capacity as a Constraint Due to Maturation Processes," in Jagdish N. Bhagwati and Richard S. Eckaus, *Development and Planning: Essays in Honour of Paul Rosenstein-Rodan* (Cambridge, Mass.: The M.I.T. Press, 1973), pp. 79-108. For discussions of absorptive capacity in the Middle East see, Keith McLachlan, *Spending Oil Revenues: Development Prospect in the Middle East to 1975*, Quarterly Economic Review Special No. 10 (London: The Economist Intelligence Unit Limited, 1972); Sam H. Schurr and Paul T. Homan, *Middle Eastern Oil and the Western World: Prospects and Problems*, Part II (New York: American Elsevier Publishing Company, Inc., 1971); Yusuf J. Ahmad, *Oil Revenue in the Gulf: A Preliminary Estimate of Absorptive Capacity* (Paris: Organisation for Economic Development and Co-operation, 1974); The International Bank for Reconstruction and Development, *The Economic Development of Kuwait* (Baltimore: The Johns Hopkins Press, 1965); and Said H. Hitti and George T. Abed, "The Economy and Finance of Saudi Arabia," International Monetary Fund *Staff Papers*, Vol. XXI, No. 2 (July 1974), pp. 247-306.

from situation to situation, but the constraint of absorptive capacity is a generic characteristic of developing countries.

Iran

Iran is one of the few oil-rich countries that will have little difficulty absorbing the added revenues generated by increases in petroleum prices. The country's experience with development planning is extensive in comparison with other oil-rich states. The First Plan was initiated in 1949 and gave equal weight to agriculture, communications, industry, and social services.[5] The Second and Third Plans encountered a variety of financial and political problems, and fell short of expected expenditures. The Fourth Plan (1968-73) appears to be the most successful in meeting its initial objectives by generating an annual growth rate of 9.4 percent and a per capita GNP of $300. Since then, the growth record has averaged 11 percent per year.[6]

This high rate of economic growth is commonly attributed to a rising proportion of GNP devoted to capital formation and high returns from productive investments made in areas where some infrastructure had already been developed. However, actual expenditures were higher than estimated allocations due largely to an expansion of governmental priorities. The constraints of absorptive capacity were manifested largely in agriculture (in terms of poor communication, poor seed, poor techniques of cultivation, lack of water, and the need for capital investments), in manufacturing industry (due to the competitive position of foreign markets and, more pressingly, the relatively small size of effective domestic markets for manufactured goods), and in manpower and management (in terms of shortages of skilled labor, a perennial problem in present development programs).

The final form of the Fifth Plan (1973-74 to 1978-79) is still unclear. So far it has been increased by 119.2% from the original allocation. Current priorities are given to (1) military expenditures (comprising 28 percent of the 1974-75 budget); (2) expenditures on industrial development (mostly direct investments in the oil sector and, to a lesser extent, in the steel industry); (3) acquisition of raw materials and industrial commodities (largely through bilateral arrangements with the advanced countries and with raw material producers); and (4) agriculture (which has been given the largest allocation in the budget under the heading of economic affairs).[7]

In addition, Iran is undertaking both extensive bilateral and multilateral assistance programs (see Chapter 5). The government seeks to expand all aspects of economic development and extend its foreign activities. Recently, observers have voiced concern over Iran's financial ability to meet its anticipated commitments, and a recent Iranian acknowledgment of the need for a $4 billion loan to meet its balance of payments problems confirms this judgment.[8]

Nonetheless it appears clear that the country's demand for revenues is high, if one views demand as representing the leadership's intents, the expressed goals for development expenditures, the availability of investment projects, and the mobilization of resources for economic growth. But there remain serious constraints of absorptive capacity reflected largely in administrative and bureaucratic problems.

Algeria

Despite differences in population size, Algeria most closely approximates Iran in its relative demand for petroleum revenues. Petroleum revenues for 1974 were \$3.7 billion, projected to 1980 at \$5.95 billion.[9] The country's experience with development planning is limited, due to a long war for independence followed by years of domestic political instability. It is only under the Boumediene regime that development planning has been regarded as an important aspect of public policy. Government expenditures for 1975 have been set at \$5.2 billion. The development budget specifies the following priorities in order of importance: education (21 percent of total expenditures), infrastructure projects (17 percent), special programs (15 percent), agriculture (11 percent), water (10 percent), and communications (8 percent). It is yet unclear whether these priorities will be met.

Iraq

In contrast to many oil-rich states, Iraq appears to have substantial economic potential over and above its large petroleum revenues. Iraq has millions of acres of cultivable land, water from two major rivers (the Tigris and the Euphrates) and a small, but rapidly growing population with skills that equal those of its neighbors. But, there are major difficulties that inhibit the expansion of this potential. These include endemic domestic political instability, which has made planning difficult, if not impossible, and chronic military disputes with its neighbors, which has made the diversion of resources from military uses politically unfeasible. There have been four development plans between 1951 and 1958; none lasted more than a year. Several more plans were initiated after the revolution of 1958 which lasted a little longer. However, actual expenditures consistently fell far short of planned levels. There were frequent changes in the bureaucratic and implementation machinery; fiscal policy did not support the plan; and marked difficulties arose in coordination among investment projects.[10] Despite these difficulties the country witnessed an annual rate of growth in GNP of 7 percent between 1950-1970.

Petroleum revenues in 1974 were \$6.8 billion.[11] The government has announced planned development expenditures of \$12.3 billion for April 1-December 31, 1975. The new Development Plan (1974-79) gives highest priority to intensive exploitation of crude oil resources, expansion of refinery capacity and the development of a petrochemical industry. Given the previous record on development expenditures it is unlikely that these plans will be realized.[12]

Iraq's capacity for productive investment in the short-term is limited because of managerial, political, and institutional problems. Large allocations to the military (averaging 50 percent of government expenditures from 1950 to 1970) are likely to persist, but greater attention is being given to the agricultural sector where financial constraints had been serious in the past. These considerations all tend to place Iraq in a somewhat intermediate position between Iran and Algeria, on the one hand, and the Gulf States, on the other, in terms of capacity for productive domestic investments.

Kuwait

Kuwait is a classical oil economy. Eighty-five to 90 percent of all employment in Kuwait is in the pay of the government. Planning for the "postoil" age has become a major policy concern, coloring all decisions on investments, savings, consumption, imports, foreign assistance, and political moves, both nationally and internationally.

Kuwait became independent in 1962. A Planning Board attached to the Council of Ministers was created in the following year. The First Development Plan covered the period 1967-68 to 1971-72. In 1969 requests from the various ministries were consolidated in a new Ten Year Plan. In the past development expenditures have fallen short of planned allocations, due largely to constraints of absorptive capacity and to administrative disorganization, confusion and inefficiency. Commitments to the Arab war effort detracted further from the execution of planned investments.[13]

At the present time, expenditures are planned in the areas of defense, industrial development, nonoil related investments, oil-based industrial and downstream expansion, agriculture and fishery and social infrastructure.[14] Allocations related to finance, banking, imports, and contributions to the other Arab states are also planned.

Kuwait has long accepted extensive foreign investments as an economic necessity. The government is aware of the limitations of absorptive capacity and, as a result, is placing the country's development plans in a larger Middle East context, thereby seeking to bypass critical domestic constraints.[15]

Saudi Arabia

The first development program in Saudi Arabia was formulated in 1949, allocating $270 million for a four-year program. Growth in the 1950s was slow and halting. The failure of government to curtail public expenditure following an unanticipated levelling off of oil revenues led to strict budgetary controls. In 1960 development programs were considered once again, with the main emphasis on the expansion of infrastructure.

The First Development Plan (1970-75) allocated an initial $9,180.7 million which was exceeded during the first three years of the plan by 34.8 percent.[16] The primary purpose of the plan was to extend infrastructure and to begin investment projects for the diversification of the economy. Defense expenditures constitute the largest single sector of expenditures. The 1973-74 budget gave 25 percent of all allocations to the Ministry of Defense and Aviation. About 11.1 percent of the total financial allocations are made to public utilities and urban development, 18.1 percent to transportation and communication, and 17.8 percent to education and vocational training.

Actual expenditures have always fallen short of planned allocations largely because of inadequate infrastructure and ineffective administration. In 1972-73 actual disbursements constituted only 50 percent of allocated expenditures. Even under the most optimistic assumptions, Saudi Arabia's total productive investments could not possibly absorb the $22 billion of oil revenues for 1974. Cumulative revenues are estimated at $133.2 billion by 1980.

The standard of living of the Saudi population is low in comparison with the neighboring states. Investments in social services have, to date, been relatively small and the government has not adopted the same welfare concerns as have the Kuwaitis or some states in the United Arab Emirates. The fear of political upheaval has constrained further the government's interest in large-scale investments in social services.

Saudi Arabia has recently announced a five-year plan (July 1975-May 1980) of $144 billion to be expended toward (1) the diversification of the country's economic base through increased agricultural and industrial production, relying heavily on governmental investments and government subsidies to industry and agriculture; (2) rapid development of manpower resources, relying upon the indigenous population growth rate of 3.4 percent per year and the migration of non-Saudi workers with an annual growth rate of 21 percent until 1980, resulting in a non-Saudi manpower base comprising 35 percent of the total workforce by the end of the plan period; and (3) the development of various regions of the country through governmental investments and social programs.[17] Given the country's population base, administrative capabilities and constraints of absorptive capacity, it is extremely unlikely, if not impossible, for the allocations anticipated in the five-year plan to be actually spent. The magnitude of government investments required to realize a total expenditure of $144 billion in five years far exceeds what is possible even under the most favorable circumstances.

Saudi Arabia faces none of the pressures of Iran, Iraq, or Algeria and the country's major concern is to find sufficient productive outlets for the investment of surplus petroleum revenues. Nor has Saudi Arabia opted for the Kuwaiti strategy of viewing its own development program in the wider context of regional development in the Middle East. This difference has led to an important debate among them regarding the disbursement of petroleum revenue and the extent to which petroleum policies ought to be guided by alternative investment strategies (see Chapter 5).

Libya, Qatar, and the UAE

Libya, Qatar, and the United Arab Emirates share the Saudi predicament of devising investment outlets for surplus petroleum revenues. Libya's planned development expenditures in 1975 are estimated at $3.6 billion, about half the country's petroleum revenues for that year and one fourth of the projected revenues for 1980.[18] Only a fraction of Qatar's oil revenues are allocated for domestic development.[19] The government's development programs are sketchy with few prospects for expansion of social services and industrial base. Qatar's decision not to join the United Arab Emirates has increased the leadership's awareness of the need to establish cooperative economic ties with its neighbors. The U.A.E. specified the following priorities for the 1973-74 federal budget: new development projects, public works, education, defense, and internal affairs (including administration, communication and transportation, health water, and electricity), in that order. The federation's petroleum revenues for 1975 were about $3.3 billion and planned development expenditures for the following year were approximately $3.26 billion.[20] Despite this apparent balance of revenue and allocated expenditures, constraints of absorptive capacity are likely to result in considerable underspending.

Egypt

Of the nonoil-exporting countries of the Middle East, Egypt's need for financial resources is clearly the most extensive in the region.[21] A large and growing population, coupled with a crippled economy due to the war burden, extensive financial debts, loss of revenues from the Suez Canal and poor planning have resulted in excessive burdens on the economy. Experience with development planning so far is not encouraging. The 1960-65 plan constituted the first draft of a National Comprehensive Plan for Economic and Social Development, which set as its goal a doubling of national income at constant prices between 1960 and 1970. The second part of the plan was never implemented. A more ambitious plan for the seven years between 1965 and 1972 anticipated total investments of around $3 billion. The uncertainties of a war situation led to its abandonment. At least two subsequent plans have been dropped. A transitional plan covering the end of 1975 was adopted and a Five Year Plan for 1976-80 is being formulated.[22]

The law of February 1974 providing directives for the investment of Arab and foreign funds and the creation of free zones represents a notable change in the country's economic orientation.[23] It provides concessions on imports, the transfer of profits, and taxes, and added guarantees against nationalization of confiscation. These directives constitute a marked departure from governmental controls of the Nasser regime and a reaffirmation of the country's new foreign policy.

Planned Expenditures and Petroleum Policies

Although the development plans of the nonoil-exporting states do not represent any direct claims on the petroleum revenues, the expected expenditures of Egypt constitute an important element in the allocation strategies of the oil-rich Arab states. Even Iran has recently made commitments for substantial investments in Egypt.[24] The intricacies of regional politics in the Middle East invariably impinge upon OPEC policies and the extent to which goals and objectives of the states in the region—oil-rich and oil-poor—are complimentary rather than conflictual.

The oil-poor Arab states, most notably Egypt, influence the policies of OAPEC; and OAPEC directives cannot be ignored in the formation of OPEC policies. Development plans represent some claim on anticipated petroleum revenues. For the poorer states, this claim is indirect. Nonetheless, the prospects for continued cohesion among the oil-exporting countries rests upon the extent to which their pricing and production policies remain complimentary and the degree to which differences in the priorities can be accommodated by coordinated action.

Constraints on Prices and Production Policies

Differences in national priorities and requirements for petroleum revenues among the Middle East states have presented OPEC with a set of constraints that are difficult to surmount. The more heavily populated members have indicated their support for higher prices even at the risk of straining the coherence of the organization. For example, Jamshid Amouzegar, Iranian Minister of Finance, has stated that his country "will not let the price of oil drop below its existing level, even if this means the break-up of OPEC."[25] Algeria and Indonesia have argued at the March 19, 1974 meetings for raising the posted price of Gulf petroleum to $14 per barrel. Nigeria and Iran endorsed this proposal.[26] President Carlos Andres Perez of Venezuela has stated that his country will maintain its price "even if others cut theirs."[27]

Saudi Arabia alone has argued for price reductions, on the grounds that the long-term stability of the petroleum market requires it. Some observers question the sincerity of the official Saudi posture.[28] The Oil Minister of Saudi Arabia, Sheikh Yamani, has asserted that Saudi Arabia would in effect set her own prices below those stipulated by OPEC directives, if other countries insisted on raising the posted prices.[29]

Kuwait and Abu Dhabi have placed in the record of the OPEC meetings of March 19, 1974 a motion to censure Saudi Arabia, accusing it of attempting to discourage oil buyers from making bids for auctioned oil.[30] They have deemed it politically and economically desirable to encourage cooperation among the members of OPEC and counter any move that might harm the organization.

Most of these arguments may reflect rhetorical postures. The outcome of the March 19, 1974 meeting was, in effect, a price freeze. Yet, there was ample evidence to suggest that Saudi Arabia had indeed attempted to lower petroleum prices in clear defiance of OPEC directives. On March 17, 1974 *The New York Times* reported an offer of oil totalling two million tons at a price of $8.50 a barrel. The companies making the offer were Exxon, Standard Oil of California, Texaco, and Mobil, all members of Aramco, which operates exclusively in Saudi Arabia. This offer was considerably lower than the current price, which ranges from $9.00 to $11.00 per barrel. The Secretary General of OPEC, Abderrahman Khene of Algeria, acknowledged that the Saudis could unilaterally change the price structure overnight. At the same time, he charged that this offer was a move to drive down oil prices. But, Khene did not officially link Saudi Arabia to this move. The cohesion of OPEC had to be maintained.[31]

The factors that contribute to the Saudi position on petroleum prices and distinguish it from other OPEC members—a small population, relatively lower requirements for petroleum revenues, and control of one-third of the world's proven reserves—necessitate a long-term perspective on petroleum policies and generate pressures for lower prices. Saudi Arabia, in effect, controls the pricing policies of OPEC—a prerogative that can be effectively exercised only at the risk of destroying OPEC. Unlike the other oil-exporting countries, Saudi Arabia does not view near term depletion as an immediate or critical constraint in its overall policy calculations. Iran, Algeria, and other large oil-exporters weigh this factor against their immediate needs for maintaining petroleum revenues. Plans for reducing their dependence on petroleum exports make depletion less of a constraint in the long run.

Some oil-exporting countries, most notably Libya, are seeking to protect their resources from rapid and unplanned exploitation. Yet, they have neither the reserves of the Saudis nor the institutional capabilities of the Iranians. Their concerns for depletion and their apparent willingness to moderate the rate of petroleum production appear to be still another consequence of the basic differentials in population, resources and technology. While the Libyan posture might be viewed in ideological terms, it is also consistent with its desire to develop workable policies for long-range resource planning. What might appear as an unwarranted ideological posture to some observers is viewed more appropriately by others as a shrewd economic move.

Differences in population size, development plans and priorities, and absorptive capacity are presenting the oil-exporting states with different policy constraints. These differences, though generating important cleavages within OPEC, may also be viewed as a potential source of strength. As long as these countries are subject to different sets of economic and political pressure, possibilities for trade-offs, compromises, and bargaining will persist.

Policies and Prospects

The new order in the Middle East appears based on a formal acknowledgment of political diversity, not on the insistence on conformity. An appreciation of the underlying diversities in their structural and economic characteristics accorded the Arab states with a new basis for interdependence. None of this was planned, or even intentional, but rather developed in response to repeated failure associated with traditional modes of political discourse in the region.[32] The prospect of tangible political and economic gains for all is a critical consideration explaining the present Arab posture. More importantly, the gains of one nation are not regarded as losses to another. These countries now aspire to effective political collaboration rather than to formal political unification as has been the case in the past.

Improved relations with the United States, Western Europe, and Japan are undoubtedly the most dramatic consequence of the 1973 war and the new policy directives. But these relations are still considerably strained. They affect as much the potential resolution of the conflict with Israel as they do the impasse over petroleum production and pricing. By early 1975 the United States had emerged in a pivotal role. Egypt, Saudi Arabia, and to some extent, Syria were opting for a strategy of partial trust in the U.S. posture. Other nations, like Algeria, refrained from endorsing this strategy. Iraq and Libya were in opposition. It became clear that failure to obtain some resolution of the Palestinian issue would inevitably weaken the position of the core leadership and strengthen that of the opponents to rapprochement with the United States.

The possibilities for reaching some accommodation with Israel rest on the conversion of the conflict from a symbolic dispute to one that involves bargaining and negotiation. Thus, the prospects for settlement coincide with and reinforce present lines of cooperation and accommodation among the Arab states.[33] The *nature* of the settlement with Israel is now becoming the focal point of the Arab-Israeli conflict.[34]

The new interdependencies influence petroleum politics and may well have an integrative effect upon the cohesion of the cartel. Indeed, Saudi Arabia might manipulate these relationships to present OPEC with significant obstacles to further increases in price. This situation places Saudi Arabia in a critical managerial role with respect to OPEC, a role consistent with its new posture in regional politics. The political constraints and objectives of the Saudis may well become critical imperatives in the formulation of Arab responses to future divisions within OPEC.

But the policies of OPEC do not depend upon the Arab members alone. Clearly, Iran exercises a major role. The country's relations with its Arab neighbors have always been uneasy. To some extent, the two groups share a common history, religion, and culture. Iran has always been concerned with maintaining its own identity and refraining from becoming embroiled in inter-Arab politics. However, the Shah's apparent desire to establish hegemony over the Gulf area has given rise to considerable apprehension on the part of the other littoral states, who refer to that waterway as the Arabian Gulf. In turn, Iran has always been fearful of a stronger Arab entity, and its relations with the Arab states had been particularly poor when Nasser announced his policy of radical Arab nationalism. With Sadat's assurances to the Shah of a more limited regional role for Egypt, relations between the two countries improved. And the improvement of Egyptian-Saudi relations contributed to the decline of tensions between the Shah and the Saudi King. The goal of preserving OPEC has bound Iran and Saudi Arabia in a common, if uneasy, alliance.[35]

Iran regards the potential emergence of stability in the Arab world as less detrimental to its own interest than the perennial instability of the past. Any direct confrontation between radical and conservative states in Arab politics would be viewed with apprehension by Iran. Yet, another dimension of Iran's relations with the Arab states pertain to their respective investments in military capability and their assessment of each other's strategic goals and objectives. Therein lies a major source of tension within OPEC (see Chapter 6). Strategic, economic, and political objectives intertwine in the Middle East and Gulf area, and seemingly extraneous factors become determinants of the petroleum policies of leading OPEC members.

The other countries of OPEC are relatively less critical to the organization's overall price strategy and production policy. Nigeria, Ecuador, Gabon, Indonesia, and Venezuela do not possess sufficient reserves to provide effective countervailing influences to the Saudi posture or to pressures from Iran. All are likely to side with Iran on the issue of increasing petroleum prices; but, none can substantially influence or manipulate any OPEC decision in this regard. And Iran itself is always subject to Saudi pressure for maintaining, if not reducing, prices. Saudi Arabia can readily effect a drop in petroleum prices without incurring any adverse economic effects. Such a move may trigger serious conflicts in the Arab world. The Saudi government may not be willing to risk its recently acquired position of leadership in the area by unilaterally lowering prices. Saudi Arabia is in the unique position of foregoing, if need be, economic gains for political ones or, alternatively, accepting economic losses in anticipation of political benefits.

Notes

1. *Facts on File, 1969*, Vol. 29, No. 1522, p. 833.
2. *The New York Times*, September 13, 1973.
3. *The New York Times*, October 16, 1973.
4. *The New York Times*, January 10, 1975.
5. Yusuf J. Ahmad, *Oil Revenues in the Gulf:* A Preliminary Estimate of Absorptive Capacity (Paris: OEDC, 1974), p. 3.
6. Ibid., p. 4.
7. Ibid., pp. 12-16.
8. *Middle East Economic Survey*, Vol. XVIII, No. 41 (1 August 1975), p. 1.
9. *Middle East Economic Survey*, Vol. XVIII, No. 14 (24 January 1975), p. 5.
10. Ahmad, *Oil Revenues in the Gulf*, p. 30.
11. *The Petroleum Economist*, Vol. XLII, No. 3 (March 1975), p. 85.
12. *Middle East Economic Survey*, Vol. XVIII, No. 32 (30 May 1975), p. 6.
13. Ahmad, *Oil Revenues in the Gulf*, p. 53.
14. Ibid., pp. 55-59.
15. Ibid., p. 65.
16. Ibid., p. 130.
17. *Middle East Economic Survey*, Vol. XVIII, No. 32 (30 May 1975), p. 1; see also, *The New York Times*, May 19, 1975.
18. *Middle East Economic Survey*, Vol. XVIII, No. 16 (7 February 1975), p. 6.
19. Ahmad, *Oil Revenues in the Gulf*, p. 104.
20. *Middle East Economic Survey*, Vol. XVIII, No. 34 (13 June 1975), p. 7.
21. The Economist Intelligence Unit, Limited, *Quarterly Economic Review, Egypt*, Annual Supplement 1974.
22. Ibid., p. 20.
23. Ibid.
24. *The New York Times*, January 5, 9, 10, 12, and 13, 1975.
25. *Financial Times*, (London), March 12, 1974.
26. *Financial Times* (London), March 8, 1974.
27. *The New York Times*, March 20, 1974.
28. See "Highlights of Testimony before the Subcommittee on Multinational Corporations of the Committee on Foreign Relations, U.S. Senate, January 29, 1975" (mimeographed), testimony of M.A. Adelman, p. 4.
29. *The New York Times*, March 20, 1974.

30. Ibid.

31. *The New York Times*, March 21, 1974.

32. James A. Bill and Carl Leiden, *The Middle East: Politics and Power* (Boston: Allyń and Bacon, Inc., 1974).

33. Maurice Harari, *Government and Politics in the Middle East* (Englewood Cliffs, N.J.: Prentice-Hall, Inc., 1962); Sylvia G. Haim, ed., *Arab Nationalism: An Anthology* (Berkeley: University of California Press, 1964) for historical background.

34. See, the statement by Egyptian President, Anwar Sadat, in *The New York Times*, July 24, 1974.

35. *The New York Times*, January 29, 1975.

5 The Politics of Capital Transactions: Strategies and Priorities

The seven Arab members of the Organization of Petroleum Exporting Countries control 75 percent of the group's petroleum reserves. Their cohesion is critical to the persistence of OPEC. Inter-Arab politics bears directly upon this cohesion. Differences in economic policies and priorities will inevitably influence the prospects of continued collaboration.

This chapter examines the history of present day economic relations among Arab states and the current debates in policy-making circles regarding the use of petroleum revenues.[a] We argue that petroleum politics is emerging as a strategy to attain control over the behavior of allies and adversaries, and that the object of such strategy by the producer governments is to maximize their individual control over indigenous resources and to increase their influence in the world petroleum market. The instruments employed are largely economic. The objectives are political. The strategy is to increase interdependencies with allies and to reduce the influence of adversaries. It is a pragmatic strategy by which economic and political concerns are only occasionally dominated by ideological ones. Finally, we show that the interests of the Arab members of OPEC have converged but also that persisting differences may compromise the cohesion of the cartel.

Economic Diplomacy

The apparent show of solidarity among the Arab members of OPEC must be viewed in the framework of the monopolistic structure of production developed originally by the major oil companies. It must also be viewed against a background of economic differences, tensions, and perennial conflict between the Arabs themselves, and of repeated failures to develop a regional economic market for commodity trade.

For nearly all of their history, economic transactions among the Arab states were confined largely to trade relations. A customs union established by the Ottoman Empire had existed as late as 1914 and provided a semblance of economic unity among the Arab states. But it was under Turkish control, and the Arabs had no direct influence over the structure of the union. Included in the union were the territories that today consist of Iraq, Jordan, Kuwait, Lebanon, Syria, Tunisia, Egypt, and Yemen and, of course, Israel, then Palestine.

[a]The collaboration of Ijaz Gilani is gratefully acknowledged.

The union was not a regional market, rather it was an arrangement of a common tariff area to facilitate trade between the Ottoman Empire and the European countries. Inter-Arab trade accounted for a rather sizable portion of trade within the region. For example, available statistics indicate that in 1910 about 45 percent of Syria's exports of approximately 2.8 million pounds sterling from the ports of Alexandria and Beirut, and Jaffa went to Egypt and other parts of the Ottoman Empire.[b] About 11 percent of Egypt's average annual imports between 1909 and 1913 came from other parts of the Empire.[1] Trade between the Sudan and Egypt accounted for a large part of the Sudan's total trade.[2] And trade among various administrative divisions of Syria appears to have been rather substantial, although much of this exchange involved the reexport of European finished goods.

Following the dissolution of the Ottoman Empire at the close of World War I, the Arab lands were divided among Great Britain and France and new states were created. Separate customs territories with different units of currency evolved in the Fertile Crescent and in the Arabian Peninsula during the 1920s. Throughout the following decade these states were oriented toward the economies of occupying European powers. Regional trade continued to be nonpreferential, but tied currencies, foreign investments, and foreign controls channelled trade to, and from, Europe. During the latter part of the 1920s about one third of Egypt's exports went to Britain, about one-fifth of its imports came from Britain. Similarly, in the Fertile Crescent about one-half of Iraq's trade, both imports and exports, was with Great Britain. The same was true for Palestine and Transjordan. By the same token, France controlled the trade of its mandate territories.

Nonetheless, the semblance of a regional market for agricultural goods and foodstuffs persisted during the 1930s. A set of official tariffs, trade barriers, and related monetary arrangements were developed during this period. They were initially conceived as an expression of statehood but gradually evolved as institutional barriers to economic cooperation. By virtue of their colonial status, some states became tied to the British currency and others to the French. By the end of the decade economic interdependence among the Arabs had seriously disintegrated. The Maghreb countries had been tied to the French, Spanish, and Italian economies well before the turn of the century, and few economic transactions with other states in the region developed. Yemen, the Sudan, and Kuwait had limited economic ties with other Arab countries; Palestine had terminated its free trade relations with Syria and Lebanon; Egypt, Saudi Arabia, and Iraq were following nonpreferential trade policies that restricted inter-Arab trade. Those free trade arrangements that persisted eventually provided the base for economic cooperation in the region between 1940 and 1945.

[b]Alfred G. Musrey, *An Arab Common Market: A Study in Inter-Arab Trade Relations, 1920-67* (New York: Praeger Publishers, 1969), p. 8. The discussion on inter-Arab economic history draws upon Musrey's study.

The immediate effect of World War II on inter-Arab economic relations was to further reduce the relative magnitude of inter-Arab trade. The creation of the Arab League in 1945 provided only a facade of cooperation. Restrictive controls and tariff frameworks that impeded regional trade persisted. Only the existence of the Anglo-Egyptian condominium in the Sudan ensured free trade in the Nile Valley. In the 1950s and 1960s numerous pacts and treaties were formulated both within and outside the framework of the Arab League to ease these restrictions, but to no avail. In 1965 inter-Arab trade continued to be merely a small fraction of each state's total commercial transactions. With the notable exception of trade in petroleum and petroleum products, and exports of agricultural products from the Fertile Crescent to Saudi Arabia and Kuwait, there had been few significant changes in trade patterns over the past 30 years, despite notable gains in industrialization made by some of the Arab states during this period.

Negotiations concerning the proposed Arab Common Market Agreements (1964-67) illustrated once again the differences in views and the varying priorities of individual states in the region. Egypt, then the United Arab Republic with a planned economy, advocated economic union throughout the region under an Economic Unity Council in Cairo. Iraq countered with a proposal for a coordinated economy of Arab states, with free trade and economic cooperation, and proposed Baghdad as headquarters. Lebanon argued for free enterprise, and requested the Arab states to abolish discriminatory legislation aimed at restricting business practices of other Arab states. Common grounds for multilateral agreement could not be found, but bilateral arrangements were established.

The predominance of petroleum in the economy of the region made the disbursement of oil revenues, not trade regulations, the major issue of economic policy. Surplus revenues gave the rich states a privilege. They sought to attain a position of dominance in Arab politics. Negotiations for the creation of an organization of Arab oil-exporting countries proceeded initially on pragmatic grounds, drawing only upon states of equal economic potential and similar political perspectives.[c] Kuwait, Libya, and Saudi Arabia satisfied these requirements in that they had the most substantial oil revenues, and all three were insulated from modernizing forces in regional politics and shared a common suspicion of the more radical states. They constituted the core group.

The 1967 war of the Arab states with Israel was the first opportunity for differences in petroleum policies and national priorities to surface. As noted earlier, some countries, notably Iran and Algeria, advocated a three-month stoppage of Arab oil exports. Others, including Saudi Arabia, Kuwait and Libya, argued for a policy of maximizing oil revenues and urged the use of oil proceeds to support the front-line Arab states in efforts to regain lost territory. At an

[c]For the notion of "minimum winning coalition" see, William H. Riker, *The Theory of Political Coalitions* (New Haven: Yale University Press, 1962).

Arab summit conference in August 1967 in Khartoum the Kuwait-Saudi-Libyan position was adopted. Their compromise was a combined offer of financial assistance, totalling $378 million, to Egypt and Jordan as a contribution to the war effort. These events replaced earlier attempts to develop viable trading partner relationships. At this point, Kuwait, Libya, and Saudi Arabia began to coordinate their policies outside the framework of the Arab League.

The Organization of Arab Petroleum Exporting Countries was formed in January 1968.[d] The new organization was an exclusive one limited to oil-exporting states. Arab producers with little export capacity were not invited. The subsequent expansion of OAPEC to other exporters was triggered by an initially unrelated event: In September 1969 the Libyan monarchy was overthrown. Cohesion of political orientation was ended, but rather than breaking the initial triumvirate, this change led to an expansion of the organization. Another radical regime, Algeria, joined early in 1970. OAPEC now provided a forum and an opportunity for the Arab oil-exporting countries to develop organization instruments for creating and regulating economic cooperation on issues other than oil. The focal point of subsequent economic transactions was not trade, but the development of aid and investment strategies.

Disbursement of Petroleum Revenues: Emerging Views

The availability of surplus revenues is providing the Arab oil-producing countries with a series of perplexing problems that may well inhibit further cooperation among them. One such problem is whether to allow the creation of surpluses at all. Indeed, they differ markedly in their approach to production policies. A substantial reduction in petroleum production would, in effect, deprive them of the surplus problem. Although the oil-producing countries are in no way united in their petroleum policies, they all share a strong appreciation of international pressures for continued drilling and maintaining high production rates.

The members of OAPEC often refer to their high levels of production as a "sacrifice" for the international community—a euphemism for the awareness of the political and military pressures to which these countries are so clearly vulnerable given their weakness militarily. They argue that the impact of this sacrifice would be reduced by oil prices sufficiently high to accommodate their development plans and to accelerate industrialization and stable investments in the West as productive value for the "postoil" age. This expression of drilling as a "sacrifice" is not simply rhetorical; the Arab oil-exporting countries regard continued production at levels beyond those needed to accommodate immediate domestic requirements as a service performed for the international community.

---

[d]See, Zuhayr Midkashi, *The Community of Oil Exporting Countries* (Ithaca: Cornell University Press, 1972), for a discussion of the origins of OAPEC.

This view emerges from all parts of the political spectrum. Thus, the Minister for Petroleum of Abu Dhabi stated:

> We have made it abundantly clear that we are prepared to produce more oil than we need because Western civilization depends on our oil and we do not want to hurt them. But you must appreciate our sacrifices and go very far toward accommodating our legitimate political and economic aspirations.[3]

And Prime Minister Jallud of Libya declared:

> Libya as an oil producer is making sacrifices. We should be exporting 800,000 b/d in accordance with our spending requirements, but in response to world energy demand we are exporting more than our requirements. This is a great sacrifice, particularly in view of currency movements. If we are making a sacrifice, others must sacrifice too.[4]

The Ba'ath Party in Iraq stated that:

> Iraq must avoid being caught in the current tendency to raise production levels in a manner which is out of line with a producing countries' financial requirements and their capacity to use the higher oil revenues effectively.[5]

From Saudi Arabia:

> Since most of these [oil-exporting] countries are required to produce more than what they need for their economic requirements, their right to establish diversified economic industrial structures must be recognized.
>
> These countries which are amassing foreign currency reserves in the process, must be given adequate safeguards against the erosion of the value of currencies and the political dangers of foreign investment.[6]

The Secretary General of OPEC, A.R. Khene, had repeatedly declared that the organization has no conservation policy as such, but that individual members would be justified in defending their own preferences and that individual interests predominate.[7]

The three-way calculations, involving concerns for depletion of reserves, depreciation of monetary holdings, and uses of financial surpluses, shape the debates among the oil-producers regarding optimum petroleum strategies. They do not view the absolute choice between "oil in the ground" and "money in the bank" as a real one. They are making the choice in the margin, and their assessment of gains and losses is colored by other than strictly economic criteria. Clearly, there is no viable alternative to some production; the debate is over the amount. A consensus among the Arab oil-exporters is gradually evolving around the following position:

> . . . as long as the absorptive capacity of any Arab country or the Arab countries collectively permits the use of these funds for speedy development we must seize

the opportunity to exchange oil for development. But, we must not exchange oil for bank deposits, which are subject to dangerous currency fluctuations, and where decision making power is not in our hands.[8]

It is a consensus predicated, officially at least, on the search for cooperative arrangements with the West, but one that seeks to influence potential agreements.[9]

There is insufficient appreciation in the West of the oil-exporting countries' gradual awareness of their own responsibility to the international community. The roots of a strategy of manipulative interdependence by OAPEC is taking shape as a calculated response to Arabs' dependence upon international financial markets of the West. This strategy is based on three premises: first, that the option of reducing (but not stopping) production below a certain level is not politically viable either domestically or internationally; second, that in return for their acceptance of the burden of continued supply at current levels, the oil-producing countries should obtain (a) higher petroleum prices, and (b) assistance in the industrialization of their economies—two necessary conditions for the development of a workable exchange calculus; and third, that petroleum is indeed a depletable resource and surplus revenues should be disbursed with diversified handling of financial portfolios. This strategy of interdependence indicates a search for both rationale and procedure in the allocation of petroleum revenues.

Directions of Capital Transactions[e]

For the oil-exporting countries foreign policy is intimately related to the politics of resource management. Resource management, in turn, involves decisions about petroleum prices, production schedules, and the use of petroleum revenues. Increasingly, investment policies and priorities will shape these coun-

[e]The following transactions are collected from: *The Banker* (London), Vols. 124-125, Nos. 575-589 (January 1974-May 1975); Business International Corporation, *Business International*, Vol. 21, Nos. 1-52, Vol. 22, Nos. 1-13 (January 4, 1974-March 28, 1975); *Euromoney* (London) (January 1974-June 1975); *The Economist* (London), Vols. 251-255, Nos. 6815-6877 (April 6, 1974-June 14, 1975); International Monetary Fund, *IMF Survey*, Vol. 3, Nos. 1-23, Vol. 4, Nos. 1-12 (January 1974-June 1975); The Middle East Research and Publishing Center, *Middle East Economic Survey* (Beirut), Vol. 17, Nos. 1-51, Vol. 18, Nos. 1-23 (October 1973-March 1975); American Academic Association for Peace in the Middle East, *Middle East Information Series*, Nos. 23-27 (May 1973-Summer 1974); *The New York Times*, September 1973-June 1975; Organisation for Economic Co-operation and Development, *OECD Observer*, Nos. 68-73 (February 1974-January-February 1975); *The Petroleum Economist (Petroleum Press Service)*, Vol. 40, Nos. 9-12, Vol. 41, Nos. 1-12, Vol. 42, Nos. 1-6 (September 1973-June 1975); The *Wall Street Journal*, January 1974-June 1975; Organization of Petroleum Exporting Countries, *Weekly Bulletin: Review of the Press* (Vienna), Vol. 5, Nos. 5-51, Vol. 6, Nos. 1-17 (February 1974-April 1975); The Morgan Guaranty Trust Company, *World Financial Markets*, May 1974-June 1975. Details on any specific transaction can be obtained from the authors.

tries' interactions with the consumer states, with each other, and with the developing world at large. At this time the magnitude of total investments, loans, grants, and assistance made by the oil-exporting states is difficult to determine with precision. Broad indications of trends and patterns can be obtained from publicly available information, yet the terms of each transaction are seldom described in detail.[f] In order to illustrate these trends, we draw upon commitments that have been reported officially by parties to the transactions and made public as of July 31, 1975. The figures cited below are probably underestimates because they represent only public commitments. Some agreements have been kept secret (particularly military transactions) and some have been unreported (because they may be relatively small). There are also some marked discrepancies in the reporting of various sources. For example, public sources in the West tend to account for commitments directed toward the United States, Western Europe, or Japan more thoroughly than do Middle East sources. The latter appear more extensive in their reporting of financial transactions within the region. Wherever possible, we have cross-checked each reported item in both sources as well as references to them in publications by international agencies.

Countries with Limited Absorptive Capacity

For those oil-exporting countries for whom major constraint is limited absorptive capability—Saudi Arabia, Oman, the United Arab Emirates, Libya, Kuwait, and Qatar—the range of priorities varies as do their transactions with different oil-consuming nations. Saudi Arabia has chosen to obtain desired goods and services primarily from the United States, Japan, and France. The government's major priorities are expanding domestic productive capability, aiding poor states, and extending loans to the International Monetary Fund and to the World Bank. Commitments to Middle Eastern states rank fourth in total dollar amounts expended. Investments in the United States constitute the single largest commitment with several billion dollars allocated to U.S. Treasury Bonds alone as of August 1974.[10] More than $1.4 billion have been committed to weapons purchases and $764 million committed to investments in United States real estate and the United States housing market. More than $6 billion are scheduled to be spent domestically with U.S. assistance.

Loans to Japan by Saudi Arabia amount to over $1 billion over a period of

[f]For aggregated estimates of OPEC disbursements in 1974 see, *International Monetary Fund, IMF Survey*, Vol. 4, No. 6 (March 24, 1975), p. 81; the Statement of the Honorable William E. Simon, Secretary of the Treasury, before the Subcommittee on Financial Markets of the Senate Finance Committee, Washington, D.C., January 30, 1975, Department of the Treasury, *News*, January 30, 1975, pp. 1-4; *The Financial Times* (London), March 24, 1975; *The Economist*, January 11, 1975, pp. 70-72; *The New York Times*, January 21, 1975; and Richard N. Cooper, "The Invasion of the Petrodollar," *Saturday Review*, January 25, 1975, pp. 10-13.

five years;[11] $800 million are committed for the purchase of weapons from France; and Saudi Arabia shared with Kuwait in a $700 million weapons purchase from the USSR.[12] While these figures appear fairly reliable, more ambiguous is the magnitude of total loans and aid to the Middle East because of the variations in the figures cited. The World Bank reported a figure of $2.4 billion; Middle East sources report $2.5 billion. Total aid to the Fourth World amounts to over $4.0 billion. Overall, as of June 1975, the Saudi government announced long-range plans to spend about $140 billion to create a national industrial base over the next five years.[13]

Of reported Saudi commitments to the West, 93 percent were in the form of investments and 7.04 percent in loans. Commitments to the Middle East were largely investments (42.2%), followed by loans (31.14%) and grants (26.19%). Allocations to the Fourth World were primarily investments (85.8%), and only marginally loans (10.26%) and grants (4.01%). Saudi Arabia's capital transactions clearly reflect a disbursement strategy directed largely toward the United States and Europe. The fact that over 60 percent of its commitments are concentrated in the West and less than 10 percent in the Middle East is further manifestation of its preferences and priorities. It is revealing however, that reported allocations to the Fourth World exceed those to Arab countries. These commitments are primarily in the forms of grants for general aid and food relief.

By contrast, Kuwaiti commitments are largely directed toward the Middle East; $4 billion have already been allocated, amounting to 60 percent of all known commitments. About $1 billion has been committed to the Fourth World, through allocations to the World Bank, the International Monetary Fund, and direct foreign investments. Beyond that, commitments are almost evenly distributed between the United States and Europe.

The Kuwaiti government has extended loans and placed investments directly in the economies of the United States, Japan, the United Kingdom, France, and West Germany, and has concluded a sizeable purchase of domestic industrial equipment with France. Weapons have been obtained from the USSR and the United States. Finally, there are some undisclosed details of investments in the West for research and development of alternative sources of energy.

Kuwait's commitments to countries of the West are primarily in the form of investments (94.2% of all reported allocations to the West) and loans (5.82%). Of allocations to the Middle East, 66.24 percent were in the nature of investments, 26.1 percent in grants, and 7.64 percent in loans. Kuwait extended mainly grants to the poor states (44.32% of all commitments to the Fourth World), followed by investments (30.95%) and loans (24.71%).

Kuwait clearly appears to behave in a way consistent with its expressed objective of circumventing the internal constraints of absorptive capacity by investing in other Arab states.[g] The relatively large commitments to the Arab

[g]For a thorough background on Kuwait's regional role see, Ragaei el-Mallakh, *Economic Development and Regional Development: Kuwait* (Chicago: The University of Chicago Press, 1968); and International Bank for Reconstruction and Development, *The Economic Development of Kuwait* (Baltimore: The Johns Hopkins University Press, 1965).

countries differ from those to the Fourth World not only in magnitude, but in terms of substance. For example, Kuwait extended loans and grants to Egypt and Syria for industrial projects and war relief, but made direct investments in Brazil, Mauritania, and Tanzania, in addition to a $20 million pledge for an African bank and $442 million to the World Bank invested in bonds.[14]

Libya's foreign commitments have been somewhat lower than Kuwait's. About 90 percent of its allocations are to the West, most of it in the form of investments. The largest commitment is a $3 to $5 billion economic and technical pact with France.[15] The country's priorities are principally for domestic investments, largely in the domestic petroleum industry. Some investments in foreign economics have also been undertaken. Investments in poor states include a deal in Zaire for a mining venture as well as negotiations with Turkey for the financing of a $600 million petrochemical complex.[16] Only 3 percent of Libya's commitments have been directed to the countries of the Middle East, in contrast to 7 percent to the poorer states.

The three remaining Arab states with relatively lower absorptive capacity have made commitments of still more modest scale. Qatar has concentrated largely on investments in Western financial markets.[17] Some efforts are being made on expanding domestic productive capacity, with France and Japan as the major participants, but these have been modest, amounting to less than half a million dollars. The United Arab Emirates have invested in the economies of oil-consuming countries in the form of real estate purchases (of undisclosed amounts) and have extended direct loans. They have also made a $10 million weapons purchase from the United States.[h] The Emirates have sought assistance for domestic development from Britain, France, and Japan, through which over $1 billion have already been committed. About $400 million have been targeted for loans and foreign investments in the Fourth World, again largely through the IMF and the World Bank.[18] In addition, the Emirates have extended loans directly to Egypt, Bahrain, Mauritania, Somalia, Tunisia, Jordan, and Syria—all in the form of development aid—totalling more than $170 million.[19] But U.A.E. preferences are clearly toward the Middle East rather than the Fourth World.

Countries with low absorptive capacities are constrained only by the necessity of creating domestic investment opportunities and the institutional and political capabilities to ensure a reasonable rate of return. The goals of Saudi Arabia appear diffuse and varied. For Kuwait they are balanced, concentrated, and allocations are evenly distributed among different recipients. For Qatar and the U.A.E. disbursement strategies are yet undecided although there appears a marked preference for financial investments in the West. These countries dramatically illustrate the predicament of most oil-exporting states: productive capacity is limited; generating political and economic demand for domestic investments is the major policy problem at hand. Without such demands, immediate pressures to increase production would become less compelling. At present, the constraints of absorptive capacity set the parameters within

[h]*The New York Times*, February 25, 1975. The United Arab Emirates have also made significant weapons purchases from France and the United Kingdom.

which other more distinctly political criteria become relevant in defining and shaping disbursement policies.

Countries with Higher Absorptive Capacity

Those oil-exporting states with relatively higher absorptive capacity have exhibited a much wider range of investments and, characteristically, have made commitments of greater magnitudes. Thus, for example, Iran has allocated over $25 billion for projects and investments involving Europe, over $12.4 billion for United States-related investments, and announced plans for an additional $15 billion agreement (including $5 billion for the sale of arms, $6.4 billion for nuclear reactors).[20] The balance has been expended toward construction projects and petrochemical and electronic plants, with about $5.7 billion for the Fourth World. Other extensive commitments have been made with France (for internal development projects in Iran), West Germany (for the same), and the United Kingdom (largely direct loans and commodity transactions).

Iran's commitments to the Arab countries and to the poorer developing states have been extensive, but not as large as those of Kuwait and Saudi Arabia. Iran has committed over $600 million of investments in industrial projects in Egypt (well in excess over Saudi Arabia's investments, although the latter has extended $1 to $1.2 billion in loans),[21] and allocated about $150 million to Syria in credits.[22] The only large investment to the Fourth World is to India for the exploitation of iron ore mines ($300 million); other commitments—to Bangladesh, Pakistan, Peru, and Senegal—are in the form of general loans.

Over 90 percent of Iran's reported commitments to the West are in the form of investments, and only 5.13 percent in loans. For the Middle East the allocations priorities are more evenly distributed: 54.75 percent of Iran's commitments to the Arab states are in loans, and 45.25 percent in investments. Most of Iran's allocations to the poor countries are in loans (73.35%), some in investments (20.8%), and very little in outright grants (5.83%). Iran has chosen to channel some of its commitments to the Fourth World both through multilateral organizations and through direct bilateral transactions. These commitments include $1,720 million to the International Monetary Fund and $200 million in World Bank bonds.[23]

In large part, Iran's priorities are, first, the development of an industrial base for the country, followed by an expansion of its military capabilities, loans for foreign countries and direct foreign investments—roughly in that order. However, the government is increasing its capital transactions on other fronts as well—the West, the Arab states, the Fourth World. There are some indications that Iran is overcommitted and that it is encountering a liquidity problem. The government's announcement of its need for a $4 billion loan to meet current balance of payments and the recent decision to withdraw the offer to purchase Pan American stock indicate a potential liquidity crisis.[24]

In comparison with Iran, Saudi Arabia, or Kuwait, Algeria's commitments have been much more modest, certainly because the country's petroleum revenues are lower but also because of the reluctance to engage in extensive investments before determining priorities. Algeria has invested about $40 million in European bonds, $40 million for the import of aircraft from the United States, $232 million in television and entertainment facilities, and $33.5 million in oil exploration. The largest commitment is for more than $1.6 billion toward the expansion of downstream energy facilities, with France and Italy among the leading participants.[25] Ninety-eight percent of all reported Algerian commitments involve countries of the West. So far, Algeria has made only negligible financial commitments or direct grants to the poorer countries and equally negligible ones to the Arab states. Algeria appears to follow a cautious disbursement strategy directed exclusively toward domestic development.

The same may be said of Iraq's capital transactions, although they are of a somewhat larger magnitude and reflect a wider set of partners and priorities. Of all reported commitments, 74 percent of Iraq's allocations are directed toward the West mainly in the form of investments, 24 percent toward the Middle East, and 2 percent toward the less developed states. In large part, Iraq has concentrated on obtaining technical assistance from Italy, France, Japan, the United States, and the Communist bloc, and priority is given to internal development projects. The relatively large-scale involvement of Japan (a loan of about $1 billion over 25 years for the extension of oil facilities) represents a departure from the pattern of other countries and may illustrate a conscious attempt to diversify its disbursements of oil revenues.[26] A grant of $3 million to Spain for oil payments reflects efforts to cooperate with peripheral countries in the West.[27] About $2,288.6 million has been announced in allocations to Arab countries in aid and loans (this figure being probably an understatement). About $176 million has been committed to the Fourth World, with India being the prime beneficiary. The precise magnitudes of allocations to the poorer states are unclear beyond the $51 million in aid to Bangladesh and an undisclosed amount targeted for foreign investments in India. Commitments to Afghanistan and Somalia have also been made. Of Iraq's commitments to the poorer states, 30.52 percent are in grants, 67.8 percent in loans, and only 1.62 percent in the form of investments.

In spite of its revolutionary posture, Iraq has come to rely upon Japan, France, and the United States for much of its development. If the government's motivations were overwhelmingly ideological, there would be more evidence of Iraqi partnership with the Soviets. There is some, but surprisingly, it does not overshadow commitments to the West. It may well be that ideological considerations are paramount only regionally, not globally; or alternatively, that Iraq is indeed adopting a more pragmatic approach to political and economic decisions by giving due consideration to investment opportunities with Western participation.

Predictably, the two other OPEC countries with relatively high absorptive capacity, Venezuela and Ecuador, have followed investment trends established by the imperatives of hemispheric politics. Petroleum revenues have created a quite different problem for Venezuela than that experienced by either Saudi Arabia or Kuwait. More than half of Venezuela's petroleum revenues is spent abroad.[28] These revenues have been invested in the World Bank, the Inter-American Development Bank (including the creation of the Venezuelan Investment Fund of $500 million), the Andean Pact Bank, in United States and West German treasury notes, in a $500 million loan to the European Economic Community (EEC), and in direct loans to poorer Latin American countries.[29] These expenditures, moreover, have been consistent with Venezuelan desires to expand her economic ties in the West and to increase her influence within Latin America generally. The agreement with Mexico, Cuba, and the USSR to create a trading company for the sale of crude oil and petroleum products to countries without an oil-producing capacity is an example of Venezuela's interest in expanding her Latin American connections.[30]

Two other members of OPEC, Nigeria and Indonesia, have relatively high absorptive capability.[i] Their predicament is to meet, not create, demand for domestic development. Indonesia has a large population and some of the institutional bases necessary to sustain large-scale investments in domestic development. Nigeria's population is much smaller and its bureaucratic institutions are generally less developed, but there are demands and opportunities for domestic investments. For example, the government has targeted $48 billion for a five-year development plan. To date, Nigeria's financial commitments have been more extensive than those of Indonesia. There are some reported transactions with the European countries, most notably France and Great Britain, of undisclosed amounts for the development of Nigeria's domestic productive capacity. Some $360 million have been allocated to poor countries. By contrast, Indonesia has made no commitments to either the Fourth World or to Europe, and has made only marginal investments in the United States. About $100 million has been targeted for internal development projects with United States assistance.

Links to Cold War Politics

Given the number of commitments of undisclosed magnitudes, it is difficult to draw precise patterns of spending of oil revenues. Nonetheless, it appears that the single most extensive commitment to the United States comes from Iran and Saudi Arabia; those to Europe come mainly from Iran and Kuwait; those to Japan from Saudi Arabia and Iraq; those to the Middle East region from Kuwait

[i]Hollis B. Chenery, "Restructuring the World Economy," *Foreign Affairs*, Vol. 53, No. 2 (January 1975), pp. 242-263, places Nigeria and Indonesia into a residual category.

(possibly as high as $4 billion), Saudi Arabia ($3 billion), and Iran ($1.8 billion); and those to the Fourth World from Iran, including allocations through international institutions, and Kuwait. Venezuela and Iraq have also made some contributions, although of a relatively marginal nature.

The overwhelming preponderance of U.S.-Saudi transactions are consistent with their respective policies in the Middle East. At least until the time of King Faisal's death, the United States saw Saudi Arabia as a stabilizing influence in the region, a possible agent for repairing United States relations with the leading Arab countries, and a major actor in any resolution to the Arab-Israeli impasse.[31] To Saudi Arabia the United States represents a guarantee against forceful expansion of Communist influence, a potential ally against the growth of radical forces in Arab politics, a major supplier of advanced technology, and a potential intermediary in any direct conflict with Iran over spheres of influence in the Gulf area.

The apparent Iranian strategy of concentrating disbursements both in the United States and in Europe is based in part on a concern for diversifying allocations as well as on a traditional relationship with the European countries, most notably France, Great Britain, and West Germany. While Iran appears to play a considerable role in the United States political strategy in the Middle East, it does so without the burden of being an Arab state. To a large extent, Iran is considered a reliable ally, in ways that even Saudi Arabia may not be. It has recently been argued that Iran could, on the basis of military superiority in the area, take on the protection of United States interests and commitments without detracting from an expansion of its own influence. (See Chapter 6 for an analysis of military issues.)

Commitments to Europe are based on the assumptions that, in the immediate future, the money market in Europe is likely to be more stable and predictable than in the United States, and that the foreign policy concerns of the individual European states are more likely to adopt flexible postures toward the oil-exporting states than would the United States. In other words, it is believed that the European states are likely to conduct their foreign policy and investment policies in pragmatic ways and that the concern for direct financial returns will be more important for the Europeans than for the United States. However, in some cases, there remains a marked preference for United States technology and manufactured goods. As long as the oil-exporting countries do not seek to expand their capital transactions dramatically, pressures to extend into the United States markets may not increase markedly. Eventually, large-scale entrance in the United States may be an economic necessity due to the magnitude of the intended investments and the financial opportunities in the United States. To the extent that Saudi Arabia or Iran encounters serious political difficulties in its United States-related transactions, the tendency to channel investments through European money markets will persist.

Western Reactions and Arab Responses

To date, the oil-exporting countries have exhibited shrewd assessment and cautionary discretion in their disposal of oil revenue. The predominant view in the West, however, is to question the ability of oil-rich states to make use of their surpluses in a "responsible" fashion. Such doubts are occasioned in part by the magnitudes of the surpluses; in part by the fact that no historical precedents exist for such phenomenal expansion of the financial base of less developed countries, since trade surplus countries have always been among the advanced industrial societies; in part by fears that this situation may signal changes in world politics; and in part by apprehension that any such changes may undermine the global power of the Western alliance. Finally, there is a genuine concern that the oil-rich states simply do not have the skills to make complex financial decisions. These latter apprehensions were expressed in an article in *Foreign Policy*:

> Not the least of the dangers posed by this extreme concentration of oil power and "unearned" money power is the pervasive and corruptive influence which this will inevitably have on political, economic, and commercial action in both the relatively primitive and unsophisticated societies and the advanced societies of the dependent industrialized nations.[32]

A member of the Commission on Critical Choices for America noted in a recent article that:

> Of the $100 billion (total OPEC oil revenues) $60 billion goes into the treasuries of not-very-stable governments in thinly populated countries, thus becoming by far the biggest accumulation of floating uncommitted capital in all history. . . . Some of the Sheikhs who collected this money have studied at Harvard. This gave them a Western education; it did not give them the experience of handling the great power that comes with the possession of great wealth. Money minus diplomacy equals uncertainty. This uncertainty is another symptom of energy disease.[33]

Some oil-exporting nations consider these expressed attitudes as another manifestation of the "white man's burden," of the persisting racism in international politics and of further evidence of the Western colonial legacy.[j] Others acknowledge the novelty of this situation and the tentativeness of their own postures.[34] But the general response among the Arab leaders is to point to the cautiousness of their capital transactions as evidence of responsible financial behavior. For example, a leading OAPEC economist, Yusif A. Sayigh, stressed the realization that the erratic movement of their funds would be counterproductive because of the rapid fall in the value of foreign currencies that

[j]For a moderate articulation of this position see, the speech of Kuwaiti Minister of Foreign Affairs Sabah Al-Ahmad Al-Jabir Al-Sabah, before the Sixth Special Session of the General Assembly of the United Nations, April 16, *Kuwait*, Vol. X, No. 10 (May 1974).

accompanies the sudden movement of large accounts of money.[35] The director of the Kuwait Fund, A.Y. Al Hamad, stated: "We clearly recognize that large and persistent balance of payments deficits of oil-importing countries, whether in the developing or the developed world, can only harm our own economic development."[36] And Sheikh Yamani of Saudi Arabia declared: "How we are going to use this money is up to us, but we have no interest in upsetting the international monetary system."[37] Even the more radical states, like Iraq, have emphasized their concern for ensuring a stable international monetary system.[38]

Partly in response to accusations of being irresponsible wealthy desert Sheikhs, Arab leaders have gone to great lengths to project an image of responsibility to the world. These efforts do not appear to be effective; indeed, they may have been counterproductive in that they accentuated Western suspicion.[39] The fact that the members of OAPEC have regarded Western proposals for recycling surplus revenues as an effort to apply a sponge to the pool of Arab financial resources, absorbing these resources and then squeezing them out in Western financial markets, simply reinforces Western hostility to the Arab states.

Leaders of oil-exporting states continually emphasize that they do not regard themselves as merely money lenders or rentiers, but seek to determine appropriate coupling of their financial resources with the development needs of their own lands. The means toward this end can best be identified, so the arguments go, by policies that take account of possibilities of both regional and international cooperation. But the specific instruments of such economic cooperation remain yet to be identified.[40] Therein lies one of the major policy issues confronting the members of OAPEC. Arab economists have talked of creating an Arab financial market with an all Arab currency unit, and substantially increasing their absorptive capacity through large-scale regional investments. The purpose of this financial market would be to handle large sums of money for future use by Arab states with the "Arab Dinar" as the common currency throughout the Arab world, and eventually as an international currency. But the more immediate objective is the expansion of their domestic productive capabilities.

The Calculus of Exchange

The concern for developing and diversifying their economies in order to ensure financial resources for future generations is shared by all the oil exporters. They all acknowledge their dependence on the United States and the European countries for the acquisition of technology and view this dependence as a central aspect of their disbursement strategy. However, they insist that those countries that wish to import petroleum must also become directly involved in the development process of the exporting states. Ironically, a primary concern in

Arab policy circles is not that the consumer countries are dependent on the producers, but that the latter are critically dependent upon the consumers for access to industrial goods.

Perceptions of dependence among the OAPEC nations are shaped in part by their colonial experiences, in part by an awareness of the marked disparity in knowledge and skills, and in part by the memories of the aborted efforts toward economic integration in the Arab World. This last consideration deserves emphasis. Three factors tend to reinforce their perceptions of inefficacy and reduce the confidence attributed to them by analysts in the West: (1) the deterioration of interregional economic trade over the past 50 years, (2) the difficulties in countering trade patterns shaped by colonial powers, and (3) the repeated failures in efforts toward economic cooperation among the Arab states.

This perception of dependence upon the oil-importing countries is consciously being transformed into a strategy of interdependence. This is done by insisting that consumer countries become involved in the economic development of the producers. Oil-exporting countries argue that, over time, their own development would allow them access to international markets that have so far been largely controlled by the industrial countries. Thus, referring to the Libyan supply of oil to Italy, the Libyan Prime Minister, Jallud said, "Italy must make Italian technology available and must help us in a manner linking oil to Libyan development plans."[41] This statement may also represent an effort to improve the terms of trade. Similarly, Sheikh Yamani declared:

> The major developed powers must shoulder the great part of the duty to make sacrifices; they must allow their less powerful partners in the international community to share with them the international markets which they dominate; they must reveal to the developing countries some of the secrets of technology which they monopolize so that the process of their development can be accelerated; and of course, they must assist the oil-producing countries in establishing alternative sources of income, which would eventually replace oil.[42]

A high ranking Saudi official has been quoted as saying that even if his country invests $10 in the developed states of the West for every $1 invested in Saudi Arabia, it would be regarded as a worthwhile investment.[43] The Secretary General of OAPEC, Dr. Ali Attiga, identified areas in which petroleum resources would be exchanged for technology and with extensive Western involvement. In descending order of importance these included:[44]

1. Petrochemical manufacturing
2. Transportation of oil
3. Expansion of infrastructure with specific emphasis on education and health services, electric power, transport, and communication
4. Development of agriculture
5. Exploration of oil, mineral, and fresh water resources

6. Development of alternative sources of energy
7. Establishment of an Arab financial market
8. Technical and educational training of manpower

The oil-exporting countries are aware that present currency values of major Western nations are somewhat unstable and may jeopardize the real financial gains accrued by higher petroleum prices; this discourages them from seeking to convert their financial resources to productive assets. Some economists in the West argue that "money in the bank" represents a more efficient use of resources than "oil in the ground." This may or may not be so, depending on interest rates. But in any case, it overlooks the political dimension of this choice and its psychological roots.

The loss of control over economic assets is one of the most critical factors in an emerging calculus of exchange. For the oil-exporting countries, investing in Western markets may be efficient, but it represents a net loss of autonomy. The political premium attached to expanding national control accounts for the apparent reluctance to employ short-term economic criteria for developing a long-term strategy of capital transactions. What might be viewed as a technical issue that could be resolved on objective grounds, adhering to established principles of economic investment, is in fact regarded largely as a political problem.

Nonetheless, most oil-exporters appreciate that, in the short run, there is no viable alternative but to invest heavily in the West. But beneath this appreciation is a debate about the long-range decision of whether they should aim for a strategy of establishing a regional economy bounded by geographical limits, or concentrate on separate economic development with each country devising its own priorities of dependence or interdependence with the consuming countries of the industrialized West. In theory, the issue revolves around the potential for individual national development, the choice of allies, and, by extension, the definition of adversaries.

The Policy Debate: A Question of Strategy

In practice, the debate over current production rates and allocation of surplus revenues is about the direction and magnitude of capital transactions. It is created by competing visions of regional political orders with alternative perspectives conditioning the priorities of different countries. In Chapter 4 we described the emerging political priorities of the Arab states; here we illustrate the economic implications of these priorities.

There are two sides to this debate: One is inward-oriented and, recalling the historical expression of the Arab states and their abortive efforts at regional cooperation, seeks to focus investments on regional and national development, establish an Arab capital market to reduce vulnerability to Western policy, and ensure that the benefits of development will be channelled to the Arab people. Its dominant motives are to avoid a return to the tent-dwelling era, compensate for past economic failures, accelerate local development, and prepare for the postoil age.

The other side of the debate is outward-oriented and, stressing OAPEC dependence on the West, argues that extensive involvement in international money markets is the price for domestic industrialization and that a policy of "opting out" of the Western economic system is not viable. It stresses that the economic security of foreign investors must be ensured and that such a commitment is necessary in order to gain access to advanced technology. In turn, the oil-exporters' investments would increase their influence in the West. The dominant motivation underlying the inward-oriented debate is to ensure orderly economic development and political stability in the region.

The two competing perspectives are represented by Algeria (for the inward-oriented position) and Saudi Arabia (for the outward-oriented position). One country is characterized by high absorptive capacity for new investments, the other by low absorption potential; one by a radical political regime, the other by a conservative monarchy; one by a technocratic elite, the other by a traditional one.

The Algerians argue for the development of a new international economic arrangement. In 1974 they persuaded the General Assembly of the United Nations to adopt a Declaration and Programme of Action on the Establishment of a New International Economic Order.[45] The Algerian position stresses the need for reordering of the relationship between industrialized states and less developed countries, and is critical of a strategy that might commit Arab resources to Western investments on a long-term basis.[46] Accordingly, the oil-exporting states should not reinforce the differences between rich and poor by aligning their economic interests with those of the industrialized West, but must concentrate primarily on their own internal development. President Boumediene declared in an interview with *Le Monde*, February 1974:

> It is criminal to let large sums remain in foreign banks when the Arabs need factories, hospitals, roads, agricultural supplies, etc. The basis of a renaissance in the Arab world lies in development, and this implies financial cooperation. Without this Arabism will be an empty word.[47]

In response, Saudi Arabian leaders complain about the lack of "well studied" Arab projects, and proceed to make a case for the outward-oriented strategy. Prince Fahd, First Deputy Premier at the time of this writing, said in an interview later in 1974:

> We often hear of the demand [to redirect surplus revenues towards development of an investment in the Arab world] and read criticism of the oil states, as if they actually preferred to invest abroad. But those who pose such questions are

forgetting the experience which Arab capital has undergone and the obstacles placed in its way. Despite this, I would ask our critics to name one well-studied Arab project that has been proposed to Saudi Arabia and which Saudi Arabia has refused to finance.[48]

There are sharp differences between the views of Sheikh Yamani and President Boumediene about the investment of surplus revenues. Yamani aspires to a better position for the oil-exporting countries in what would essentially be the same international economic order. Boumediene envisions a fundamental change in the present economic system and a reassessment of the predominance of the industrialized countries of the West. Far from representing the idiosyncracies of two individuals, these views illustrate significant differences in national priorities and perspectives, and in structural characteristics such as population size and economic development.

The outward-oriented strategy assumes that the oil-exporting countries must operate effectively in the Western economic system and that large-scale changes in the world economy will not occur in the near future and are perhaps even undesirable. The optimal tactic is to become integrated within that system and to pursue policies that would increase Western involvement in Arab economic development. It is not the structure of the system that is to be manipulated, but the relative positions of its members. Surplus revenues afford the oil-producing states with a unique opportunity for effective intervention in the international economic system. In the longer run, strategies of interdependence with the West, within a Western economic system, would have beneficial effects for the development of the oil-rich states. The concepts of regionalism and regional development are amorphous at best, and illusionary at worst. National priorities must be conceived in national terms.

Sheikh Yamani is reported to have summarized the outward-oriented strategy in a closed session of OPEC by stating that whether they like it or not, the oil-producing countries are themselves part and parcel of the Western economic system, and therefore any lasting damage to that system also constitutes a threat to their own long-term interests, particularly when the present level of oil prices gives such a significant competitive advantage to the Communist bloc, which is self-sufficient in energy resources.[49] This statement incorporates three important features of political orientation in the traditional oil-exporting states: concern for safeguarding the structure of the existing international system and the dominance of the West in that system; a desire to regulate economic transactions with the West; and a desire to minimize, or at best neutralize, the potential influence of the Communist bloc. Fear of communism remains the single most critical focus of Saudi foreign policy and it is compatible with Western interests. In short, the outward-oriented strategy seeks to obtain a more favorable position within the existing international framework.

By contrast, the inward-oriented strategy is predicated on the view that transformation of the international system is not only desirable but necessary, given recent changes in the economic potentials of oil-exporting nations. The critical global political issues involve international inequalities, not East-West conflicts. Political gains can be brought about only by concentrating on economic development. A coordinated posture among the Arab oil exporters is an effective tactic for mobilizing resources for growth. The guiding premise is one of revolutionary change, both national and international. Boumediene best summarizes the inward-oriented strategy:

> For the first time in contemporary history, the advanced world feels that its destiny is tied to the Arabs and that the era of economic dependence of the Arabs on the West has gone.[50]

And further,

> If the Arabs can unify their points of view and capabilities at the lowest common level and can build with speed and strength an Arab-African bridge, they will be able to change—both politically and economically—their relations with a large number of countries in their favor in record time and in a most fruitful way. . . .
>
> We should also make the best possible use of our potential, not to harm the interests of others, but to defend our own interests and our future.[51]

It is often tempting to explain the debate in terms of differences in political orientations or in absorptive capacity. But explanations based on either ground alone will be misleading. The case of Kuwait best illustrates the traps attending simple explanations.

On the debate over the use of petroleum revenues, Kuwait is closer to Algeria than to Saudi Arabia. However, its political orientation, though slowly becoming more modern, is cautiously and haltingly still conservative. The country's absorptive capacities are similar to those of Saudi Arabia. And it shares none of the Algerian enthusiasm for revolutionary change or for reordering international economic relations. This "mix" has, in turn, led to a strategy of investing in the Middle East and supporting regional development projects. The Crown Prince and Prime Minister, Sheikh Jabir al-Ahmed al-Sabah, stated:

> Our Arab countries, with their great economic capacity, will have wide scope for investment in the coming years. There is no doubt that Arab monetary surpluses will be of great assistance to the Arab countries in strengthening and diversifying their economies and raising the standard of living of their peoples. Priority must especially be given to projects of a regional nature which serve our ultimate aim of achieving Arab unity.[52]

For Kuwait, the Algerian-Saudi debate represents a facile and possibly counterproductive statement of alternatives. Investment priorities must be viewed first in the context of national development then, depending on economic constraints, on regional development. Capital transactions with the

West ought to be regarded primarily as instrumentalities and not as objectives in their own right and only when regional investment opportunities are exhausted. Integrating the country's economic structure within the larger Western economic system must be viewed only as a tactical issue, if at all. This vision of priorities is not new for Kuwait. The country has a relatively long record of financial transactions in the Middle East. Kuwaiti financial institutions in the area are regarded by neighboring states as having a respectable record on both economic and political grounds.[53]

The orientation of the Arab oil-exporting states toward the Fourth World is based in part on some concern for the impact of higher prices on economic development, and in part on the desire to neutralize any attempt by the advanced states to mobilize poorer countries in opposition to higher prices. Furthermore, to the extent that the oil-exporters choose not to ignore the Fourth World in their strategic calculations, they can avail themselves of potential outlets for investments and technological exchange. For the more radical oil-exporters for whom changing the international economic order is a serious objective, supporting poorer states becomes an attractive political option. Yet, the oil-producers are apparently sensitive to problems of imposing political control or even employing petroleum revenues for political influence. They remain uneasy with their role as donors. So far they have approached the poorer states with caution.

The full range of problems associated with investments in the Fourth World are yet to emerge. In anticipation, the oil-producing countries are insisting that they continue to be regarded as Third World states and that OPEC is part of the less developed world. While the oil-exporters have few economic plans for the Fourth World, the total resources they have committed to it are even larger than those allocated for regional development in the Middle East. It now appears that OPEC aid commitments in 1974, totalling about $9.5 billion, actually exceeded the funds provided by the 22 OECD nations in loans and grants to the poorer states. However, actual disbursements were at about 25 percent of official commitments.[54] Some 75 percent of these disbursements were allocated to Muslim countries. The oil-exporters are presently arguing for a three-sided arrangement on loans to the less developed countries, with OPEC countries agreeing to lend money to the other developing countries based on the financial guarantee of the advanced states. So far, however, allocations to the Fourth World have been largely in the form of capital investments, not loans or grants.

Pragmatism in Economic Policy

The largest transactions by the Arab oil-exporting states can be explained largely by economic expediency, the political implications of which vary from state to state. Among the Arab states, we find much of the same trends manifested in economic interactions as we have found in political ones discussed in length in Chapter 4, where we argued that the emerging cooperation in the Arab World is increasingly based on two important factors: the dispersion of political power, and an emerging political pragmatism. One represents the new structural realities in the region; and the other reflects a new style of diplomacy and new directions in regional politics.

The same pragmatic considerations dominate the capital transactions of the other members of OPEC. For example, Iran is using its surplus revenues as direct instruments of foreign policy. Investments in the Arab World (most notably in Egypt) are all part of Iran's plans to consolidate its position in regional politics, improve relations with Arab states, and obtain assistance from the West for accelerated domestic development. Venezuela's concern for its position in Latin America has been noted earlier.

The dispersion of power among the Arab oil-exporters will reinforce the cohesion of the group and, possibly, increase incentives for maintaining the strength of OPEC. To the extent that economic cleavages among the Arab states continue to be cross-cutting rather than reinforcing, the shared motivation may tend more toward collaboration than conflict. These cleavages, brought about by the dispersion of economic power, are manifested in several ways and are consistent with the political trends described earlier.

First, those states strong in military and domestic political capabilities are most in need of added revenues but do not have surplus petroleum revenues. The largest surplus revenues are held by countries that lack both the military strength and attendant domestic infrastructure to mobilize political capabilities.

Second, the traditional patterns of donor-recipient in financial relations among the Arab states are being reversed in that the old leadership of the Arab world is now in a dependent economic position. Egypt is increasingly reliant upon the conservative states whose political stability may be endangered by extensive domestic investments. Syria, also a recipient country, is acquiring recognition as the moral and ideological leader in the region. The major donors, Saudi Arabia, Kuwait, and the U.A.E., all of whom have been traditionally weak both economically and politically, are now acquiring a new role in Middle East politics as a result of their economic power.

Third, earlier dependencies persist when considering both the differentials in technology and skilled manpower, and the use of these differentials as a basis for economic transactions. The agreement between Egypt and Kuwait of January 1974 by which Kuwait will participate in financing joint Egyptian-Kuwaiti projects, is illustrative of recognized economic interdependencies,[55] as are the agreements to set up a joint Egyptian-Kuwaiti investment company with an initial capital of $200 million[56] and a joint Egyptian-Saudi Arabian investment company with a capital of $100 million.[57] The purpose of these ventures is to couple the skilled manpower of Egypt with the capital of the oil-exporting countries to mutual gain.

Fourth, differentials in absorptive capacity provide an economic rationale for policies intended to reinforce these economic and political dependencies. Individual economic constraints are recognized and are being employed as the basis for joint policies designed for mutual advantage.

For the first time in the history of the region the riches controlled by some countries are no longer an embarrassment in their political relations, rather a powerful resource to be employed judiciously for economic and political advantage. The extensive nature of economic transactions makes the emerging pragmatism a trend shaped by necessity rather than by choice.

Both conservative and radical oil-exporting states are becoming political technocrats with an operating style of technocratic pragmatism. A Kuwaiti financial advisor states succinctly the case for nonideological approaches to capital transactions:

> The investment of these funds must be carried out according to principles which will preserve their value; give us a good yield, and also allow for selection of those types of investments that will safeguard the political interests of the Arab world and serve its national causes.[58]

On the issue of assistance to the other Arab states, the pragmatic posture is best reflected as follows:

> [We are] contributing to the strengthening of the Arab economy—which offers excellent markets and returns—on a sound and objective commercial investment basis.[k]

A shared realism lies at the core of Arab efforts to define criteria for capital transactions. Thus, the Arab oil-exporters interact with the international oil companies in accordance with the principle of maximizing gain and minimizing losses. Al-Hamad of the Kuwait Fund for Arab Economic Development states:

> The MNCs [multinational corporations] are essentially, it is true, only profit-motivated enterprises and it would be idle to expect them to have as regards our countries, or any other country . . . development aims as such. However, . . . it is up to the host countries themselves to apprise according to the merits of each individual case, the contributions that the MNCs can, eventually make towards furthering national objectives.[59]

Again, both conservative and radical states deliberately seek to reduce fears of nationalization and to reassure foreign investors of the integrity of any commitments made. An Iraqi official states:

---

[k]From a statement of the Kuwaiti Minister of Finance and Oil, 'Abd al-Rahman al-'Atiqi, to the Kuwaiti National Assembly. According to the *Middle East Economic Survey*, this was the most comprehensive and detailed survey of Kuwaiti investment policy yet to be made public. The statement covered the size and distribution of and rate of return of Kuwaiti investments both internally, regionally, and globally. *Middle East Economic Survey*, Vol. XVII, No. 35 (21 June 1974), p. i.

If there is any fear of nationalization, it has now become clear that this will not happen, particularly if this takes place within a coordinated plan from which everyone benefits.[60]

Even those states that favor nationalization argue their case on pragmatic grounds and, according to the Algerians, ". . . not as a matter of [rigid] ideological choice but . . . as a [practical] means of liberation, aimed primarily at freeing our natural resources from foreign domination and placing them under national control, thus giving their exploitation a national character."[61] Expansion of national control over disbursement, capital transactions, and investment policies is a common policy objective for all the oil-exporting countries. So, too, the Saudis have repeatedly emphasized their pragmatic policies and that their "door is open to anyone with the willingness and ability to pay us the true value of our oil. We have no inhibitions and do not hold any predetermined preferences; our choice of a country from among those that come forward will be determined solely by that country's capabilities. . . ."[62] A statement of this nature must be placed in the context of traditional Middle East politics where rhetoric has tended to prevail over rationality. It illustrates once again the emerging pragmatism in public policy.

But it is on the issue of inter-Arab economic cooperation that there is the most realistic and acute recognition of potential pitfalls. The new pragmatism has reduced but not eliminated the conventional ideological content of regional politics. Specific gains to donors underlie each individual commitment made to recipients. These gains are reflected both in the terms of aid and investment and in specific institutional developments. Egypt, with its higher absorptive capacity, is receiving the most investments, but at close to the market rate of interest and with guarantees stipulated by the donors.

Recent decisions made by the Arab Fund for Economic and Social Development reveal a persistent strain between economic and political concerns. It has granted loans to Egypt and Algeria at interest rates of 6 percent,[63] in contrast to loans to the IMF Oil Facility at 7 percent,[64] and to Europe and Japan at 10.5 percent.[65] By contrast, loans to the Sudan were extended at 4 percent. It should be higher given the country's economic weakness and attendant risks. This lower rate should be interpreted in political terms, invoking the necessity for cooperation rather than the use of strict economic criteria in the assessment of risk. The Sudan case indicates the continued, though reduced, persistence of traditional features of regional politics.

Further examples of emerging pragmatism are found in official statements regarding the establishment of joint ventures. In contrast to earlier concerns for establishing a unified Arab state encompassing the individual political entities, there is now a recognition of the legitimacy of national sovereignty. This fact may not be startling in its own right, but when viewed in the context of inter-Arab politics where the historical goal had been to create a larger Arab nation, formal recognition of individual sovereignty is a significant concession to an evolving realism. One example of this trend is the recent Sudanese-Saudi Arabian joint venture agreement for exploiting mineral resources in the Red Sea. The agreement formally recognizes the legal jurisdiction of each country over parts of the Red Sea.[66] Another example is the Investment Guarantee Agreement ratified by 12 Arab countries, which provides the necessary guarantees to protect Arab investments against nationalization or confiscation in the signatory countries, and is viewed as a particularly important instrument in assuaging the fears of the more conservative Arab governments.

Institutional Development

The first formal institution for inter-Arab cooperation was the Arab League. It was based on the assumption that in a unified Arab nation, each member state would carry equal political weight. This assumption reflects neither economic nor political differentials. In recognition of new realities, the oil-rich states have bypassed the Arab League Economic Unity Council and established several agencies, mostly under the national control of major donors. Some are assigned specific tasks; others assume a broader development mandate. For example, the Arab Company for Shipping and Repair was established to implement OAPEC's project for a dry dock in Bahrain and has subsequently expanded its membership to Saudi Arabia, Libya, Bahrain, Iraq, and Kuwait, with the mandate to extend operations in other countries. By contrast, the Arab Fund for Economic and Social Development (AFESD) was established to finance general development projects in the area; so far $213 million has been expended out of a total pledged capital of $273.8 million. Initially members included 16 Arab states and loans have been extended to South Yemen, Egypt, Syria, and Tunisia.

The new pragmatism is reflected not only in the development of institutions with specific tasks and a restricted membership, but in their acceptance by the Arab League. OAPEC and AFESD are now operating as autonomous bodies affiliated with the Arab League. The leadership of these new organizations is drawn from the new class of Arab technocrats, rather than from army officers or traditional elites as in the past.[1] Table 5-1 lists the purposes, membership, and recent activities of Arab institutions for economic transactions.

In sum, the Arab oil-exporting states are developing a pragmatic approach to the problem of disbursing surplus oil revenues. There are differing strategies, views, and priorities, but these differences do not yet overshadow possibilities of continued collaboration. Political objectives are placed in an economic perspective, and an emerging pragmatism is replacing the ideological concerns of the

[1]For biographical sketches of OAPEC leaders see, Mikdashi, *The Community of Oil Exporting Countries*, pp. 219-222; also see, Robert Stephens, *The Arabs' New Frontier* (London: Temple Smith, 1974).

past. All the oil-exporting countries are concerned with assuring the judicious management of surplus revenues and retaining discretionary power over financial allocations and disbursements.

Table 5-1
Major Institutional Developments in Arab States

Abu Dhabi Fund for Arab Economic Development	Established in July 1971 to provide development loans at low interest rates. It recently increased its capital from \$125 to \$506 million. A statement issued 26 May, 1974 declared that the increase was made to permit the fund to expand its activities in granting loans to Arab, African, and Asian states. Total loan disbursements were less than \$1 million in 1974 and are expected to increase substantially in 1975. Rates of interest range from 3 to 4.5% per year, extended so far only to Arab League members.
Arab Bank for Industrial and Agricultural Development in Africa	Set up in January 1974 by the OAPEC countries at a meeting with members of the Organization of African Unity (OAU) in Cairo to assist in the industrial and agricultural development of OAU states. Members are Libya, Iraq, Algeria, U.A.E., Qatar, Lebanon, Tunisia, Egypt, Jordan, Mauritania, Palestine, and Kuwait. OAPEC countries have increased the capital of the bank to \$210 million with an expected increase to \$400 million.
Arab Company for Shipping and Repair	Established to implement OAPEC project for a dry dock in Bahrain. Kuwait and Iraq joined in May 1974 bringing total membership to seven—Saudi Arabia, Libya, Bahrain, Iraq, Kuwait, Qatar, and the United Arab Emirates.
Arab Energy Institute	Proposed at a meeting of OAPEC oil ministers in July 1974 to conduct nuclear research, study the possible use of solar energy, and search for new uses for oil. Its intent is to reduce Arab dependence on imported technology.
Arab Financial Company	Established in Beirut in April 1974 with a capital base of \$2.6 million to carry out financial operations, including the creation and development of investment activities in the Arab world. Shareholders: 1. Arab Organizations: Kuwait Investment Company (18%), Investment Promotion Group (18%), Beirut Riyad Bank (9%), Banque Europeènne Pour le Moyen-Orient (9%). Total = 54%. 2. Non-Arab Organizations: Banque de l'Union Europeènne, France (18%), Manufacturer's Hanover Trust Co., U.S., (18%), The Bank of Tokyo, Ltd., Japan (10%). Total = 46%.
Arab Fund for Economic and Social Development (The Arab Fund)	Established in May 1968 and began operations in February 1972 with a membership of 17 Arab countries and a capital base of \$347 million. Its purpose is to finance development projects in the Arab world. So far \$213 million has been paid out of a total pledged capital of \$273.8 million at interest

Table 5-1 (cont.)

	rates of 4 to 6% per annum, including recent loans to South Yemen, $24.3 million, Sudan, Egypt, and Algeria, $69.3 million, Syria, $6.8 million, and Tunisia, $6.8 million. Most projects are financed cooperatively with the Kuwait Fund, the Abu Dhabi Fund, and the World Bank.
Arab Investment Guarantee Organization	Set up in April 1974 by the Arab League Economic Unity Council in Cairo. The participants are Egypt, Syria, Lebanon, Iraq, Sudan, Abu Dhabi, Algeria, Libya, Tunisia, Qatar, Jordan, and Kuwait. The agreement provides for the necessary guarantees to protect Arab investments against nationalization or confiscation in the signatory countries. It is also designed to encourage mobility of capital funds employed in financing development projects in these countries. The capital of the organization is set at $33.8 million.
Arab Maritime Petroleum Transport Company	Sponsored by OAPEC to create an oil tanker fleet controlled by Arab states. Members are Saudi Arabia, Kuwait, Abu Dhabi, Libya, Iraq, Algeria, Qatar, and Bahrain. It recently placed an order for the construction of two 278,000 ton tankers from a French shipyard.
Arab Petroleum Investment Company	Established in September 1974 by OAPEC Special Committee to participate in the development of oil projects and industries as well as subsidiaries with preference to joint Arab projects. Capital authorized at $676-1,014 million. Actual allocations are $169-338 million. Priorities are given to joint ventures between member governments for oil-related projects.
Islamic Development Bank	Established in December 1973 by the delegates to the Islamic Finance Ministers Conference, including Algeria, Egypt, Chad, Guinea, Indonesia, Jordan, Kuwait, Qatar, Lebanon, Libya, U.A.E., Malaysia, Mauritania, Morocco, Niger, Oman, Pakistan, Saudi Arabia, Senegal, Somalia, Sudan, Turkey, North Yemen, Tunisia, and Mali. Its initial capital was set at $1 billion to finance development in Islamic countries and increased to $2.4 billion. Large non-Islamic states are also eligible for loans.
Kuwait Fund for Arab Economic Development (KFAED)	Established in 1961 to fund development projects in Arab countries. Since 1961 it has disbursed $426 million to Arab states. The fund helped establish the Arab Fund for Economic and Social Development. In April 1974 Kuwait increased KFAED capital to $3,380 million and is the major lending institution of the Kuwaiti government. Loan commitments totalling $160 million to several African and Asian countries have been reported as of April 1975. Interest rates range from 3 to 4%. During its first years of operation KFAED extended over 40 loans to 12 Arab countries including projects in transportation, agriculture, and power generation.

Table 5-1 (cont.)

The Iraq Foreign Development Fund (The Iraq Fund)	Established in June 1974 with a capital of $169 million to provide medium long-term loans to assist in financing developments in Arab countries and in poor states. The first loan was extended to Afghanistan. Data for 1974 are not available.
The Saudi Development Fund (SADF)	Established in September 1974 with a capital of $2.8 billion to provide project loans to developing countries. SADF loans are to be repaid in Saudi Arabian riyals and any loan is not to exceed 7% of the fund's capital or exceed one-half of the total cost of the project. SADF stipulates that contracts provide guarantees against nationalization of SADF assets in borrowing countries. There are reports of loans to Egypt in 1974, totalling $161 million for partial financing of development projects.
Special OAPEC Fund for Arab Nonoil Producers	Established in June 1974 as a Special Fund with allocations of $80 million for 1974 to be distributed to 6 countries: Sudan ($37.5 million), the Yemen Arab Republic ($11.0 million), the P.D.R. of Yemen ($11.3 million), Morocco ($8.2 million), Somalia ($7.3 million), and Mauritania ($4.7 million). Loans are interest-free, repayable after 10 years following a 10 year grace period.
Special Arab Fund for Africa	Established in March 1974 with a capital of $200 million and administered through the African Development Bank for oil purchases by African states and to assist in the development of oil resources in Africa. Loans carry 1% interest rate, repayable over 5 years after 3 years of grace. Loan recipients are selected by the Organization of African Unity in cooperation with the Arab League. Sixteen African countries received the loans in 1974.

Notes

1. Alfred G. Musrey, *An Arab Common Market: A Study in Inter-Arab Trade Relations*, 1920-67 (New York: Praeger Publishers, 1969), p. 8.

2. Ibid.

3. Press Conference by Abu Dhabi Minister of Petroleum and Industry, Mana' Sa'id al-Otaiba, *Middle East Economic Survey*, Vol. XVII, No. 7 (7 December 1973), p. 3.

4. Libyan Prime Minister Major 'Abd al-Salam Jallud, *Middle East Economic Survey*, Vol. XVII, No. 15 (1 February 1974), p. i.

5. President Ahmad Hassan al-Bakr's remarks contained in a political report submitted to the Eighth National Conference of the Arab Ba'ath Socialist party, which was held from 8 to 12 January 1974, as reported in the *Middle East Economic Survey*, Vol. XVII, No. 21 (March 15, 1974), p. 5.

6. Address byShaikh Ahmad Zaki Yamani at the Sixth Special Session of the United Nations General Assembly as reported in *Middle East Economic Survey*, Vol. XVII, No. 27 (26 April 1974), p. 21.

7. Address by Dr. Abderrahman Khene, Secretary General of the Organization of the Petroleum Exporting Countries at an international conference on "Oil and Money" in London on 18 April 1974, as reported in *Middle East Economic Survey* Vol. XV.II, No. 29 (10 May 1974), p. 5.

8. Interview by Dr. Ali Ahmad Attiga, the Secretary General of the Organization of Arab Petroleum Exporting Countries, which appeared in the July/August 1974 issue of the Beirut monthly, *Qadaya Arabiya* as reported in *Middle East Economic Survey*, Vol. XVII, No. 51 (11 October 1974), p. ii.

9. See, the Solemn Declaration issued by the Conference of the Sovereigns and Heads of State of the OPEC Member Countries, *The New York Times*, April 1, 1975.

10. *The New York Times*, September 20, 1974.

11. *The New York Times*, September 18, 1974; *Middle East Economic Survey*, Vol. XVII, No. 48 (20 September 1974).

12. *The Economist*, January 5, 1974.

13. *Middle East Economic Survey*, Vol. XVIII, No. 32 (30 May 1975); *The New York Times*, May 19, 1975.

14. *Middle East Economic Survey*, Vol. XVII, No. 21 (15 March 1974); *Boston Globe*, August 23, 1974.

15. *The New York Times*, February 20, 1974; *Middle East Economic Survey*, Vol. XVII, No. 18 (22 February 1974).

16. *The New York Times*, January 18, 1974; *Middle East Economic Survey*, Vol. XVIII, No. 11 (3 January 1975); *Middle East Economic Survey*, Vol. XVIII, No. 12 (10 January 1975).

17. *Middle East Economic Survey*, Vol. XVIII, No. 11 (3 January 1975).

18. See, for example, the *Middle East Economic Survey*, Vol. XVII, No. 30 (17 May 1974).

19. See, for example, the *Middle East Economic Survey*, Vol. XVII, No. 15 (1 February 1974); see also, the *Middle East Economic Survey*, Vol. XVIII, No. 33 (6 June 1975).

20. *The New York Times*, March 5, 1975; *Middle East Economic Survey*, Vol. XVIII, No. 20 (7 March 1975).

21. *Middle East Economic Survey*, Vol. XVII, No. 32 (31 May 1974); *Middle East Economic Survey*, Vol. XVIII, No. 6 (29 November 1974).

22. *Middle East Economic Survey*, Vol. XVII, No. 31 (24 May 1974).

23. *Middle East Economic Survey*, Vol. XVII, No. 29 (10 May 1974); *Middle East Economic Survey*, Vol. XVIII, No. 19 (28 February 1975); *Middle East Economic Survey*, Vol. XVIII, No. 23 (29 March 1974).

24. *The New York Times*, July 27 and August 15, 1975.

25. *Middle East Economic Survey*, Vol. XVII, No. 12 (11 January 1974), No. 14 (25 January 1974), No. 29 (10 May 1974), No. 38 (12 July 1974); *Middle East Economic Survey*, Vol. XVIII, No. 12 (10 January 1975), No. 14 (24 January 1975), No. 24 (4 April 1975), No. 26 (18 April 1975), and No. 27 (25 April 1975).

26. *Middle East Economic Survey*, Vol. XVII, No. 44 (23 August 1974).

27. *Middle East Economic Survey*, Vol. XVII, No. 13 (18 January 1974).

28. *The New York Times*, April 27, 1975.

29. *The New York Times*, April 25, 1975; March 5, 1975; April 1, 1975.

30. *The New York Times*, March 26, 1975.

31. *The New York Times*, March 26 and 30, 1975.

32. Walter Levy, "An Atlantic-Japanese Energy Policy," *Foreign Policy* (Summer 1973), p. 166.

33. Edward Teller, "The Energy Disease: Diagnosis and Prescription for an International Ailment," *Harpers*, Vol. 250 (February 1975), p. 16.

34. See, Jahangir Amuzegar, "Philosophy, Views and Objectives of the Oil Exporting Countries," Statement before the Advanced Seminar on Energy Economics and Management, Northwestern University, Evanston, Illinois, June 24, 1975 (mimeographed).

35. From an abridged text of a talk given by Dr. Yusif A. Sayigh at a meeting of the Energy Committee of the North Atlantic Assembly in Brussels on 21 October 1974 as reported in *Middle East Economic Survey*, Vol. XVIII, No. 12 (19 January 1975), p. 4.

36. Abdlatif Y. Al-Hamad in his address given to the Convention of the Bankers' Association for Foreign Trade, San Diego, 10 April 1974, in Abdlatif Y. Al-Hamad, *Investing Oil Revenues* (Kuwait Fund for Arab Economic Development, April 1974), p. 19.

37. Shaikh Ahmad Zaki Yamani, *Middle East Economic Survey*, Vol. XVII, No. 15 (1 February 1974), p. 3.

38. See the interview with Dr. Sadoon Hammadi, Iraq's Minister of Oil and Minerals, in *Middle East Economic Survey*, Vol. XVII, No. 9 (21 December 1973), p. 1.

39. See Thomas O. Enders, "OPEC and the Industrial Countries: The Next Ten Years," *Foreign Affairs*, Vol. 53, No. 4 (July 1975), pp. 625-637.

40. Abdlatif Y. Al-Hamad, "Arab Capital and International Finance," *The Banker*, Vol. 124, No. 575 (January 1974), p. 25.

41. Libyan Prime Minister Major 'Abd al-Salam Jallud, at a press conference in Tripoli, Libya on 23 January 1974 as reported in *Middle East Economic Survey*, Vol. XVII, No. 15 (1 February 1974), p. i.

42. Shaikh Ahmad Zaki Yamani, "Producer-Consumer Relationships in the Oil Industry: A New Era," *Middle East Economic Survey*, Vol. XVII, No. 30 (17 May 1974), p. 4.

43. Christopher Tugendhat, "Oil—How to Avoid a Catastrophe?" *The Banker,* Vol. 124, No. 576 (February 1974), pp. 101-102; see also, *The Petroleum Economist*, "The Race for Industrialization," Vol. 41, No. 9 (September 1974), pp. 324-328.

44. Dr. Ali A. Attiga, secretary general of OAPEC, "The Role of OAPEC in Promoting Cooperation between its Members and Oil Importing Countries," *Middle East Economic Survey*, Vol. XVII, No. 30 (17 May 1974), pp. 6-8.

45. See Resolution 3201 (S-VI) adopted by the United Nations General Assembly on 1 May 1974, as reported in *Middle East Economic Survey*, Vol. XVII, No. 31 (24 May 1974), pp. i-iv.

46. Dr. Ali Ahmad Attiga, in an interview published in the July/August 1974 issue of the Beirut monthly *Qadaya Arabiya*, as reported in *Middle East Economic Survey*, Vol. XVII, No. 51 (11 October 1974), p. ii.

47. President Boumediene of Algeria in an interview with *Le Monde* on 5 February 1974, as reported in *Middle East Economic Survey*, Vol. XVII, No. 16 (8 February 1974), p. xi.

48. Prince Fahd ibn 'Abd al-'Aziz of Saudi Arabia in an interview in the Beirut daily *al-Anwar* on 25 October 1974, in *Middle East Economic Survey*, Vol. XVIII, No. 1 (25 October 1974), p. 4.

49. Shaikh Jabir al-Ahmad al-Sabah, Crown Prince and Prime Minister of Kuwait, *Middle East Economic Survey*, Vol. XVII, No. 18 (22 February 1974), p. 8.

50. *Middle East Economic Survey*, Vol. XVII, No. 35 (21 June 1974), p. 3.

51. President Boumediene of Algeria in an interview with the Beirut daily *al-Nahar* on 19 October 1974, as reported in *Middle East Economic Survey*, Vol. XVIII, No. 1 (25 October 1974), p.,5.

52. Ibid.

53. Ragaei el-Mallakh, *Economic Development and Regional Cooperation: Kuwait* (Chicago: University of Chicago Press, 1968), pp. 232-237.

54. International Monetary Fund, "Financial Assistance from Oil Exporting Countries to Developing Countries," May 8, 1975 (mimeographed).

55. *Middle East Economic Survey*, Vol. XVII, No. 15 (1 February 1974).

56. *Middle East Economic Survey*, Vol. XVII, No. 41 (2 August 1974).

57. *Middle East Economic Survey*, Vol. XVIII, No. 32 (30 May 1975).

58. Mr. Khalid Abu al-Sa'ud, advisor on financial affairs to the Kuwaiti Ministry of Finance and Oil, in an interview in the Beirut weekly, *al-Hawadith* on 18 October 1973 as reported in *Middle East Economic Survey*, Vol. XVII, No. 18 (22 February 1974), p. i.

59. Al-Hamad, "Arab Capital and International Finance," p. 28.

60. Mr. Saddam Husain, vice president of Iraq's Revolutionary Command Council, in an interview with the Kuwait daily *al-Siyash* on 5 March 1974, as reported in *Middle East Economic Survey*, Vol. XVII, No. 20 (8 March 1974), p. ii.

61. President Boumediene in his address to the Sixth Special Session of the United Nations General Assembly as reported in *Middle East Economic Survey*, Vol. XVII, No. 27 (26 April 1974), p. 10.

62. Yamani, "Producer-Consumer Relationships in the Oil Industry: A New Era," p. 5.

63. *Middle East Economic Survey*, Vol. XVII, No. 26 (19 April 1974), p. 13.

64. International Monetary Fund, *IMF Survey*, Vol. 4, No. 7 (April 14, 1975), p. 97.

65. *Business International*, Vol. 21, No. 50 (December 20, 1974), p. 402.
66. *Middle East Economic Survey*, Vol. XVII, No. 31 (24 May 1974), pp. 1-2.

The Search for Control: Economic Coercion and Military Force

Debates on price and production policies, alternative recycling proposals, and different strategies of capital commitments are all manifestations of efforts to control petroleum transactions. This chapter examines the uses of economic and military force as means of attaining control over the global energy system. The question of control is viewed from two perspectives: first, that of the oil-exporting countries, in terms of (a) their strategic calculations, and (b) their use of economic sanctions; and second, that of the oil-importing countries, in terms of (a) the possibility of counterembargos, (b) the development of a joint energy posture to counter the power of the Organization of Petroleum Exporting Countries, and (c) the use of military force.

To some extent both exporters and importers recognize their mutual interdependencies. Both realize that manipulating these interdependencies is a question of strategy and not a principle of value in its own right. Both are involved in a general search for allies and adversaries, partisans and neutrals. Various arguments for buttressing existing international institutions, for developing new ones, for involving the West in the development of the oil-exporters, for involving the importers in the economies of the exporters, for assisting the development of poorer states, for reorganizing the international economic system—all reflect power struggles to enhance national postures, to organize economic markets, and to maximize political gains and minimize attendant losses. It is the discrepancy between preferred objectives and empirical realities that pose both producers and consumers with mirror-image problems. The instrumentalities available to each differ as do their potential effectiveness. But the search for control in a situation of perceived loss of control is a shared predicament. In addition, the discrepancies between overt manifestations of policy (actual behavior) and statements of intent (professed behavior) yield further clues into the bounds of permissible behavior for each state. What is not said can often assist in interpreting what is indeed meant. Modes of communication are not always formal; messages are often implicit rather than explicit. In an environment where formal rules of interaction are yet to be developed, nations behave on the basis of mutual expectations.[1]

The use of military force as a means of reducing interdependencies and increasing national autonomy has, so far, remained largely in the background of current debates among the oil-exporters and the oil-importers. Force is generally resorted to when parties to a conflict perceive no other lower cost alternative to obtaining their objectives; it always presumes some calculation that anticipated gains will outweigh expected losses. The issues at hand are undoubtedly complex in that they involve consideration of the options available to the consumer countries in their attempts to increase control, and the options available to the producers as they seek to extend control not only over petroleum decisions but over the entire military-strategic dimensions of their own foreign policies as well. Observers agree that the oil-importing countries could in fact employ force successfully, but they disagree as to their intent to do so. In addition the large-scale transfer of sophisticated weapons into the Middle East is placing in doubt the conventional wisdom regarding the military weakness of the oil-exporting countries. Iran is rapidly becoming one of the dominant military powers in the region, presently competitive with Israel and, in the longer run, possibly also with Soviet and United States capabilities in the area.

The use of military force as a means of controlling energy flows assumes complex proportions as Middle East conflicts and regional politics are taken into account. The large-scale flow of armaments into the area may well increase the probability of local conflict. The cohesion of the oil-exporting countries may be disintegrating under a set of regional pressures. In the event of a serious inter-Arab dispute or a military confrontation between Iran and Arab states, OPEC would surely be destroyed.

Strategic Assessments of Producer Countries

The military calculations of oil-exporting countries in the Middle East are closely related to their weapons acquisitions. The flow of military hardware in the region since the rise in oil prices in the aftermath of the October 1973 war is truly dramatic,[2] but its impact remains a matter of dispute among strategic analysts. The rise of Iranian military capability is universally recognized and accepted reluctantly by the Arab states. Less clear, however, is the apportionment of motivation for such purchases in terms of the three conflict systems converging in the Middle East—inter-Arab, Arab-Israeli, and Soviet-American—and in terms of domestic as well as local strategic objectives. So, too, there remain uncertainties regarding the implications of such flows for the cohesion of OPEC, and for the coordination of policy in the event of another oil embargo.

The most extensive military purchases from the West have been made by Iran and Saudi Arabia. Those from the USSR have been made by Egypt, Algeria, Iraq, Syria, and, marginally, Kuwait. Of these, the Iranian purchases are the most substantial in light of their military potential. Iran purchased 30 F-14 fighters in January of 1974 at a cost of $900 million.[3] In February an additional 30 F-14 fighters as well as 50 Air Force F-15's were contracted for.[4] Eight months later is was disclosed that Iran and the U.S. Department of Defense were negotiating a cash sale of $4 billion for communication equipment, and in October 1974

McDonnell-Douglas Aircraft in the United States announced a letter of intent signed by Iran for the purchase of 36 F4E Phantom fighters, with an estimated cost of $150 million.[5] In November of that year Iran awarded Northrup Corporation an $8 million contract for aerial target drones.[6] These figures are illustrative of the magnitudes involved and the degree of Iranian commitment to military purchases, but the specifics might well change in months to come. In addition, there are serious utilization, training, and management problems which may delay effective usage.

In October 1974 Saudi Arabia awarded Raytheon Corporation a $260 million contract to modernize the country's Hawk air defense system.[7] In January of the next year a $750 million agreement was negotiated with the United States for the purchase of jet fighters and the training of pilots.[8] Critics of United States arms sales to Saudi Arabia point to the potential long-term implications of these sales for regional politics and of the destabilizing effect; and to the apparent Saudi strategy of overtly arguing for lowering petroleum prices but at the same time keeping prices high. Critics also point to the obvious United States conflicts of interests in the area, in terms of simultaneous support for Iran, Saudi Arabia, and Israel when conflict may break out between any two of them at any point. Supporters of the United States strategy of military assistance to Saudi Arabia argue for its intended stabilizing effect and for its potential contribution to the reduction of petroleum prices. Both critics and supporters of the United States posture predicate their arguments on some implicit notions of control and of the costs attached to the strategy. But there are differing interpretations of who controls whom, to what degree, with which policy instruments, and to what intended effects.

Saudi Arabia has also negotiated an $800 million arms deal with France for the purchase of tanks, planes, armored cars, and the like.[9] The only Saudi transaction with the USSR is a joint purchase with Kuwait amounting to $700 million in armaments.[10] Neither details on the nature of the commitment nor on arms specifications have been made public.

The Saudi purchases interject a critical element in the country's military potential and could affect its actual capabilities in the not too distant future. These purchases are sufficient to allow for a limited use of force in adjacent territories in the Arabian Peninsula, but they are not comparable to Iranian purchases either in magnitude or in potential impact on the strategic balance in the Gulf.

Changes in budgetary allocations to the military yield further indication of the commitments undertaken since 1973. Table 6-1 compares the defense budgets of eight Arab states, Iran, and for illustrative purposes Israel as well, noting expenditures in 1973, expectations for 1975, and changes between the two. The actual significance of these changes is unclear largely because of delays involved in making effective use of budgetary allocations.

There are numerous explanations for each state's expanding financial commit-

Table 6-1
Middle Eastern Defense Budgets, 1973 and 1975
(In Millions of U.S. Dollars)

Country	Actual 1973	Estimated 1975	% Increase
Algeria	100	404	304.00%
Egypt	1737	3117	79.44%
Iran	2010	3225	60.44%
Iraq	338	803	137.57%
Jordan	119	142	19.32%
Kuwait	n.a.	167	–
Libya	145	402	177.24%
Saudi Arabia	1090	1808	65.87%
Syria	216	460	112.96%

Note: In 1973 Israel's military budget was $1.474 million; in 1975 it rose to $3.688 million, representing an increase of 150.2% over this two-year period.

n.a. = not available.

Source: International Institute for Strategic Studies, *The Military Balance*, 1974-75, Various Issues; Dale R. Tahtinen, Arms in the Persian Gulf (Washington, D.C.: American Enterprise Institute, 1974).

ments to the military.[11] For Iran, it is conventionally believed that fear of Soviet power has long dominated the country's foreign policy concerns, reinforced by perceptions of a vacuum in the area created by the withdrawal of British forces and the reluctance of the United States to assume a strong position in the Gulf area or the Indian Ocean. Memories of the Persian Empire provide further impetus for Iran's increasing military capability. The dominant imperative in regional politics, however, is to ensure Iran's military superiority in the Gulf and to reinforce this policy through the use of economic and diplomatic means. Financial support to Egypt and the settlement of the border dispute with Iraq are illustrative of a comprehensive foreign policy strategy.[12] This strategy dictates the necessity to neutralize sources of opposition to Iranian strength. Efforts to exclude super-power presence in the Indian Ocean (articulated in terms of a "zone of peace"), to reduce incentives for nuclear proliferation in the Middle East (articulated in terms of a "nuclear-free zone"), and to retain the option of developing nuclear capability must be viewed in those terms.[13] A cornerstone of this strategy is to ensure passage through the Straits of Hormuz to protect critical oil fields.[14]

The control of internal dissidence in Iran is another, but only a marginally important, rationale for the country's military buildup. However, critics of the Iranian government argue that maintaining domestic order is a major political goal for the regime and that these military purchases bear directly upon its ability to exert force internally.[15] Government supporters, on the other hand, point only to external factors as causing these large-scale military purchases. Finally, the influence of bureaucratic factors must not be ignored in accounting for the large purchases from the United States. This is the one area where past decisions have been regarded as successful by both donor and recipient, each believing that their individual goals are converging, possibly reinforcing their respective positions in the Gulf region. Iran has acquired a sophisticated understanding of bureaucratic politics in the United States and is employing the extensive arms purchases as a vehicle for strengthening diplomatic and economic cooperation.

The characteristics of the Saudi policy generate important constraints on its foreign policy and on the possibilities for mobilizing its military capabilities. The leadership's immediate concerns in the Gulf are necessarily more limited. However, Saudi Arabia aspires to a military role throughout the Arabian Peninsula. But large-scale investments in the training of military personnel and the formation of attendant infrastructure have been made only recently. There are significant gestation periods in the development of effective capabilities, which reduce the immediate significance of budgetary allocations and current arms purchases.

A dominant Saudi objective so far has been the safeguarding of political stability in the region, with a prime interest in supporting Egypt's new posture. A $1 billion Saudi gift to Egypt in August 1974 was made in recognition of stabilizing objectives of the Sadat government. Clearly, Saudi Arabia's immediate concerns with inter-Arab and petroleum politics stem from its aspiration to economic leadership in the Arab World. The Arab-Israeli conflict may well be of secondary importance. Saudi military purchases are not yet seriously intended to influence differential capabilities between Arabs and Israelis, but to increase the country's credibility in Arab politics and buttress its posture within the Organization of Arab Petroleum Exporting Countries and, ultimately, within OPEC.

Differences in the preferences and priorities of Saudi Arabia and Iran have been debated extensively by observers in the West. The prevailing wisdom is that the political differences between the countries are strong and that Saudi preferences for lower oil prices are motivated in part by fear of Iranian expansion in the Gulf area,[16] in part by a concern for the diplomatic power accrued to Iran from petroleum revenues, and in part by Saudi Arabia's increasing involvement in Arab development. There is much speculation that the disintegration of OPEC will result from potential conflicts between Iran and Saudi Arabia. Nonetheless, there remains a marked degree of cohesion between the two countries, undoubtedly aided by common gains obtained so far. Saudi Arabia's interest in the Arabian Peninsula do clash, but only tangentially, with Iran's border objectives in the Gulf area and the Indian Ocean. In addition, the Saudis are not involved in regional problems emanating from the Indian-Pakistan conflict and do not share Iran's fear of the effects of this conflict on its relations with the Arab states.[a] On balance, Saudi Arabia has found it necessary to emphasize the economic dimension of its foreign policy to the relative subordination of military factors.

In sum, for the oil-exporting countries of the Middle East, strategic calculations remain strictly regional. There the key military issue is not the use of force for manipulating energy interdependence, but the expansion of military capabilities for regional political control, the expansion of weapons systems, and the implications of such flows for changing the military-strategic calculations in the area. Motivations for weapons acquisition are mixed and calculations diffuse. But the fact remains that the strategic policy is providing an increasingly critical input into petroleum politics, the magnitude of which is not yet fully appreciated. So far, however, the oil-exporting countries have relied by necessity on economic, not military, force in their dispute with the oil-importing countries.[b]

Economic Sanctions as Instruments of Force: Oil Embargo and Production Cutbacks

The ability of some oil-exporting countries to employ economic sanctions as an instrument of force has been demonstrated in the embargo of 1973 coincident with the fourth Arab-Israeli war. The Arab oil-exporters had previously considered the possibility of an economic move as a necessary correlate of any military venture against Israel. The 1967 effort was the first, albeit abortive, effort toward economic and military cooperation among the Arab states. The embargo six years later resulted in higher petroleum prices for everyone and more than temporary cutbacks in production by some states.

Some observers argue that it was only after the war broke out that the economic implications of an embargo became clear and economic directives were allowed to take precedence over political ones. Others maintain that the war was only an excuse, and that the oil-exporting countries had found a convenient opportunity for raising prices. Both positions are probably correct. For some OPEC members, most notably the Arab states, the embargo was motivated by their conflict with Israel. For other members, the 1973 war and the oil embargo were convenient means of increasing petroleum prices. Once prices were raised, maintaining the cohesion of OPEC became a paramount policy consideration for all the oil-exporting states, and the initial motivation for the price rises receded in importance.

[a]*The New York Times*, January 22, 1975. Nonetheless, Saudi Arabia has not been indifferent to the countries of South Asia. See, *The New York Times*, January 2, 1975.

[b]Although an embargo is not per se an act of war, the United States government concluded that Saudi Arabia had violated a 1933 treaty with the United States by using the embargo in a discriminatory manner. See, *The New York Times*, December 19, 1973.

The events of October 1973 appeared to reflect a logic of their own. When violence broke out in the Middle East, the entire framework of petroleum transactions was fundamentally affected. The story of the oil embargo is closely entertwined with the development of OPEC price policy. Indeed, the interconnections are so strong that recounting the embargo story inevitably entails a survey of the evolution of OPEC pricing policies.

On the sixth of October, the Egyptians crossed the Suez canal marking the beginning of another war in the Middle East. Ten days later the Gulf producers increased posted prices by an average of 70 percent; other members of OPEC immediately followed suit. On October 17, members of OAPEC resolved to cut back oil production by 5 percent in relation to the levels of September 1973, and to reduce production by an additional 5 percent per month until such time as Israel withdrew from the territories occupied in 1967. Two days later Libya unilaterally initiated a total embargo on oil deliveries to the Netherlands. In a similar move, Iraq nationalized the Dutch share of the Basrah Oil Company. At the same time, however, Iraq denounced the OAPEC decision to cut back production, claiming that it would harm only Western Europe and Japan, which had been supportive of the Arab states. This position marked the first official dissent on embargo within OAPEC. It is significant that Iraq, a more radical state, had taken that posture. Even more important is the fact that, at the time, Iraq was not denounced by the other states. The evolving rules within OAPEC were to seek only broad cohesion and allow maximum latitude for individual responses—a consideration that became consistent with, and indeed reinforced, an emerging political pragmatism in the region.

On October 26, *The New York Times* estimated that the total cutback in production had reached a level of 4 million barrels per day, approximately 20 percent of the prewar flows. Several days later, Sheikh Ali Khalifa al-Sabah, head of the price commission of OPEC, voiced a new fear among the Arabs, namely, that the United States would undertake military action against the oil-producers. On November 5, OAPEC announed that each of its 11 members would reduce oil production to 75 percent of their September 1973 output, with a forecast of an additional 5 percent drop in December. *The Middle East Economic Survey* reported that total cutbacks had reached 28.5 percent of September production.[17] The European Economic Community responded to these developments by issuing a joint statement calling on both Egypt and Israel to return to the cease-fire lines of October 22. This statement included an additional call to Israel to "end the territorial occupation which it has maintained since 1967," adding that peace was incompatible with the "acquisition of territory by force."[18]

On November 18, 1973, OAPEC announced that the 5 percent reduction scheduled for December would not be implemented in appreciation of the stance taken by the European Economic Community, but that embargo against the United States and the Netherlands would continue. Three days later Secretary of State Kissinger warned that the United States might have to consider retaliatory action if the Arab move continued "unreasonably and indefinitely."[19] The immediate response from Saudi Arabia was that further production cutbacks would be made—as much as 80 percent—if the United States, Europe, or Japan planned any countermoves, clearly implying massive destruction of oil wells should the West use military force. On December 6, again Kissinger articulated the implicit threat regarding "What the U.S. might do if other countries treat us unreasonably. . . ." Three days later nine Arab oil ministers agreed on a further 5 percent reduction to take effect on January 1, 1974. However, Iraq announced that it planned to increase its oil production in spite of the other Arab cutbacks.

Throughout, Iran assumed the role of impartial observer, calling upon the Arabs to remove the embargo, but applying little diplomatic or political pressure. In December, Iran announced the sale of crude petroleum at $14.00 to $17.50 per barrel. Six Persian Gulf producers announced that the price of oil would double on January 1, 1974; and OAPEC declared that starting the new year, production cutbacks would be reduced from 25 percent to 15 percent. Venezuela announced the intent to cut production levels by around 10 percent in 1975. At the same time, other members of OPEC initiated an increase in prices. Non-OPEC members followed suit. On December 26, Canada announced an increase of $0.30 per barrel. In January of 1974, OPEC offered to freeze its prices over the next three months. The first efforts to lift the embargo against the United States began in January, supported primarily by Egypt, and opposed by Libya and Iraq. Two months later, on March 17, the boycott was lifted. On June 15, OPEC again decided to freeze prices. In July the embargo against the Netherlands was also raised. Since then production has been reduced, with the exception of Iran and Iraq, to about 85 percent of the September 1973 level.

The other members of OPEC have persisted with their refusal to initiate any significant roll back in prices. As of this writing the declines have been marginal. Indonesia even announced a rise in prices from $10.80 to $11.70 per barrel. (For illustrative purposes, see Table 2-2 for prices as of March 1975.)

So far, at least, the cohesion of OPEC had been retained. The directive that economic benefits must not be jeopardized for political gain resolved the impasse between the Arab oil-producers and the United States. The Arabs had chosen not to make the demand for immediate evacuation of occupied territories a necessary condition to the termination of the embargo; they exhibited a willingness to accept signals for potential evacuation as a sufficient condition. More important, however, they had become aware of the limitations of economic force as a policy instrument. The key political objectives could not be attained solely through economic coercion. And clearly the non-Arab members of OPEC benefited from the economic consequences of the embargo.

By the turn of the year, in January 1975, economic and political motives had become blurred and the underlying objectives increasingly ambiguous. Some obvious benefits had accrued to every oil-producing state, including those we have designated earlier as de facto members of OPEC. So, too, the Arab states had attained some limited political gains—many of them merely symbolic. And the major importers were beginning to appreciate the potential impact of economic force exercised by select oil-exporting countries. As long as the other oil-producers made no concerted effort to counter the strategies of OAPEC, net gains could be obtained and the cohesion of OPEC protected. By the middle of 1974 it had also become clear that political developments were such as to reinforce the strength of the cartel. But no one had the illusion that this cohesion would continue indefinitely: partisans as well as detached observers question only the timing of the impending breakup. Any subsequent embargo may not produce either the economic or the political cohesion that had characterized the use of economic coercion in October 1973.

Of the many options available to consumer countries in their efforts to exert control over petroleum transactions and break up the cartel, the three examined here—counterembargo, unified energy posture, and the use of armed force—are all confrontation stances. The first is economic, the second largely diplomatic, and the third military. All three share a common recourse to coercion and force. As such, they differ from other consumer options examined earlier, such as the development of alternative sources of energy (in Chapter 1) or financial measures and recycling proposals for reducing the impact of increased oil payments (in Chapter 3).

These three confrontation options are accompanied by a different set of costs and benefits and differing probabilities of success depending on the goals specified and the criteria employed. Further, they have different time horizons both in terms of performance and potential consequences.

Counterembargo as an Option for Consumers

Some analysts have suggested that the oil-importing countries could employ trade to influence the policies of the oil-exporters. This view is based on the dual considerations that the oil suppliers concentrate their trade on one or two advanced countries and that there is a high degree of economic penetration of the producing countries by the industrial societies. These facts are undoubtedly correct. However, the extent to which the industrial states may effectively employ trade as an instrument of political and economic control depends not only on trade asymmetries, but on the options available to the oil-exporters and the extent to which they can substitute one trading partner for another.

The oil-exporting countries obtain electric machinery, nonelectric machinery, transport equipment, and cereals and flour from the West, primarily the United States, Britain, France, West Germany, and Japan.[c] The United States accounts

[c]The data on trade patterns are from the United Nations, *World Trade Annual, 1964* and *1971* (New York: United Nations); and the International Monetary Fund, *International Financial Statistics, 1964* and *1971* (Washington, D.C.: International Monetary Fund). We have used the most systematic figures available. More recent data tend to confirm these patterns.

for 25 percent of all world transactions in electric machinery, 31 percent of nonelectric machinery, 30 percent of transport equipment, and 63 percent of cereals and flour. It sends only 5 percent of its exports in electric machinery (electric appliances, television and radio equipment, and general electronic equipment) to the oil-exporting countries, primarily to Venezuela, Iran, and Saudi Arabia; 7.5 percent of its exports in nonelectric machinery go to oil-exporters; and about 5 percent of all its exports in transport equipment (primarily railroad equipment, cars, trucks, aircraft, boats, and ships). But these types of industrial goods are also exported by the other advanced states. They could always make up for any United States denial of these commodities to the oil-producers. This option is available also with respect to cereals and flour. The oil-exporting countries accounted for 8.7 percent of all exports of cereal and flour by the United States in 1972. At one point food may have been thought to represent a potential leverage in the United States' interactions with the oil-producing countries.[20] But Canada and Australia already provide alternatives to the United States. In addition, the magnitude of total such exports to OPEC countries is so small, relative to world trade in cereals and flour, that other states readily fill any gap created by a United States refusal to supply food and cereals.[21]

In sum, while the oil-exporting countries are indeed highly reliant upon the oil-importing states for the imports of capital-intensive goods and agricultural goods, there are options available with respect to trading partners. This fact markedly reduces the ability of the consumer countries to employ trade as a leverage for changing the behavior of the oil-exporting countries—*unless they act in unison.* There are no leverages in the area of commodity trade for any single oil-importing nation. But this is a general assessment; it does not take account of substitution possibilities, market conditions, or opportunity costs.

There is always the possibility of inter-consumer competition for supplying commodity goods to the producers as the oil-consuming nations seek to offset their balance of payments deficits associated with oil imports. The advanced countries have no alternatives to OPEC as major suppliers of crude oil, whereas the members of OPEC individually and collectively have both the alternatives and the means to secure access to any desired commodity. For this reason, a counter-embargo is an implausible strategy in response to the petroleum cartel.

Coordinated Energy Strategy as an Option for Consumers

The development of a coordinated energy policy is a consumer response to OPEC which has recently been given considerable attention both in the United States and in Western Europe. Various recycling proposals, described in Chapter 3, reflect the evolution of official thinking in this regard. More recently,

Table 6-2

Percent of Imports of the Major Oil-Exporting Countries from the United States, United Kingdom, France, Germany, and Japan

(In Percent of Dollar Value of Total Imports)

Exporter	United States		United Kingdom		France		Germany		Japan		Rest of World[a]	
Importer	1964	1971	1964	1971	1964	1971	1964	1971	1964	1971	1964	1971
Algeria	8	6	3	5	70	41	2	10	1	3	16	34
Indonesia	10	22	3	3	3	1	8	9	18	38	59	26
Iran	19	25	11	9	6	4	17	19	7	12	40	28
Iraq	14	4	14	8	1	6	7	4	4	3	60	73
Kuwait	17	12	17	10	2	5	8	6	11	12	45	52
Libya	20	11	17	9	6	13	10	8	3	6	45	51
Nigeria	9	11	28	26	4	3	8	9	11	6	40	44
Saudi Arabia	23	20	10	11	2	4	7	6	9	16	49	41
Venezuela	47	40	5	4	2	4	7	9	5	7	34	34

[a]World is defined as the OECD countries, Israel, Yugoslavia, Australia, and New Zealand, and excluding Turkey.

Sources: International Monetary Fund, *International Financial Statistics, 1964* and *1971* (Washington, D.C.: International Monetary Fund); United Nations, *World Trade Annual, 1964* and *1971* (New York: United Nations).

however, this thinking has taken a more forceful tone as a response not only to the challenge of the cartel but to the overall energy crisis of the West. The most notable institutional development in this regard is the new International Energy Agency (IEA). The story of the IEA to date indicates the problems and the prospects of developing a joint consumer energy strategy, and the reactions of the oil-exporting countries to a stance they may regard as confrontational.

International Energy Agency

The International Energy Agency was first proposed in June 1974 at a meeting of the Washington Energy Coordination Group as a United States plan to pool emergency oil supplies among the 12 participating members. A European position was worked out simultaneously through the OECD, which was initially opposed to the sharing principle. Differences of views centered around the "criteria for defining when a crisis existed and sharing should begin. . . ."[22] By July, a compromise was worked out between oil-rich consumers like Norway, which sought to view sharing as a political decision, and oil-poor countries, which argued for the development of automatic sharing procedures regardless of the political implications. The 12 nations also agreed to constrain domestic demand for petroleum by 7-10 percent of current volume, in the event of another crisis. The details of the agreement were made public in September of that year. It proposed that states affected by any embargo would receive supplies from a common pool when their oil imports dropped by more than 7 percent. The draft of September 1974 committed the 12 OECD nations to create the International Energy Agency in November. Despite a façade of agreement, there remained strong differences among the OECD states.[23] Sweden, Switzerland, Austria, Spain, Turkey, and New Zealand have recently applied for membership to the Energy Coordination Group, bringing total national participation to 17.

Norway is a major dissenter. It refused to join in any plan to share oil. This for two reasons: The country received only 4 of a total of 136 votes in the plan; and it feared pressures to increase the rate of exploitation of its North Sea fields. Norway found its interest conflicting with those of the other OECD members.

France, too, opposed the 12 nation energy consumer's group because "it could conflict with efforts of the nine members of the Common Market to create their energy policy."[24] However, France agreed to consultation among the oil-consuming states to clarify their positions toward the oil-exporting countries in a meeting between Gerald Ford and Giscard d'Estaing. The agreement on consultations among oil-importing nations represented a French concession to the American position, which had been that the major consumer countries should work out a joint position first before entering into any tasks with the oil-exporters.

The United States has argued for consideration of three main issues by the IEA: finance planning, conservation, and new energy sources. The main question in the area of finance planning pertains to the financing of $25 billion solidarity fund as discussed in Chapter 3. On this issue the United States stood in sharp opposition to West Germany. The United States regarded the Bonn proposal as too favorable to the oil-exporters; Bonn viewed the Washington plan as inflationary. In the area of conservation, the issue is one of developing agreed upon targets for reducing energy consumption. There are no significant differences of views. In the area of new energy sources, the main differences revolve around the floor price for oil. Observers have noted that initial reactions among the oil-consuming countries to the floor price were halting and tentative but not unfavorable. The United States appeared to favor common minimum prices since these would enable the persistence of high domestic prices as a spur to production. The West European countries and Japan preferred to make direct subsidies to their energy industries and to import their oil as cheaply as possible.[25] The European Economic Community was considering a counter-proposal to the Kissinger floor price plan. It argued for a flexible floor price predicated on an annual review of market conditions, and three different floor prices for the United States, Europe, and Japan. This plan obtained limited approval; it was not accepted by the OECD. The only strong support came from West Germany.

Diplomatic Impacts of the IEA

Agreement on the International Energy Agency was a prelude to consultations among various parties to global energy transactions. The formula for representation to an eventual preparatory conference for basic negotiations on oil supplies included 10 participants: four oil-exporting nations (Saudi Arabia, Iran, Algeria, and Venezuela); three oil-importers (the United States, Japan, and the European Economic Community); and three less developed states (India, Brazil, and Zaire). The first formal meeting between exporters and importers of crude petroleum was held on April 7, 1975. In the course of agenda discussions, Algeria pressed hard to expand the issues to be considered to the entire range of raw materials problems. A week of deliberations produced no agenda. The Algerian position was supported by Saudi Arabia, Iran, Venezuela, Zaire, India, and Brazil. The United States strongly opposed any expansion of the agenda to include all raw materials.

The United States has subsequently called for a new meeting between oil-importers and oil-exporters and has conceded to some Algerian arguments by indicating its willingness to consider arrangements for greater price stability for raw materials exported by developing states. This is the first clear concession of the United States toward the recognition of demands by less developed states.

Secretary of State Kissinger declared: "Our economic well-being depends on a structure of international cooperation in which the developing countries are, and perceive themselves to be, participants. The new problems of our era–insuring adequate supplies of food, energy, and raw materials–require a world economy that accomodates the interests of developing as well as developed countries."[26]

New International Economic Order

The story of the International Energy Agency and subsequent developments reflects the transformation of the international system and the evolution of political and economic pressures for a new international economic order. The deliberations in the General Assembly of the United Nations during the session in 1974 revolved around the economic and political consequences of global changes resulting from the petroleum crisis. The oil-exporting states, led by Algeria, succeeded in mobilizing support for a resolution calling for the establishment of a New International Economic Order.[d] The advanced countries opposed this move.[27] However, agreement was reached to call a Special Session of the General Assembly for September 1-12, 1975. The purpose of this Special Session would be to examine the economic and political ramifications of global changes occasioned by the petroleum crisis, the development of a consumer response to the general energy situation, and the evolution of some concerted postures on the part of the nonindustrialized states.

While these developments have as yet only symbolic effects, the fact that an atmosphere has been created whereby economic issues of global significance could be debated in an open forum may well establish an important precedent for future interactions between the advanced industrial states and the relatively poorer countries. Nothing specific may emerge in the immediate future, but these developments may well herald new times in which international economic issues are actively debated and shaped by states other than the advanced countries of the West. Therein lies the immediate and more pressing significance of calls for a New International Economic Order. It is ironic, however, that the genesis for this movement can be found in consumer attempts to adopt a confrontation stance vis-à-vis the oil-exporting states. Several stories of subsequent strategies, moves, and countermoves become entertwined, with the net result being a general recognition of the need to confront global economic problems in a context of global deliberations.

[d]See, the speech by Algerian President Houari Boumediene to the Sixth Special Session of the United Nations General Assembly on April 10, 1974, in the *Middle East Economic Survey*, Vol. XVII, No. 27 (26 April 1974), pp. 2-16. For the text of Resolution 3201 (S-V1)–"Declaration on the Establishment of a New International Economic Order"–adopted by the General Assembly on May 1, 1974, see the *Middle East Economic Survey*, Vol. XVII, No. 31 (24 May 1974), pp. i-iv.

Military Force as an Option for Consumers

The use of military force as a means of breaking up the cartel remains as yet an implicit policy option for the consumer countries, most notably the United States. In January 1975, Secretary of State Kissinger declared:

We should have learned from Vietnam that it is easier to get into a war than to get out of it. I am not saying that there's no circumstance where we would not use force. But it is one thing to use it in the case of a dispute over price, it's another where there's some actual strangulation of the industrialized world.[28]

Although United States officials frequently deny the possibility of force, it nonetheless persists and is so perceived by the oil-exporting countries. In resorting to force, nations essentially make the decision to emphasize the strategic dimension of their foreign policies and employ military instrumentalities for obtaining other than military objectives. Articulating goals, procedures, anticipated costs, and potential consequences become of paramount importance in any decision to use force. The more specific the goals are, the easier it is to determine appropriate procedures, criteria of performance, and associated costs and, possibly, some of the anticipated consequences. In light of the political sensitivity of these issues, such discussions are rarely conducted in the public domain.

It is alleged that during the Arab oil embargo of 1973-74, the United States had drawn up contingency plans for landing marines in the oil fields and had selected Abu Dhabi as their site.[29] The possibility of such an event is enhanced by the relative weakness of the polity in question. The actual decision to send the marines may never have been seriously entertained, but the use of force is gradually surfacing in United States academic and policy-making circles, and the costs and benefits of such a course of action increasingly evaluated.[e]

[e]See Andrew Tobias, "War–The Ultimate Antitrust Action," *New York*, Vol. 7, No. 41 (October 14, 1974), pp. 35-40; Stockholm International Peace Research Institute, *Oil and Security* (Stockholm: Stockholm International Peace Research Institute, 1974); Dennis C. Pirages, "Strategic Implications of the Energy Crisis," Paper presented to the International Studies Association, Washington, D.C., February 19-22, 1975; William E. Griffith, "The Great Powers, the Indian Ocean, and the Persian Gulf," Paper prepared for the Conference on the Persian Gulf and the Indian Ocean in International Politics, The Institute for International Political and Economic Studies, Tehran, March 25-27, 1975; Daniel Yergin, "The [Economic Political Military] Solution," *The New York Times Magazine* (February 16, 1975), p. 10; Robert Tucker, "Oil: The Issue of American Intervention," *Commentary*, Vol. 59, No. 1 (January 1975), pp. 21-31; Miles Ignotus, "Seizing Arab Oil," *Harpers*, Vol. 250 (March 1975), pp. 45-62. See also, the excerpts of the press conference by the United States Secretary of Defense, John Schlesinger, on 14 January 1975, in *Middle East Economic Survey*, Vol. XVIII, No. 13 (17 January 1975), pp. i-ii; the statements by U.S. President Gerald Ford and United States Secretary of the Treasury in *Middle East Economic Survey*, Vol. XVIII, No. 14 (24 January 1975), pp. iii-iv; the interview with the United States ambassador to Saudi Arabia, James Akins, with the official Saudi Press Agency on 12 March 1975, in *Middle East Economic Survey*, Vol. XVIII, No. 21 (14 March 1975), pp. 3-4. U.S. Secretary of State Henry Kissinger gave unqualified assurances to the Saudi Arabian

The use of military force would involve the occupation of key oil fields in one of the Gulf States, notably Saudi Arabia. The logistics imposed by geographical constraints are such that attaining control of oil fields in no way ensures the protection of such control. The operational costs are reputed to be manageable given the present United States global commitments, but there will be inevitable political costs and constraints, both international and domestic.

Among the potential international consequences of a United States show of military force are possibilities of (1) Soviet military intervention, despite Saudi Arabia's reputed opposition to communism; (2) dissension among the Western Alliance, most notably led by France whose opposition for such a move is based upon extensive experience with interventions in the Middle East; and (3) the anticipated outcries from an outraged "world opinion." The first of these consequences might conceivably be countered by possible United States concessions to the expansion of Soviet military capability in the Indian Ocean, even extending to the Gulf area. The second can be countered by an effective United States delivery of reduced petroleum prices, perhaps as low as $3 to $4 per barrel. And the third has rarely been an effective lever on superpower politics and poses less of a constraint on United States policy than the need for political concessions or the delivery of economic goods.

On the domestic side in the United States, the constraints on such a venture are fewer. Faced with continued high petroleum prices, a shrewd administration might effectively enlist support for an interventionist policy by arguing that force is employed not for political gain but to ensure the survival of Western industrial economies. In those terms, the anticipated gains would be portrayed as specific, high, and attainable, and the projected costs as manageable, foreseeable, and credible. In situations where symbolic political explanations would be more effective, military force could also be justified in terms of its potential for safeguarding Israeli territories (despite the possibility of a viable Sinai settlement) or for safeguarding the American way of life in the United States.

The use of military force as a viable consumer option is marred only by the need to identify criteria of success in the larger context of the energy crisis. If these were defined strictly in terms lowering petroleum prices, the attendant tactics would differ than if the criteria were to sustain the long-term occupation of the oil fields, or to identify and/or impose agreed upon procedures for production, pricing, and distribution of petroleum over the longer run. By the same token, if the objective were defined in terms of a discrete short-term outcome, it's implications would be different than if long-term structural changes or institutional development in the world petroleum market were envisaged.

Government that the United States had not inspired any of the printed speculation concerning an invasion of Saudi Arabia, in *Middle East Economic Survey*, Vol. XVIII, No. 22 (21 March 1975), p. 1. For the Arab response to Kissinger's original statement concerning the use of force in the event of strangulation in the January 13, 1975 issue of *Business Week*, see *Middle East Economic Survey*, Vol. XVIII, No. 12 (10 January 1975), pp. viii-xi and *Middle East Economic Survey*, Vol. XVIII, No. 13 (17 January 1975), pp. iii-iv.

This use of force also necessitates the search for means of terminating military activities. Generally these involve regularized methods of interaction whereby force would be replaced by agreed upon (and possibly enforced or enforceable) procedures for political exchange among the parties to the conflict. Developing routinized procedures of interaction means more involvement, more interdependence, and more constraints on the behavior of the military intervenor as well as the target states. The success of military force as a policy option defined by other than battlefield criteria of performance may well require a long-term involvement. The inevitable consequence of the use of force as a means of reducing the constraints of energy interdependence may be, in effect, to increase these constraints by necessitating a longer term military presence in the oil-exporting states.

More important, a military strategy complicates the immediate possibilities of accommodation with OPEC. The oil-exporting countries are sensitive to the reality of a military intervention and their reactions to consumer proposals are colored accordingly. For example, Yusif A. Sayigh of OAPEC stated:

> The search for forms of cooperation cannot be carried out in the context of allusion to confrontation.[30]

And Boumediene reiterated:

> It is difficult to conceive that we can at the same time brandish such threats and call it international cooperation. One cannot really wish for such cooperation using the language of force and interfering in order to impose solutions contrary to their interests.[31]

The net result of a consumer military option would be to increase the cohesion of the cartel. In a situation where the oil-exporting states perceive a common military threat, the logical and inevitable outcome is to enhance mutual support and consolidate their ranks.

In sum, while the general consensus among military and strategic experts is that military force is indeed a viable option on technical grounds, it is likely to create political problems the resolution of which might be difficult, if not impossible, in the short run. In addition, Western occupation of large oil fields may well need broader tactical and administrative support, which could require a larger presence in the oil-exporting states. Whatever gains might be accrued in terms of lowering petroleum prices in the short run, such a strategy would be to increase and not reduce prevailing constraints created by petroleum related transactions in the longer run.

Coercion and Interdependence

The use of military force might restructure the constraints on national behavior or impose a different set of rules and regulations, but it will not eliminate the predicaments posed by the structure of interdependence. The same may be said with respect to the development of a joint consumer energy policy. The story of the International Energy Agency indicates that any efforts to coordinate the energy policies of oil-importing nations will invariably elicit a response from the oil-exporting countries. This response will, in turn, give rise to the necessity for the coordination of policies and postures between oil-importers and oil-exporters. Calls for a New International Economic Order reflect further the new interdependencies created by the petroleum crisis of October 1973. The interconnections between political and economic features of this crisis point to the complexity of the issues at hand and the inadequacy of piecemeal solutions.

Notes

1. See, Thomas C. Schelling, *The Strategy of Conflict* (Cambridge: Harvard University Press, 1960); Morton Deutsch, *Resolution of Conflict: Constructive and Destructive Processes* (New Haven: Yale University Press, 1973); Erving Goffman, *Strategic Interaction* (Philadelphia: University of Pennsylvania Press, 1969).

2. International Institute for Strategic Studies, *The Military Balance* (London: International Institute for Strategic Studies, 1971-74); Dale R. Tahtinen, *The Arab-Israeli Military Balance Since October 1973* (Washington, D.C.: American Enterprise Institute, 1974).

3. *Wall Street Journal*, January 14, 1974.

4. *The New York Times*, February 26, 1974.

5. *Wall Street Journal*, January 14, 1974.

6. *Wall Street Journal*, November 7, 1974.

7. *Wall Street Journal*, April 9, 1974.

8. *The New York Times*, January 10, 1975.

9. *The New York Times*, December 5, 1974.

10. *The Economist*, January 5, 1974.

11. Shahram Chubin, "Iran Between the Arab West and the Asian East," *Survival*, Vol. XVI, No. 4 (July/August 1974); see also, Rouhollah K. Ramazani, "Emerging Patterns of Regional Relations in Iranian Foreign Policy," 1974 (mimeographed).

12. *The New York Times*, January 4, 8, 9, 10, 12, and 13, 1975; and March 7, 1975.

13. George H. Quester, "Can Proliferation Now Be Stopped?," *Foreign Affairs*, Vol. 53, No. 1 (October 1974), pp. 87-88; see also, *The New York Times*, October 9, 1974.

14. *The New York Times*, May 7, 1975.

15. *The New York Times*, June 3, 1974 and March 22, 1975.

16. *The New York Times*, January 29, 1975; and February 3 and 7, 1975.

17. Facts on File, *Energy Crisis, Volume 1*, 1969-1973 (New York: Facts on File, Inc., 1974), p. 202.

18. *The New York Times*, November 18, 1974.

19. Facts on File, *Energy Crisis, Volume 1*, 1974, p. 205.

20. See, U.S., Congress, House, Committee on Foreign Affairs, *Data and Analysis Concerning the Possibility of a U.S. Food Embargo as a Response to the Present Arab Oil Boycott*, 93rd Cong., 1st sess., November 21, 1973, p. 1.

21. U.S., Department of Agriculture, Economic Research Service, *Foreign Agricultural Trade of the United States*, October 1974, p. 15.

22. *The New York Times*, July 10, 1974.

23. *The New York Times*, September 21, 1974.

24. *The New York Times*, October 16, 1974. See also, the interview with the French Minister of Foreign Affairs, M. Jean Sauvagnargues, in the *Middle East Economic Survey*, Vol. XVIII, No. 14 (24 January 1975), pp. i-ii.

25. *The New York Times*, February 6, 1975.

26. *The New York Times*, May 29, 1975.

27. See, excerpts of the speech by the United States Secretary of State, Henry Kissinger, to the Sixth Special Session of the United Nations General Assembly on April 15, 1974, in the *Middle East Economic Survey*, Vol. 17, No. 26 (19 April 1974), pp. 10-12.

28. *Business Week*, No. 2363 (January 13, 1975), p. 69.

29. See, "American Intentions in the Middle East: Haikal's Controversial Article," *Journal of Palestine Studies*, Vol. 3, No. 3 (1974), pp. 167-169.

30. Yusif A. Sayigh, "Arab-European Cooperation: Its Prerequisites and Framework," *Middle East Economic Survey*, Vol. XVIII, No. 12 (19 January 1975), p. 1.

31. Excerpts from President Boumediene's letter to United Nations Secretary General Kurt Waldheim, *Middle East Economic Survey*, Vol. XVIII, No. 1 (25 October 1974), p. xii.

7 Political Correctives for Economic Assumptions: The Case of OPEC

The fact that a multiplicity of factors influence the policies of the Organization of Petroleum Exporting Countries suggests that a purely economic perspective is an inadequate explanation for the cohesion of the cartel. The interaction of economic and political motivations is a distinguishing feature of this cartel. Any predictions of its demise based on economic grounds alone are likely to be incorrect if not misleading. This chapter seeks first, to summarize the different interests that OPEC satisfies for its members and to evaluate the extent to which the pursuit of these interests enhances rather than detracts from the cohesion of the organization; second, to review cartel policies on price, production, and market shares; third, to determine how applicable conventional economic criteria are in explaining and predicting the cohesion of OPEC; and fourth, to develop plausible scenarios for the breakup of OPEC. We argue that, to a very large extent, the strength of OPEC is maintained by political factors that reinforce and support economic sources of cohesion, and that the disintegration of the cartel will stem from endogenous influences and from the erosion of common political objectives.

The Importance of OPEC for its Members

OPEC serves different purposes for different members. Not all member nations are motivated solely by profit-maximization nor do they all define their gains in economic terms alone. OPEC has become a repository of technical skills upon which its members can draw and from which information is available to them on an equal basis. It serves as a forum, greatly facilitating interactions among oil-exporting states. In recent years participation in OPEC has been employed as a means of legitimizing the role of its members in the world petroleum market. For some nations, joining OPEC has even been regarded as status-raising, enhancing a small state's position in international politics. Both Ecuador and Gabon have benefited politically from their membership and Syria's application may be regarded in part as a means of strengthening the country's posture in regional as well as international politics. More important, however, membership in OPEC has been used as a means of pursuing objectives other than those related to oil.

The motivations of OPEC members are too diffuse to be strictly defined. Conventional economic goals, such as profit maximization, only partially account for the behavior of individual OPEC nations which have systematically begun to use OPEC as a forum for a wide range of issues over which they seek to increase control. The embargo of October 1973 is an excellent example of the convergence of political and economic objectives. The Arab-Israeli war of 1973 provided an opportunity for the demonstration of economic power by the Arab states, which resulted in economic gain for all the oil-exporting countries. These gains further reinforced the pursuit of the initial political objectives of the Arabs and prompted the demands for further economic gains by all oil-exporting countries. Another example is Algeria's demand for the restructuring of international economic relations and its seeming ability to mobilize countries of the Third and Fourth World toward this end. The effectiveness of the Algerian leaders in articulating their position was facilitated by the use of OPEC as a vehicle for the pursuit of objectives other than the control of petroleum prices. So, too, the Saudi concern for protecting the organization from the outbreak of overly divisive conflicts indicates the country's interest in employing OPEC as a means of maximizing stature and power in regional politics.

The agreement between Iran and Iraq to limit the Kurdish liberation movement is another such example.[1] It indicates a willingness to resolve conflicts that could jeopardize both countries' relations with other Middle East members of OPEC. Any violence between the two countries would impel the Arab states to take some stand on the dispute. Libya and Algeria may be expected to support Iraq. Saudi Arabia and Kuwait might be predisposed toward Iran. The political divisions in OPEC would have to surface. The new policy directions that each state had so laboriously sought to foster would be endangered. The thin layer of cohesion would be strained beyond immediate repair. The same rationale may in part explain Syria's willingness to consider a more moderate posture vis-à-vis Israel. Similar calculations may account for the fact that the debate on strategies for the disbursement of petroleum revenues has developed into overt political disagreements.

Three factors account for the differing importance of OPEC to its members and the different degree to which they regard the pursuit of economic gain as the primary objective of the cartel. First, there are major structural and economic differences among the oil-exporting states. Second, the members of OPEC differ in their concern for protecting their national autonomy. And third, there are cultural differences. Each of these factors yields integrative as well as disintegrative influences upon the cohesion of the cartel, and contributes to rendering a purely economic assessment of its survival potentially misleading at best.

Structural Differences

As noted in previous chapters, the members of OPEC are too diverse in their economic characteristics and political objectives to attach any comprehensive or common valuation to the maximization of profit or to calculations for discounting future value. In some cases, the emerging strategy is even one of satisficing rather than maximizing.[a] It is ironic that the sources of the strength of OPEC can be found in structural differences among its members and that these differences also harbor the roots of its weakness.

Differences in population size, petroleum reserves, level of knowledge and skills, and absorptive capacity—described in Chapters 1, 2, and 4—have given rise to differences in the extent to which immediate financial gains are pursued rather than placing added value upon future profit. The comparison of OPEC members presented in Table 2-1 now allows for some broad generalizations yielding clues into the cohesion of the cartel.

Oil-exporting countries with high known reserves and relatively high absorptive capacity seek to obtain the highest possible price *and* increased production *and* increased market shares. On these grounds, Iran and Iraq may have the fewest incentives for moderating their economic demands to preserve the cohesion of OPEC. Immediate gains are pursued possibly at the expense of long term benefits. Yet, both countries have so far sought to protect the organization and to employ a relatively privileged position for pursuing political objectives.

To Iran, OPEC is clearly a means of increasing financial revenues. It is also a political instrument for enhancing its own position in the region and in international politics more generally. Amity with Saudi Arabia, the other leading member, has led to substantial political payoffs. By supporting OPEC policies, Iran has attempted to alleviate Saudi fears regarding Iran's potential expansion in the Gulf. By reassuring the Saudis, Iran has also been able to improve the earlier strained relations with the other Arab states, most notably Egypt and Iraq. Iran's relations with these two states had been poor—for different reasons and with different consequences—and support for a strong OPEC has had substantial side benefits, which the Iranian government has been quick to exploit.

For Iraq, OPEC also means an assurance of higher petroleum revenues. OPEC provides Iraq with the possibility to expand areas of common interest with other littoral states. The identification of common economic gains has prompted the leadership to seek an improvement in its relations with Iran. The maintenance of a cohesive OPEC has necessitated the search for means of reducing regional tensions. OPEC is a means of exerting influence, particularly vis-à-vis Egypt and Saudi Arabia. OPEC has also increased the leadership's concern for enhancing the role of technocrats in determining national policy and it has presented the country with the opportunity to chart more stable development plans than had been the case in the past. In addition, OPEC provides Iraq with another forum for exerting political influence regionally, over and above OAPEC and the Arab League. An expansion of the country's political and economic concerns has, by necessity, led to a search for international influence.

Oil-exporting countries characterized by relatively low known reserves and

[a]For the development of the notion of satisficing see, Herbert Simon, *Models of Man* (New York: John Wiley & Sons, Inc., 1957).

relatively high absorptive capacity seek the highest stable prices possible *and* increased market shares, but seek only limited if not marginal increases in production. Their petroleum policies are motivated by a shorter time horizon; economic gains and losses are calculated in more immediate terms. They may well be the most vulnerable members of OPEC since their domestic needs are greatest and the time period to depletion lowest. They are most likely to deviate from group practices if sufficient economic pressures were felt. They have few common political ties, no cultural similarities, and no shared memories of a common colonial past. There are strong cleavages in this group. Differences among them may be as great as those between them and the other members of OPEC. Aside from shared interests dictated by their common structural characteristics, membership in OPEC is evaluated differently for the five countries in question.

For Algeria, OPEC represents an institutional forum for expressing the leadership's views on the reorganization of the international economic order. It is a means of placing demands upon the industrial societies and providing a vehicle for organizing the non-industrial states in their potential confrontation with the advanced powers. Algeria regards membership in OPEC as a necessary component of its foreign policy, but only a means to an end, and not an end in itself. Clearly, however, that organization is instrumental in providing the Algerians with higher petroleum revenues. But the government is beginning to look beyond economic considerations to the broader political gains that OPEC could yield.

For Indonesia, OPEC is primarily a vehicle for increasing its petroleum revenues. It is also a means of enhancing its technical capacities in the petroleum area and increasing its bargaining position vis-à-vis the major importers. Indonesia appears to have no immediate political objectives to pursue through its membership in OPEC, nor does it integrate its petroleum policies as closely to other foreign policy objectives as do the oil-exporting states of the Middle East.

The same may be said of Nigeria. Like Indonesia, it is confronted by relatively lower petroleum reserves and relatively high claims for petroleum revenues. As noted earlier, neither country can influence the behavior of OPEC; they are essentially price followers and their petroleum policies will be determined largely by the directives of the organization. As with Indonesia, Nigeria has not integrated its foreign policy objectives with its petroleum policies.

Gabon and Ecuador, the two most peripheral members of OPEC, have also a relatively narrow range of interests. For them, the organization is largely a means of increasing their petroleum revenues. Regional goals cannot be pursued directly through their membership in OPEC. Yet, there is some indication that the leaders of Ecuador place high value on allegiance to the cartel for domestic political purposes as well as economic ones.[b] For Gabon, foreign policy

[b]Even in the face of sharply reduced demand for Ecuadorean crude, Ecuador was initially reluctant to reduce oil prices. *The New York Times*, December 9, 1974.

objectives remain as yet to be fully articulated. So far, petroleum policies are closely tied to the goal of profit maximization; OPEC serves the purpose of enhancing this goal.

Countries with relatively limited absorptive capacity have reasons to delay the generation of oil revenues, and for them OPEC serves still different functions. Libya, Kuwait, Saudi Arabia, and the United Arab Emirates all have small populations. Kuwait and Libya face an additional constraint in that their known reserves are not expected to last beyond the turn of the century.[c] Their interests will thus not coincide with those of Saudi Arabia and the U.A.E. Libya and Kuwait have reason to cut back productions and to maintain high prices. The fact that they differ in their views of Arab politics in no way detracts from the pursuit of the dual goals of maintaining high prices and moderating production.

Libya's role in the initial formation of OPEC in 1960 was negligible at best, but its importance in effecting the October 1973 move was substantial. Since then the country has taken an active interest in the policy deliberations of the oil-exporting states. Libya has argued for moderation in production schedules and for bringing petroleum policies in close alignment with foreign policy objectives.

Kuwait's foreign policy is closely integrated with its petroleum politics. It has employed OPEC as a means of protecting its growing influence in the Middle East. This influence is largely economic and its political prestige stems from a strategy of large-scale investment in Arab lands. OPEC has also accorded Kuwait with an international role that transcends regional bounds. To the extent that this widening of the country's political and economic interests persist, Kuwait will continue to value OPEC over and above its concern for enhancing economic gain.

Only Saudi Arabia and the United Arab Emirates can employ the fact that they do not have immediate domestic claims against petroleum revenues for political leverage in exerting influence over cartel policies. Further, Saudi Arabia has the most flexibility in terms of price, production, and market shares. Its conservative leadership has so far found a policy of caution to be most consistent with its structural characteristics. It may be the most adaptive to the demands of other states and can afford, both economically and politically, to accommodate group constraints. These factors may allow Saudi Arabia the luxury of subsuming economic objectives to political ones, or, alternatively, interjecting a greater political input into economic decisions than may be possible for the other states.[d]

[c]Kuwait is optimistic about the size of its reserves. In an interview with the French news agency AFP, Kuwaiti Oil Minister 'Abd al-Muttalib al-Kazimi stated that Kuwait's reserves will last 70 to 110 years. This estimate includes drilling for oil fields directly beneath Kuwait City. *Middle East Economic Survey*, Vol. XVIII, No. 44 (22 August 1975), p. 1.

[d]In an interview with Oriana Fallaci of the Italian weekly *L'Europeo* on August 22, 1975, Saudi Minister of Petroleum and Mineral Resources Ahmad Zaki Yamani stated that "Saudi Arabia can do a great deal, since it is the world's leading oil producer. We can produce more than eleven million barrels a day or we can limit production to three and a half million

As noted earlier, membership in OPEC has given Saudi Arabia a new international prestige, which exceeds by far its diplomatic and military capabilities. In addition, it has allowed the Saudis to widen the range of political objectives that could be tied to petroleum politics and pursued in conjunction with economic gain. Membership in OPEC enabled Saudi Arabia to follow regional objectives and enhance its position vis-à-vis the other Arab states in ways that are not tied to conventional political discourse in the Middle East. Finally, the success of OPEC has encouraged the Saudis to promote a regional organization of petroleum exporting countries, one in which they would have a dominant role. OAPEC allows Saudi Arabia to reinforce its ascendancy in regional politics and to develop a power base from which to consolidate its new role. In Chapter 4 we described the change in Saudi Arabia's position and its present role of leadership in the Arab world. Some of this change must be attributed to its adherence to OPEC and to the care with which the country has sought to protect the organization from undue pressures.

For the United Arab Emirates, membership in OPEC is valued largely in economic terms. The federation continues to pursue regional goals and its interest in OPEC is closely mirrored by its concern for the continued viability of OAPEC. As noted in Chapter 5, the federation has recently begun to extend its economic interests throughout the Middle East. But this decision is yet tentative, and reflects the states' present embarrassment of riches rather than a well defined policy objective.

Concern for National Autonomy

A second factor that accounts for differences in the importance of OPEC to its members is the extent to which they view the pursuit of national autonomy as a major policy directive. Some of the oil-rich countries were former colonies. Memories of a dominated past are strong in shaping present dispositions and fear of control emerges as the single most important determinant of political behavior and, by extension, of petroleum policies. Algeria, Iraq, and Libya are perhaps most concerned with national autonomy. Venezuela and Ecuador share this same fear but its roots differ, as do its manifestations. In Saudi Arabia the desert tradition of individualism has persisted despite past domination by the Ottomans. By contrast, Iran's memories of past glories yield hopes for future Empire. It is not fear of domination that persists as the major value, but the desire to reestablish a regional hegemony that had once been strong. Iran's political dispositions are thus shaped by the dual concerns of rapid economic development and the extension of influence in the Gulf area. For Iran,

---

barrels a day. This makes us powerful vis-à-vis the producing countries as well as the consuming countries." But, Yamani pointed out, "to leave OPEC, even for us in Saudi Arabia, would do us serious damage." *Middle East Economic Survey*, Vol. XVIII, No. 45 (29 August 1975), p. ii.

maximizing economic gain is accorded added valuation in light of its regional political objectives. In this case, political and economic goals are mutually reinforcing resulting in pressures for increasing production and keeping prices high.

Cultural Differences

Cultural differences among the members of OPEC also shape their views of the organization and of its purposes. Cultural factors give content to political objectives, and are instrumental in allocating relative weights to different national goals, and accentuate political differences among member countries. For example, cultural differences between Arabs and non-Arabs within OPEC has often been regarded by outside observers as a potential source of tension. While Iran is frequently mistaken for an Arab country, there are sharp cultural differences, which sometimes become manifested in political terms. So, too, the cultures of Indonesia, Ecuador, and Venezuela have little in common with the Middle East states, providing further grounds for predictions of the breakup of the cartel. But most of the organization's members share a common cultural heritage, which they have successfully employed to repair frequent political rifts. A shared language, culture, and history, sometimes cushion political tensions.

Clearly, the cohesion of OPEC cannot be sustained on cultural grounds alone. But, on balance cultural differences are only marginally relevant in placing strains upon the cartel. The distinctive characteristic of OPEC in this regard is that the integrative effects of a common heritage by seven states appear to exceed the disintegrative influences generated by cultural differences.

The Diversity of Interests

To a large extent OPEC has been successful so far primarily because of the diversity of interests of its members. This diversity has been reflected in the multipurpose nature of the organization and widened its appeal to the constituent states. As a result, the persistence of different and sometimes conflicting interests has become a source of bargaining and negotiation, and possibly of mutual accommodation. The hypothesis that structural, economic, and cultural diversity among the members provide the basis for cohesion appears increasingly plausible.[e] OPEC seems to be organized as a loose coalition in which any subgroup may align on a specific issue but is free to align differently others. The bounds of permissible behavior appear to be broad and the degree of formal cohesion low. This feature provides a means of adjusting to differences and may well be an important source of strength for the cartel.[2]

[e]For the role of selective interests for the cohesion of groups see, Mancur Olson, *The Logic of Collective Action* (Cambridge: Harvard University Press, 1965).

Price, Production, and Market Shares

Joint policies on prices, production schedules, and market shares are essential for maintaining OPEC. Obtaining agreement over price has, to date, been relatively easy. At the same time, however, there is evidence of some price cuts since the freeze of January 26, 1975. Perhaps the most significant reason for these declines is the reduction in world petroleum consumption in 1974. That reduction was 3.2 percent in 1974, with the most significant declines in Western Europe (9%) and North America (5%).[3] This lessening of demand for crude has softened the oil market such that absolute as well as relative declines in price have taken place.

There have been specific reductions in the posted prices of crude in Libya, Algeria, and Abu Dhabi. Both Libya and Algeria had previously been receiving price premiums due to the proximity of these nations to the European market. The priority given to low sulphur crude has been lessened and the depressed tanker market has reduced shipping rates to the point where the premiums are unnecessary.

Prices have also declined in relative terms because of world inflation. The prices of Western foods and industrial goods have risen considerably since the oil price freeze. The decline in the foreign exchange value of the U.S. dollar reduced the purchasing power of oil-exporting countries which accept payment in dollars.[4] Some states are now agreeing to link their currencies to the Special Drawing Rights of the IMF in order to avoid the effects of a dollar devaluation. Efforts to index oil prices to the prices of certain key commodities represent means of compensating for inflation.[f]

In addition, a number of oil-exporting states, including Iraq, are allowing credit extensions of 30, and as much as 90, days for the payment of oil. Such extensions can effectively cut the price of crude, from $10.00 a barrel to $8.50 a barrel.[5]

These declines in oil price do not yet signal the disintegration of OPEC. In fact, some nations have specifically sought OPEC approval for their price reductions.[6] If demand continues to decline, pressures for further price reductions may intensify to the point where they may seriously threaten the cartel. But to date these declines could well reflect the search for viable pricing policies that would accommodate the requirements of individual members. The tolerance for deviance may be an emerging policy directive, one that would reduce the need for enforcement mechanism or overt sanctions to assure the cohesion of OPEC. The important issue for the continued success of the organization is not only the actual price that is agreed upon but rather the manner in which the agreement is reached and the strength of the consensus. Agreement on a lower price in no way signifies the failure of OPEC; the critical factor is the agreement, not the exact price that is agreed upon.

---

[f] *The New York Times*, February 2, 1975. The United States government appears willing to discuss the possible indexation of petroleum prices. *The New York Times*, February 4, 1975.

Reaching agreement on production schedules is considerably more difficult. The different needs of different producers dictate different schedules. Since production has a direct effect on price, regulating output becomes a major determinant of OPEC's price-setting. Production cutbacks may be necessary to maintain high prices. So far, Saudi Arabia has been willing to undertake significant cutbacks to assist in sustaining OPEC directives. But the excess capacity of exporting countries with high petroleum reserves makes this arrangement tenuous at best. The temptation either to cut prices or to raise production increases the necessity of developing means for enforcing production cutbacks by all OPEC members.

Market allocation is the third consideration in cartel policy. So far, the need to obtain formal agreement on such allocations has not been pressing. Established patterns of imports and exports over the past 25 years and changes in these patterns, noted in Chapter 1, have led to regularized and structured allocations that have not been severely shaken by the creation of OPEC. For example, Venezuela continues to focus on the United States market; Indonesia centers its exports around Japan; Algeria focuses extensively on France; and Nigeria on the United States and Great Britain. The regularities of flows in the world petroleum market has provided the basis for the structured transactions between the members of OPEC and the consuming nations of the West. The fact that market allocation continues to be made by the multinational oil companies means that OPEC is not faced with the burden of regulating exports to the consumers or of reaching an agreement on market shares.

The service rendered by the oil companies in this regard constitutes another source of strength for the cartel. At the same time, however, to the extent that individual oil-producers seek to increase their autonomy in the petroleum market by creating national oil companies, the coordinating function of the companies will be reduced and competition within OPEC for increasing market shares will arise. It is ironic that the success of the oil-exporting countries in their attempts to constrain the international oil companies constitutes an important potential for weakening the cartel.

The diversification of oil imports by the consuming nations, that had strengthened the cartel in its initial stages, may now prevent an OPEC agreement on market allocations. Both Iran and Iraq exploited the 1973 embargo to increase their market shares.[7] This move is consistent with the fact that producers have tended to expand their production during periods of difficulties in the oil fields of neighboring states. For example, the Kuwaiti fields were developed during the Iran embargo of 1951-53, and those in Abu Dhabi when Iraq attempted to ameliorate its position vis-à-vis the multinational oil companies in 1961.

It may well be, as economists tend to stress with respect to earlier cartels, that the root of OPEC disintegration will lie in competition for market shares. Difficulties in reaching price and production agreements could be relatively minor in comparison with those occasioned by market competition. In addition to the usual difficulties in predicting the behavior of oligopolies, the special problem in predicting either the outbreak or the magnitude of such competition in OPEC is that nation-states, unlike individual firms, pursue multiple objectives of which profit maximization is only one, and often not the most important, objective.

OPEC as a Cartel: An Assessment of Economic Criteria

So far we have attempted to identify political factors bearing upon the cohesion of OPEC. It remains for us to specify the ways in which these considerations may have impinged upon narrow economic criteria for evaluating the stability of the organization. In Chapter 2 we listed the economic conditions most favorable for the success of cartels. At this point we can evaluate the evidence at hand and assess OPEC's performance according to these criteria. To recapitulate, the criteria are:

1. The existence of few sellers.
2. The dominance of one seller.
3. An agreement about appropriate market shares.
4. A similarity of costs incurred in the production process.
5. A similarity in the sellers' predictions of the demand for the product.
6. The stability of that demand.
7. A similarity in ways and rates of discounting future profits.
8. The shared perceptions of risk.
9. Unorganized consumers for the product.
10. A compatible valuation framework by which sellers seek to maximize profits. and buyers seek to minimize the cost of goods purchased.

The first cited condition pertains to the number of sellers. Although the international oil companies are the actual sellers of petroleum, the 13 OPEC states control 70 percent of the world's known petroleium reserves and 52 percent of world production, and account for 85 percent of the world's exports. But of the thirteen, three states, Saudi Arabia, Kuwait, and Iran, control 48 percent of the world's reserves, 29 percent of production, and 43 percent of total world exports. For all practical purposes, then, thesc three states constitute the core group. Two of them have common political objectives, which they have employed to reinforce economic linkages. The concentration of oil in the Middle East gives the oil producers major strength.

Thirteen sellers is a relatively large number, given the existence of only five major consumers. Other importers are small in relation to total world consumption and are presumably not influential in the global petroleum market. Moreover, their near-total dependence on external sources for petroleum makes their reliance on OPEC oil more significant than might be warranted on the ground of market size alone. With the exception of the United States, all the oil-consuming countries draw heavily upon external sources for meeting their petroleum requirements. Thus, while OPEC does not strictly meet any numerical criteria of success for a cartel, the relative strength of three members given the concentration of consumer needs, serves to render the number of sellers as an integrative rather than disintegrative influence.

The second cited condition for the success of a cartel pertains to the size distribution of the sellers and the existence of a dominant producer. Saudi Arabia is undoubtedly the major oil producer, and has the highest known petroleum reserves. This condition is clearly met.

Third, there has appeared to emerge some rough agreement regarding market shares, but this agreement is predicated on the coordination performed by the international oil corporations. New sources of petroleum may change established patterns of transactions, although not in the immediate future. There is no reason to believe that any of the newer discoveries will become commercially viable prior to the next decade. Furthermore, in the case of persistently high demand, there is also no reason to believe that new exporters will not share the same interests as OPEC, at least in the short run or as long as the market sustains both higher prices and new entrants. Canada, Norway, China, and Mexico all appear to follow OPEC pricing policies. They do not, however, follow coordinated production schedules. This situation may eventually force OPEC to reallocate its own reduced production among member states. So far, fringe producers have contributed to the stabilization of the market. There are, as yet, no incentives for marked price reductions; even recent declines within OPEC appear more in the nature of a search for stable prices than as indicators of the impending dissolution of the cartel.

Since the international oil corporations continue to perform an allocative function in the world petroleum market, they have relieved OPEC of a potentially destabilizing problem by continuing to regulate market shares. State-owned oil companies may change this situation by bringing governments in direct competition for market shares. But there are geographic bases for some market allocations that are represented by regularized patterns of oil flows.

Fourth, there are no similarities in costs of production for the individual exporters. Different qualities of crude oil, different transportation costs, and production difficulties in some fields (most notably in Indonesia, Nigeria, and Venezuela, which are the most formidable to drill) make any common valuation of cost difficult at best. Clearly OPEC does not meet the similarity of costs condition for the success of a cartel, nor are opportunity costs the same for all members. However, cost differences in petroleum production are not important, since costs constitute a small proportion of price for all the producer states.

Fifth, there are shared perceptions of aggregate demand for crude petroleum. All exporters agree that in the short run the demand for oil will remain high and, further, that the demand for oil as a fuel will not slacken considerably for at least another 7 to 10 years, despite the decline in world energy consumption of 3 percent from 1973 to 1974. The resulting surplus is a conjunction of two extraordinary circumstances: first, enforced conservation in major consumer countries aided by a succession of mild winters; and second, an economic recession in the major importing nations, the worst since the depression of the 1930s. A return to more normal conditions may well bring about the more customary levels of demand.

Sixth, the stability of consumer demand for petroleum, another condition for maintaining the effectiveness of OPEC, appears assured. Demand has increased steadily at a rate of 4 percent per year over the past 25 years. As long as demand remains fairly high, the incentives for price cutting, increasing production, and competition over market shares will be reduced accordingly. If it stabilizes at a lower rate or even declines intra-OPEC differences will crystallize and the probabilities of disintegrative actions will increase. In the absence of alternative sources of energy, the demand for petroleum will continue to be high or, at the very least not decline sufficiently and rapidly enough to affect OPEC price and production schedules substantially in the immediate future.

The seventh condition for the success of a cartel, similarities in rates of discounting future profits, does not hold for the members of OPEC. There are major differences in their assessments of the trade-offs between present and future gains. Clearly, some oil-exporting countries have been motivated most directly by the prospects of immediate gains, while others have preferred to stress future benefits.

Some oil-exporting countries have made investment decisions that they now regard as erroneous and appear to be reassessing not only these decisions, but their own preferences for discounting future profits. For example, during the first quarter of 1975, Iranian petroleum exports declined by 1.3 million barrels per day.[8] By halting all secondary development projects and imposing priorities on all projects, Iran openly admitted a major miscalculation in its determination of future profits.

Uncertainty in the market, yielding further ambiguities in discounting calculations, is increasing significantly due to differential inflation rates and differential economic growth. While such differences have been somewhat dampened by the recent OPEC switch to the Special Drawing Rights of the IMF, such uncertainty will make estimates of future profits more conservative and possibly increase the primacy of short-term gains.[9] At the very least, they will contribute to further assessments and debates among the members of OPEC regarding the value of present versus future benefits.

The inward-outward policy debate on the disbursement of petroleum revenues described in Chapter 5 illustrates the types of political and economic factors that shape national orientations toward the present and the future, and the extent to which differences in such orientations are determined by structural factors and, in turn, influence patterns of international economic transactions.

Despite frequent rhetoric to the contrary, the economic behavior of the oil-exporting countries lacks both general design and specific directions. There are five distinct although not mutually exclusive strategies that illustrate economic differences among the members of OPEC. First, conservation through cutting back on petroleum exports. This option is becoming more prevalent, particularly for Libya and Algeria. Second, an internal development strategy, in terms of accelerating expenditures on imports. This approach is pursued to varying degrees of magnitude by all oil-producing states, most notably Iraq. Third, a Middle East strategy aimed at regional development. Only Kuwait pursues this option. Fourth, an investment strategy, involving extensive capital transactions abroad, primarily in the West. Again, the larger producers, Iran and Saudi Arabia, have adopted this option. Fifth, an aid strategy, in terms of assistance, loans and grants to the Fourth World. All the oil-exporting countries exhibit varying degrees of commitment to this strategy, with Saudi Arabia being the most generous.

The "oil in the ground" versus "money in the bank" debate bears on the extent to which the value of petroleum in the ground would increase at a rate equal to the market rate of interest. If the value of oil in the ground grew more rapidly than the market rate of interest, it would make economic sense to conserve this resource. However, if the value of oil in the ground grew more slowly than the rate of interest, it would pay to exploit known reserves immediately. This calculation—however sketchy, incomplete, and potentially misleading it might be—takes into account only economic factors, namely, the differential value of oil versus the rate of interest. In addition, the relevant consideration may not be the bank rate of interest, but the opportunity cost; that is, the rate of return on the invested funds in the best possible uses. For Saudi Arabia and Kuwait it may be deposits in banks, for Algeria and Iran, probably not. Different members of OPEC bring to bear on this issue a host of related considerations that are not readily translated in economic terms. For example, Saudi Arabia's commitment to the preservation of OPEC might lead to it overlooking the economic advantages of accelerating the present rate of production. Libya's radical regime might place the value on preserving a valued good for future generations, even though it might appreciate the ground at a rate lower than the market rate of interest. Algeria might regard its policy ambiguity with respect to national priorities sufficiently compelling to prevent it from making substantial commitments to pursuing immediate gains. There are numerous other examples. The point is that the members of OPEC do not share the same criteria for discounting future profits. Indeed, the differences are dramatic.

Eighth, there are some shared economic and political risks, which all OPEC members face when confronting other oil-exporting and the major oil-consuming states. The major economic risk to persistently high prices and production cutbacks lies in the development of alternative sources of energy. This is not likely to affect the world petroleum market in the immediate future. The more important risk pertains to the development of alternative sources of petroleum and to the accelerated increase in the export capacities of the newly discovered fields. Cautious estimates for such developments converge around five to eight years. More optimistic assessments range from three to five years. But no one has predicted substantial changes in the next one or two years. Lastly, the members of OPEC all share the common risks associated with creating significant economic instability in the world.

There is another set of risks, common to all OPEC states, namely, those associated with staying or not staying in the cartel. Such risks are particularly important for countries with high claims against petroleum revenues and small known reserves. Accelerating production or lowering prices would lead to a more rapid depletion of reserves.

There are also different political risks tied to a policy of undermining the cartel. For example, Saudi Arabia might jeopardize its newly acquired leadership of the Arab world. Iran would incur strategic losses and possibly endanger its recent improvement of relations with the neighboring states. Algeria would risk its new posture as a radical state seeking to propel a reorganization of the international economic system and possibly endanger its newly acquired leadership among similarly inclined states of the Third and Fourth worlds. Kuwait's risks would be similar to those of Saudi Arabia, in addition to endangering its investments in the Arab states. Furthermore, any marked deviation from OPEC would antagonize the Palestinian population of Kuwait, possibly placing added burdens on the national leadership. In many cases, therefore, the political costs of deviating from OPEC directives would be great.

Ninth, OPEC is confronted with a set of unorganized buyers. Despite frequent attempts to promote coordination, the consumers of the West have yet to develop united postures. These buyers have different needs for imported oil, ranging from Japan's 98 percent dependence on external sources to the 35 percent dependence of the United States, most of which remains from reliable sources. These differences have given rise to strategic, political, and economic implications for the consumer countries as a group. There are no common grounds for collaboration other than over some notions of lower prices and assured supplies. Even within such areas of vague agreement, there are divergent views as to the proper policy responses. The various recylcing proposals described in Chapter 3 represent the search for ways of controlling the new interdependencies. Despite their lack of cohesion, the oil-consuming nations are gradually becoming more organized, but far from sufficiently as to threaten the existence of OPEC.

Finally, a fundamental tenet of economic theory is the existence of a common valuation framework, not only among the members of a cartel, but also between the cartel and the buyers. This tenet stems from the behavioral assumption that sellers maximize profit and buyers minimize purchase costs. From the evidence so far, the story of OPEC and its interaction with the consumer countries appears to indicate that this dual premise is simply inapplicable. The oil-exporting countries are not simply seeking to maximize economic profits; they are maximizing some composite goal of which profit is an important, and perhaps the most critical, factor but it is not the only one.

In sum, six of the ten conditions for the success of a cartel hold for OPEC. Only two of these are exogenous, in that they pertain to market conditions and the characteristics of the buyers. The consumers are still too disorganized and their policies and priorities remain to be specified. Alternative sources of petroleum are not likely to become fully operational for another three to five years. Countries with potential export capacity are likely to require at least that much time for increasing their production to substantially cut into OPEC shares of the market. They as yet do not constitute a threat to the cartel. All petroleum producers, be they members of OPEC or not, presently gain from the cartel price policies. And the international oil companies continue to perform the market coordinating function that is so central to the maintenance of OPEC. With time all of these factors may change, but at present they contribute to the success of the cartel.

Of the four conditions that do *not* hold in the case of OPEC three pertain to factors endogenous to the group. Yet, OPEC remains a strong organization. Much of its strength can be attributed to the political feelings that integrate the group and compensate for the disintegrative economic influences. These factors are regarded as distortions from an economic perspective; yet, they are profoundly significant–if not determinant–in explaining the success of a cartel that appears not to conform to the economists' criteria of success. On economic grounds alone one would not expect OPEC to survive much longer. On political grounds, one would be more cautious in making such an assessment.

The exclusively economic character of previous cartels can explain the disintegration of such agreements in the past. In such cartels there is an inherent tendency to internal price cutting and to the breakdown of market allocations. But OPEC may well yield a story different from that of earlier producer cartels for the following six important reasons: (1) It controls a product that is irreplaceable in the short run and for which demand is growing; (2) the producers vary extensively in their requirements of added revenues; (3) agreement on price is necessary, but price maintenance does not depend upon rigid coordination, nor are the incentives for price cutting uniform; (4) cartel policy appears to be made in recognition of political and economic diversities among the members, not with the insistence on conformity; (5) OPEC does not, as yet, employ overt sanctions, thus making it easier to tolerate minor deviations from group directives; and (6) seven of its thirteen members are tied not only by prospects of common economic gains, but also by shared political objectives. It is the *conjunction* of these factors that has made frequent predictions of the cartel's demise somewhat premature.

Finally, it may well be that a cartel perspective is not the most useful one in explaining or predicting the behavior of OPEC.[g] There are too many factors that are overshadowed by such a perspective, yet remain critical in predicting its eventual demise.

The Break-up of OPEC

In the long run market conditions will no longer favor the cartel; new sources of petroleum will be available, the consumers will develop effective strategies in response to OPEC, and new sources of energy will become commercially viable. Since three of the four conditions for the success of a cartel that do not hold for OPEC pertain to the internal features of the group, we must conclude that the most immediate sources of disintegration will be endogenous, and that they will come from political and economic competition among its members. This competition will develop to the extent that individual gains are no longer consistent with collective gains. Internal dissension will eventually result in conflict over price, production schedules, and the allocation of market shares.

On the assumption that the breakup will come from within rather than from factors external to the cartel, at least four scenarios appear likely from both economic and political perspectives. The sequence with which they are presented here is intended to suggest differing degrees of probability.

The first scenario involves strains between Iran and Saudi Arabia, the two dominant members of OPEC. Their economic and political interests are dissimilar and their recent record of compromise may not persist. Iran's requirements for increased petroleum revenues may necessitate an accelerated production schedule and larger market shares, but it is unlikely that they will lead to price cutting. In turn, Saudi Arabia might choose to exert influence upon Iran (and upon the organization more generally) by unilaterally reducing prices and/or increasing its petroleum production. Saudi Arabia has the greatest maneuverability in each of these regards, a fact that escapes none of the members of OPEC.

By way of ensuring against a Saudi exercise of economic power, Iran has sought to improve its political relations with the Arab states as a whole. Iran's improved relations with Egypt must be viewed not only in their bilateral context, but in terms of the potential payoffs of such a move to Iran, given Egypt's dominant role in Arab politics. So, too, the rapprochement between Egypt and Saudi Arabia, a by-product of inter-Arab politics, has reinforcing effects upon the new detente between Iran and Saudi Arabia.

[g]For an economic analysis of cartels see, Davis B. Bobrow and Robert T. Kudrle, "Theory, Policy and Resource Cartels," September 1974; Ervin Hexner, *International Cartels* (London: Sir Isaac Pitman & Sons, Ltd., 1946); William Fellner, *Competition Among the Few: Oligopoly and Similar Market Structures* (New York: Alfred A. Knopf, 1949); Roger Sherman, *Oligopoly: An Empirical Approach* (Lexington, Mass.: Lexington Books, D.C. Heath and Co., 1972); and Martin Shubik, *Strategy and Market Structure: Competition, Oligopoly, and the Theory of Games* (New York: John Wiley & Sons, Inc., 1959).

The second scenario for the break-up of OPEC involves conflict between Algeria and Saudi Arabia. There, again, differences in the economic and political interests of the two countries are strong. The policy debate on the disbursement of petroleum revenues described in Chapter 5 is indicative of the differences in orientations that, when reinforced by economic differences, and placed in the context of inter-Arab politics, may well become explosive. Saudi Arabia represents the traditional elements in the Middle East. Algeria is the spokesman for the revolutionary and radical influences. In recent years the two countries have been able to develop at least a facade of cooperation. If the new directions in regional politics described in Chapter 4 are entrenched at the present time, the possibilities of conflict between Algeria and Saudi Arabia may be forestalled. If these directions are temporary or fragile and more traditional modes of inter-Arab politics are resorted to, then the Algerian-Saudi situation is a prime candidate for the break up among the oil-exporting states.

The third scenario is based on potential conflict between Kuwait on the one hand, and other Middle East producers on the other. Kuwait has been the most cautious in its petroleum exploitation policies and in its strategy for the disbursement of petroleum revenues. It has the greatest experience with regional economic transactions and its national development plans are closely predicated upon the persistence of regional cooperation. Kuwait is not likely to jeopardize the cohesion of the oil-exporters in any unilateral move. But its response to policies of other states that it might regard as being destructive to OPEC could, in itself, trigger further disintegrative effects. It is unclear precisely how this might occur. But so far, considerably more attention in both policy making and academic circles of the West has been given to the dominant members of OPEC and comparatively less to Kuwait. The position of this country in OPEC politics remains as yet not fully understood. However, Kuwait has as least as much flexibility as does Saudi Arabia in opportunity costs associated with manipulating prices, production schedules, or the allocation of market shares. How it chooses to exercise this flexibility may in itself become a source of strain.

The fourth scenario involves strains that might well be posed by the behavior of Iraq. So far Iraq has been engaged in minor price deviations. None have been serious and none have caused any overt commentary from the other members of OPEC. But the situation will not persist. Iraq will not be allowed to continue cutting prices, nor will any substantial expansion of its market shares be condoned. Political disputes with Iran, Kuwait, and Saudi Arabia have, for all practical purposes, been resolved. But the resolution is new. It may not yet be institutionalized. Economic disputes may well flare up into political ones again, making a presently volatile situation, potentially very disruptive.

Another Arab-Israeli war will almost certainly strain the organization. Pressed for petroleum revenues, Iran is not likely to support the Arabs. The non-Middle East producers will not participate in any embargo. The fringe exporters will be in an advantageous position. Saudi Arabia and Kuwait's maneuverability and influence upon OPEC policies will be neutralized. Another Middle East war would almost inevitably destroy OPEC.

The Balance Sheet

It is a peculiar convergence of circumstances that has allowed OPEC to exercise the kind of influence it did in October 1973. Some of these circumstances have been created by the increasing petroleum demand of the consumer countries, some by the oil-exporting states themselves, and some by the policies of the international oil companies.

So far, OPEC has succeeded in developing an apparently viable institution to meet some basic needs of oil-exporting countries. It has succeeded in manipulating prices and in raising them beyond any previous level. And it has been recognized as an international group, with the status, rights, and privileges of an international organization.

But OPEC has failed in its attempt to identify the priorities of its members and to reach an agreement regarding the structure of these priorities. It has failed to unify their petroleum policies. And it has failed to devise ways of stabilizing petroleum prices. So far, the members of OPEC have not needed to disrupt each other's markets. But every cartel or price fixing agreement depends on a critical interdependence among the members, in that no party will try to increase its share of the market by offering lower prices or better terms of sale. It remains unclear whether the appreciation of this interdependence is sufficiently strong among the members of OPEC to forestall the development of internal dissension.

Regardless of when OPEC breaks up, or how, all parties to petroleum transactions have come to recognize their common predicament. Everyone is caught in a web of interdependence. Managing this interdependence has become a primary policy concern for both importers and exporters of crude petroleum. Therein lies the most important lesson from our recent petroleum experience.

Notes

1. *The New York Times*, March 7, 8, 9, 11, 12, and 13, 1975.
2. See, Davis B. Bobrow and Robert T. Kudrle, "Theory, Policy and Resource Cartels," an expanded version of a paper presented to the American Political Science Association, Chicago, Illinois, August 29-September 2, 1974, p. 10.
3. International Monetary Fund, *IMF Survey*, Vol. 4, No. 10 (May 26, 1975), p. 160.
4. *The New York Times*, June 11, 1975; see also, June 20, 1975.
5. *The New York Times*, February 19, 1975.
6. *The New York Times*, March 2, 1975.
7. *The New York Times*, November 14, 1973; and December 18, 1973.
8. *The New York Times*, January 26, 1975; May 28, 1975; June 17, 1975; July 20, 1975; and August 15, 1975.
9. *The New York Times*, March 25, 1975.

A Synthesis: The Structure of Energy Interdependence

This book has described and analyzed petroleum exchanges and the complexity of ties that bind nations in their attempts to meet energy requirements. We argued that many of these exchanges cannot be explained solely by a narrow economic analysis and that political objectives are often paramount. Indeed, the interaction between political motivations and economic instrumentalities provides much of the intricacy of petroleum politics. This chapter presents a brief synthesis of the international interdependencies generated by the flows of energy across national boundaries.

Energy Interdependence

The structure of energy interdependence is created by many linkages emanating from asymmetries in production and exchanges, vulnerabilities and sensitivities, shared interests, the costs of pursuing national objectives, and the efforts to increase control over international transactions. The energy predicament of all nations emanates from the multiple effects of the increases in petroleum prices in conjunction with the discrepancies between those effects and the way they are perceived by various actors. Different views of the impact of higher oil prices lead to different definitions of the problem and its solutions. The absense of a shared perspective on the petroleum problem precludes a common view of alternative solutions. While political difficulties may lie in the minds of men, the complexities of interdependence provide little assistance in aligning perceptions with underlying realities. In addition, the analyst's predispositions toward what "ought to be" often contaminate his analysis of "what is."

By beginning with basic petroleum flows and tracing their implications we tried to be explicit about political issues at the sources of prevailing value judgments, many of which are not grounded in empirical realities. This procedure has drawn attention to the increasing constraints on national behavior at each stage of subsequent exchange. For example, imports and exports of petroleum define basic transactions and fundamental dependencies; these are modified by total commodity trade and by the alternatives available to importers and exporters; and finally, petroleum exchanges have created surplus revenues in producing countries that necessitate large-scale capital transactions.

These linkages define a situation in which a broad range of each nation's policies are influenced by those of other nations. The common policy response to mutual constraints is one of seeking to decrease the scope, range, and domain of activities and issues that are currently *not* under one's own control. But at each stage of petroleum-related exchanges, the costs to each nation of exercising *direct* control becomes higher; at each stage a country has progressively less direct control over its environment, over the consequences of its own activities, and over the behavior of other states. The efforts to reduce the impact of constraints on control often become increasingly counterproductive and inconsistent with the original policy intents. The net impact of the foregoing is an ever widening range of actions and issues that require *joint* responses and that defy manipulation through unilateral intervention.

The essense of political interdependence can thus be found in those issue areas that lie beyond each nation's control and beyond the control of others, and that require common responses. This situation in itself defines the predicament of interdependence in international politics: When joint responses are required to bring about desired outcomes or shared utilities, the need for coordination in itself constitutes a necessary and sufficient condition for interdependence. The roots of this predicament lie in the asymmetries generated by the flows of petroleum across national boundaries and by higher petroleum prices.

Structural Asymmetries

The flow of petroleum reflects structural and behavioral differences among nations. Higher petroleum prices have consolidated these differences and given rise to a series of economic and political repercussions that, increasingly, constrain national autonomy in international politics. We have termed these differences as *asymmetries* to indicate the initial inequalities which provide the basis for evolving interdependencies in energy transactions. These inequalities constitute the basis of the world-wide energy crisis and have given rise to yet other asymmetries that provide one context for petroleum; they shape the basic realities within which oil-importing and oil-exporting nations interact, and define the leverages that each may exert upon the other. By themselves asymmetries indicate only the initial transactions generated by energy needs but with institutionalized flows they become the basis for defining potential vulnerabilities. It is these vulnerabilities that assign political meaning to structural asymmetries in petroleum-related transactions and create the initial motivations for the search for policy alternatives.

Vulnerabilities

Consumers are vulnerable to possibilities of oil embargos. They have become sensitive to the actions of the producer countries, to the possibility of being denied access of a critical source of energy, and to the fact that this denial may be shaped by political objectives and not by considerations of narrow economic rationality. They are also vulnerable to the manipulation of petroleum revenues and to the investment preferences of the producing countries. Where and how the members of OPEC invest their surplus revenues will inevitably have an economic impact on the consumer countries; the latter may not be able to control the direction of such investments entirely.

The consumers continue to remain vulnerable to increases in petroleum prices; they are also sensitive to difficulties in planning associated with accommodating to price uncertainties. Many of these vulnerabilities have led to political disagreements among the oil-importing countries. These disagreements may, at some point, contribute to political instability in the West. Differences among the oil-consuming nations in approaches to OPEC and in their preferences for ways of recycling surplus petroleum revenues point to potential sources of discord among the Western allies. French support for, and initial United States opposition to, indexing petroleum prices reflect only minor differences. The United States' desire to provide leadership in structuring a common posture for the importing countries may not be acceptable to the Europeans or to Japan. Indeed, the very premises upon which consumer cooperation is to be established are themselves the subject of strong debate.

On their part, the exporting countries are becoming sensitive to the possibility of depleting nonrenewable energy resources. They differ in magnitudes of known reserves and in perceptions of risk associated with accelerating production, but they are all aware of their dependence upon geological constraints that cannot be readily manipulated in short order. Exporter countries are always vulnerable to military intervention. In addition, OPEC is sensitive to internal political and economic discord.

The economies of the oil-exporting countries are highly dependent on trade with the West and on continued access to industrial goods, advanced technology, and associated services. The fact that such goods and services can be obtained interchangeably from many of the advanced countries does not negate the reality of this dependence, but only its potential use by the West as a means of influencing the policies of the oil-exporting countries.

So, too, the international oil corporations have become increasingly affected by the growing strength of OPEC, as well as by the direct involvement of consumer governments in petroleum-related decisions. The maneuverability of the oil companies is being constrained. Although they are viewed by some as being agents of the producers, by others as agents of the consumers, everyone recognizes that the activities of the oil companies are severely restricted.

The countries of the Fourth World in turn are vulnerable to the effects of higher petroleum prices; they are the most drastically affected by price increases. In a fundamental way, their economic fate is controlled by decisions made elsewhere.

In short, all parties in petroleum transactions are vulnerable to international financial dislocations occasioned by increases in petroleum prices. The higher prices have accentuated the economic problems occasioned by worldwide inflation. The impacts may be differential, but no state can effectively "opt out" of the economic constraints imposed by increases in petroleum prices. These vulnerabilities determine the importance of petroleum and related financial transactions to various states. They suggest the types of instrumentalities nations may be willing to employ in order to manipulate such vulnerabilities. The political importance assigned to separate features of resource-related transactions that are often asymmetric signal the presence of mutual constraints. It is because of a near-universal recognition of increased vulnerabilities that shared interest becomes politically important. The search for common interest may thus be created by the reality of structural asymmetries and associated vulnerabilities. With reciprocal vulnerabilities the costs of eliminating constraints become higher, and by extension, the pressures or predispositions for defining shared interests also increase. In the absence of a willingness to incur whatever costs are necessary to reduce constraints on national behavior and related vulnerabilities, the search for shared interests becomes a major policy imperative.

Shared Interests

The perceived vulnerabilities of nations, which result in a concerted awareness of their shared interests, may increase collaboration among members of antagonistic groups, but they may also heighten the concern for pursuing independent actions. A shared interest in intragroup cohesion characterizes all parties in the world petroleum market. For example, it is to the individual interests of the producers that the strength of OPEC be maintained; to some extent short-term individual gains have even been sacrificed for common benefits.

On their part the oil-importing nations have a shared interest in stable and ensured sources of supplies. This assurance is regarded as fundamental as reducing the price of petroleum. There are also some common interests expressed in various recycling proposals. The premises underlying these plans differ; yet, the major concern of most proposals is for developing regularized means of attracting, channelling, and controlling OPEC investments in the Western industrial economies, and only marginally in the Fourth World. There is also a common interest in increasing the control of oil-importing countries over the investment strategies of the exporters.

These communalities of interest are only partially shared by the exporters who recognize the importance of developing viable procedures for recycling petroleum revenues but differ with the consumers regarding the underlying premises and predispositions, particularly regarding suggestions that OPEC investments be controlled by the West.

Both oil-importing and oil-exporting countries have a common interest in a stabilized international economic situation. Dislocations benefit no one. The effect of instability may be differential. The gains may be unequal. Yet, the losses associated with international economic instabilities affect both producers and consumers. The risk of triggering international economic disruptions appears to be one that producer countries are reluctant to make. Their recognition of the gains to all parties of a stabilized world economy shapes their concern for protecting that order.

Yet, there remain marked differences between oil-exporters and oil-importers (and within each group) regarding their conceptions of a *preferred* international economic order and the extent to which the present system may be manipulated to bring prevailing realities in closer alignment with their preferences.

So, too, there are some shared interests that bind exporters and importers that transcend their individual preferences regarding petroleum prices, production or distribution. Members of the Organization of Arab Petroleum Exporting Countries are linked by common language, culture, and colonial experience. They are united in their opposition to Israel, but they differ on the terms of the prospective settlement. They also have some shared interests in the resolution of fundamental inter-Arab conflicts; yet, they differ on their priorities and preferences regarding the terms of such solutions.

The oil-importing countries of the West are linked by common military and strategic concerns vis-à-vis the perceived Soviet threat and by shared economic concerns for the well-being of the Western bloc; yet, they differ regarding their concern for the viability of the Western alliance in the form of NATO. They differ regarding their preferences for individual rather than shared postures toward OPEC. And they differ in the extent to which they attribute responsibility for the present crisis to the unilateral price increases of OPEC. Everyone is now seeking to identify the optimum policy instruments; yet, everyone remains sufficiently unclear about ways of obtaining desired outcomes. Confusion regarding means prevails, and it is even not clear whether proposed policies are designed to modify empirical realities or whether they are viewed as ends in themselves.

The most dramatic example of confusion regarding means, ends, instrumentalities and expected outcomes is found in the United States where official rhetoric alternates between Project Independence and Project Interdependence. Each term implies a different assessment of instrumentalities and different preferences for ends and outcomes. However, each seeks to increase the scope, range, and domain of international outcomes susceptible to United States control or, at a minimum, to reduce the control of other states over outcomes viewed as critical to the United States. The issue of the cost to be incurred in the pursuit of national objectives is a critical foreign policy imperative.

Costs

Structural asymmetries, attendant vulnerabilities, and shared interests all ultimately involve the costs broadly conceived that nations are willing to incur in order to minimize those constraints on national autonomy regarded as threatening. The definition of autonomy itself is ambiguous since different nations have different conceptions of the degree of autonomy desired or the extent to which constraints would be tolerated. The autonomy sought by the United States is fundamentally different in degree and in kind from that required by Canada, Japan, or the West European countries. National capabilities define the extent of possible autonomy. But autonomy is also defined by the perceptions of costs to be incurred—either in the pursuit of national objectives or in the tolerance for the constraints on objectives.

It is particularly difficult to obtain a clear assessment of the calculations undertaken by each state, given the multiplicity of factors that influence costs. There is no common denominator to aggregate different kinds of costs—economic, military, strategic, environmental, or other. Higher energy prices are only one aspect of the cost calculations. The price of petroleum is an unsatisfactory indicator of the costs of obtaining that resource since price may not reflect other often political and strategic features of the transactions that as yet defy ready quantification.

Thus, for example, there are costs to be incurred by oil-exporting countries in their efforts to secure political autonomy, both vis-à-vis each other and in relation to the Western powers, most notably the ex-colonial states. In this case these may be so high as effectively to preclude the active pursuit of such an objective. There are also costs associated with political interdependencies among exporters. For the members of OPEC, at least, seeking to increase cohesion is undertaken at the expense of the pursuit of individual national goals. Each state has found it necessary to modify its regional political objectives and to take account of joint goals. In some cases, this has necessitated a fundamental change in national orientation and in political priorities.

There are undoubtedly economic costs to be incurred by the oil-importing countries in any concerted effort to secure autonomy in meeting their energy requirements. These costs are impressive and consumers vary among themselves regarding the extent they entertain such a possibility as being worthy of discussion at all. Japan, for example, has always been extremely dependent on external sources for meeting its energy requirements; energy autonomy is not regarded as a viable policy option; the costs of autonomy would simply be too high. By contrast, the United States has been, and continues to be, the least dependent on external sources relative to other consumer countries, yet places high value on the goal of autonomy and has assigned significant negative value to reliance on external sources for meeting its energy needs.

There are also costs associated with economic interdependence among consumer countries and differing assessments of costs to be incurred in the course of manipulating the interdependence. The effort to manipulate economic transactions for political gain presents yet another perspective on the question of cost. For some consumer countries, there are political costs related to a strategy of accommodation with the exporters. There are similar constraints upon the producers and differences in political orientations make these constraints even more salient. The shared objective of protecting the base of cohesion itself becomes an input in attendant costs.

For oil-importers and oil-exporters to coordinate activities for the development of a stable international economic system would involve incurring significant political costs. The advanced industrial states would, by necessity, acknowledge the importance of the resource producers and accommodate to demands for changing terms of exchange. Any such changes will inevitably affect their respective assessment of military and strategic calculations.

There are further costs associated with more substantial assistance to the Fourth World. For the consumers this would involve a decision to include the interests of the poorer states any recycling proposals and to incorporate their assessments in structuring demands upon the exporters. For the oil-exporters this would also mean broadening the basis of debate and allocating to the poorer states the same acknowledgment of legitimate role in world politics that they themselves are seeking to obtain from the industrial countries of the West.

Ultimately, however, the issues of asymmetries, vulnerabilities, shared interests, and costs can only assist a nation in determining its national priorities. The discrepancy between a country's preferred position and its actual position in the international energy system gives rise to the concern for reducing this discrepancy and increasing its control over energy-related transactions.

Control

The underlying controversy between oil-exporters and oil-importers involves different conceptions of and preferences for modes of control over price, production, and distribution of petroleum, and for control over the consequences of such decisions. Exporter countries seek to attain control over production decisions and reduce the influence that consumer counteractions might have. Similarly the importers wish to influence this decision and increase their control over the factors that ultimately influence production decisions. The producers also seek to maintain control over price and to exert influence over the factors that will continue to shape future prices. They wish to attain some control over the recycling processes proposed by the consumer countries and participate in the development of any agreement.

A background consideration from the consumers' perspective is the concern for maintaining control over their own energy requirements and increasing their own abilities to influence the demand side of the exchange. Their apparent unwillingness so far to substantially alter their own consumption habits is becoming an issue of domestic concern, as is the development of domestic policies for manipulating demand. Their goal of breaking up the oil cartel is an attempt to gain control not only of price, but also over production schedules.

In short, each nation is exhibiting both generalized as well as more specific concerns over the apparent constraints on national autonomy. Nations differ in their ability to establish control over their own environment or to reduce the undesirable consequences of the actions of others. But in the process of seeking to increase national control, each state may be generating outcomes over which it may have even *less* control. The range of issues that can be manipulated unilaterally are reduced accordingly. The result is an increase in the scope and range of issues whose manipulation requires coordinated policies. The process of seeking to increase control may in itself result in the further reduction of national autonomy. The trap of interdependence is to be found in the predicament that actions designed to produce one kind of effect by necessity result in outcomes reinforcing the situation whose modification was initially desired. At each stage, the probabilities of unilaterally affecting international events decrease markedly, making it more difficult to undertake direct interventions and produce direct results.

The Policy Paradox

Conflicts between oil-importers and oil-exporters, and differences within each group reflect different perceptions of reality and different views regarding optimal solutions to common problems. The dispute at the core of present controversies pertains to the authoritative allocation of values in the world petroleum market and to different conceptions of control over the petroleum transactions. Therein lies the paradox: Because of the interdependencies binding nations in their attempts to meet their energy needs, any effective allocation of authority throughout the system cannot be done unilaterally. No state alone can impose its conception of order or control upon the others. Yet, any successful coordination of behavior can only be undertaken in the belief that it enhances national autonomy. Only through the pursuit of autonomy is coordination possible politically, and only through some coordination can the dispute over control be resolved. It is because of the constraints on national autonomy imposed by the structure of international interdependence that the regulation of petroleum transactions require coordination among parties to these transactions.

This coordination requires operational rules of behavior to accommodate competing national objectives and directives. It is thus a regime response to worldwide interdependence. There are other possible responses to the energy crisis, but they are based on alternative assumptions and preferences. These include domination by a single state; domination by a group of states; autarky or isolation, which essentially attempts to negate the ties that bind nations and "opt out" of attendant interdependencies; and world order arrangements, among others. The use of force by energy importers may be a response consistent with each of these options, but the costs will be high if the objectives are not clearly specified and if criteria for success are ambiguous.

The Regime Solution

The search for international agreements to coordinate the flow of energy across national boundaries requires the development of mutual expectations between nations. These expectations may be implicit or explicit; they represent a set of lowest common denominators that are agreed upon by parties to a transaction; the agreement must be based on consensus, not on coercion. The underlying element of voluntarism is critical for the operational organization of an agreement or regime. This voluntarism may be real in that no threats of sanction are evoked; or it may be illusory, in that it is realized in anticipation of potential sanction. These expectations must be routinized, but not necessarily in terms of formal international institutions.

These critical attributes of a regime response to global interdependence do not depend on the development of a set of concrete organizations; it is a response to global interdependence based on a recognition of the costs of pursuing national autonomy. It is an attempt to minimize these costs through international coordination and the development of shared expectations between nations. The trap of interdependence emerges from the paradox noted earlier: The ties that bind nations make it difficult to regulate transactions voluntaristically; yet, without the element of voluntarism, the costs of regulations may exceed anticipated gains. Policies directed toward increasing national autonomy, if actively pursued as such, would effectively reduce such autonomy and render the problem of control even more salient than it may have been regarded earlier.

The residuals in international transactions—those issues whose resolution require joint, coordinated, and collaborate responses—necessitate an effective division of labor that recognizes the possibilities of partial control by almost every state. This control is differential and incomplete. It cannot by itself generate the desired outcome. The net effect of such a situation resembles a mutual hostage syndrome in which partial control is accompanied by the acquisition of new ways of influencing the behavior of others.

Confronted with the need to accommodate to mutual constraints, each state is faced with the problem of predicting the actions of other states, searching for behavioral expectations, reducing uncertainty, and obtaining the basic minimum information necessary for rational planning. These requirements generate the search for ways of controlling the behavior of other states. This search is manifested in probes for rules upon which the institutionalization of collective behavior can be based. These rules are about the *distribution* of energy resources, the *price* of exchanges, and the nature of the *regulatory mechanisms* to institutionalize any agreement between importers, exporters, and intermediaries. Disputes over the control of these three factors is the major policy issue at the heart of the current energy "problem."

The question of *distribution* pertains to the allocation of petroleum and to the disposition of petroleum revenues. The parties to petroleum-related transactions obviously have differing conceptions of appropriate distribution. For example, in initiating production cutbacks, exporting countries are invariably affecting the pattern of distribution, thereby having an impact on all consumer countries. The impact is differential, the effects of which are reinforced further by differences in their views of appropriate distribution.

The issue of *price* stands as the ultimate trace of patterns of distribution. Price is essentially a medium of interaction reflecting the convergence of demands, the recognition of these demands, and the formulation of strategic objectives. The price of energy represents the operational values of the dominant actors in an energy system, and the manipulation of price indicates a concern for restructuring the basis of exchange. The price increases of October 1973 were a clear statement of protest and desire of the oil-producing nations to obtain larger revenues—for a variety of interrelated economic and political reasons. The question of a "just" price raised by both U.S. Secretary of State Kissinger and OPEC officials reflects the desire of all parties in energy transactions to maximize gains and minimize liabilities. But costs and benefits are defined differently by different nations, and these differences are reflected in alternative conceptions of a "just" price.

Finally, there is the question of the *regulation* of petroleum flows and of related transactions. Regulation is intimately related to price and distribution. The economic interdependencies generated by higher petroleum prices suggest that regulating general as well as specific economic transactions is emerging as an important policy imperative for all parties. Again, there are differing conceptions of what needs be regulated and how. Alternative proposals for recycling petroleum revenue indicate the differences in various conceptions of regulation and the extent to which consumer countries were willing to share discretionary power with the oil-exporting nations. To a large extent this willingness is not forthcoming from the oil-consuming nations. But there are some indications of direct consultation about price, distribution, and regulation between producers and consumers of crude petroleum.

For the first time in the history of the West, there is an awareness of the need to take account of the demands of oil-exporting nations when searching for means of resolving global economic problems. The story of the International Energy Agency reflects this search for regulation and subsequent developments indicate a gradual move toward including other less developed states in international deliberations. There is the search for international means of regulating energy transactions. The contents of shared expectations are yet to be worked out as are the institutional basis of collective action. But the shared predicament posed by the energy crisis–how to meet national energy requirements without generating undue economic and political dislocations–is now cast in a framework that clearly recognized the constraints upon national autonomy imposed by ties that bind nations in efforts to meet their energy needs.

In conclusion, a regime solution to the paradox of interdependence involves an identification of policy imperatives, of who controls major decisions, and of what the distribution of gains and losses will be. Any agreements–or lack thereof–between importers and exporters of crude petroleum will provide important precedents for regulating an international system based on alternative sources of energy.

Part III: Epilogue

9 The Structure of Interdependence for Alternative Sources of Energy

This chapter anticipates the potential structure of interdependence for future energy systems based on alternatives to petroleum. We consider first coal, natural gas, and nuclear power and then the more esoteric possibilities. Our observations are, by necessity, indeterminate given the technological and economic uncertainties associated with each alternative to petroleum. We assume that the higher the price of crude petroleum, the more likely it will be that the consumer countries will make greater investments toward the development of other sources of energy.

Different sources of energy will highlight different types of inequalities among nations, defining resource-rich and resource-poor differently, and give rise to different sets of national options and priorities. For any alternative to petroleum, the advanced states will control technological development; they will in effect become the producers of energy. As a result, asymmetries in technology are likely to overshadow asymmetries in access to the critical underlying resources, particularly in the case of uranium but also with respect to coal and natural gas.

The global institutional arrangements governing transactions in energy have yet to be developed to any significant degree. It is clear that the national governments will assume a primary role in such arrangements. Whatever agreements importers and exporters of crude petroleum might develop in the immediate future, it is unlikely that such arrangements could be transferable to other sources of energy. Thus, the question of developing viable regimes for energy transactions will continue to be relevant in the years to come.

Structural Asymmetries and Vulnerabilities

It is safe to say that the structure of interdependence in a world drawing upon alternatives to petroleum as basic sources of energy would be fundamentally different from that of today. Structural asymmetries, vulnerabilities, shared interests, costs, and the search for control may differ appreciably. Present assessments may be speculative at best; yet, available evidence regarding control and distribution of various energy resources yields important clues into potential interdependencies.

For the industrial countries to invest in the development of alternatives to petroleum is to make some commitment toward autonomy of action in the energy field. In many cases, this autonomy will be costly—in political, economic, and environmental terms. But it might have global implications that transcend national boundaries, possibly giving rise to new types of interdependencies.

At the present time, there appears to be little likelihood of intricate structural asymmetries in coal transactions. Indeed, for countries with extensive coal reserves, a coal-based energy system would simply increase energy autonomy and lead to few, if any, higher order interactions or transactions. In this regard, a coal-based energy world would differ substantially from one based on petroleum. Coal would enable the development of strategies of independence in energy policy. But it would not necessarily ensure that this independence would extend to other issue areas. Unlike petroleum, therefore, there would be no ready spillover effects across issue areas, either favorable or unfavorable.

A U.S. commitment to a coal-based energy system could generate new types of interdependence and eliminate old ones. For example, the economic and financial problems occasioned by petroleum imports would disappear, thereby increasing United States international monetary flexibility. However, the possibilities of transferring gasification technology to other countries—most notably those allied with the United States—would forge new linkages among them. Reliance on coal would reduce balance of payments deficits associated with the cost of importing petroleum. Under favorable technological circumstances, exports of coal could be employed further to offset the United States balance of payments. Developing additional coal mines might also yield domestic economic benefits, most notably in providing employment in the depressed mining areas. In the event that the United States would become a major supplier of coal, it would find itself in a pivotal position, not an implausible possibility given the magnitude of the country's reserves. In addition, coal would present none of the security-related problems associated with access to petroleum. Since the world's largest reserves of coal are found in the USSR, potential competition between the United States and the USSR for security of access would also not be at issue. The reliance on coal could also have a positive effect upon United States relations with Western Europe and Japan by reducing competition for Middle East oil. But such an eventuality might also broaden the gap between United States interests and those of its allies in terms of policies toward the oil-producing countries.

In short, there is little international trade in coal. For the United States there are practically no international vulnerabilities associated with conventional uses of coal. Technological processes of liquification and gasification have been known for some time, although there has been and continues to be the need for considerable refinement in these techniques.

Although there are similarities in the production, consumption, and flows of coal and natural gas, the attendant vulnerabilities differ considerably. Despite its large domestic production, the United States' dependence on external sources for natural gas is likely to increase, particularly if governmental regulation of prices persists and if coal gasification technology does not improve appreciably. The potential strength of OPEC countries in influencing price, production, and distribution of natural gas might become an important factor in international transactions of this source of energy. The Organization of Petroleum Exporting Countries could become a major exporter. In the longer run, its influence would increase if it coordinates with the USSR, an event that appears unlikely at the present time but may become plausible in the future.

A nuclear-based energy system would reduce the United States' dependency upon petroleum and its interdependence in a global petroleum system. But, as with coal and natural gas, it would still not eliminate United States reliance upon oil as a major source of energy in the foreseeable future. Reliance on nuclear power could reduce the balance of payments deficit associated with the costs of importing petroleum. For example, the value of United States reactor exports increased by 40 percent between 1971 and 1973. In 1973 the total value of nuclear exports was almost as large as the overall value of such exports for the 11 years between 1959 and 1970.[1] It is anticipated that by 1985 the value of United States exports in nuclear reactors will range between $2.0 and $2.8 billion.[2] This estimate may be low. However, the very high capital costs associated with the development of nuclear energy plants and the probable increase in the costs of exported goods manufactured with high energy costs may well provide negative effects on the balance of payments.

The United States will undoubtedly have a pivotal position in any global energy system based on nuclear power and in the development of rules and regulations for interaction among nations. However, there are problems ahead. The use of nuclear power could have at least four undesirable consequences: (1) the expansion of nuclear nations in conjunction with the persistence of inadequate safeguards, (2) terrorist use of plutonium itself, in the manufacture of nuclear weapons or in sabotage of nuclear plants, (3) well-publicized environmental consequences, and (4) uncertainties about the adequacy of uranium supplies in the United States. Such developments accentuate the possibility that one nation's security will be another's insecurity.

The Swedish International Peace Research Institute (SIPRI) estimates that by the early 1980s the present nonnuclear countries will have 26,000 kilograms of Plutonium-239 available to them every year.[3] Other estimates state that several thousands of kilograms will be present in civilian fuel cycles by 1980.[4] With the exception of France, the countries of Western Europe and Japan do not have high reserves and they continue to be dependent on the United States for enriched uranium. To counter potential dependence on the United States, Western Europe is purchasing enrichment services from the USSR and is working on centrifuge technology to enrich its uranium. Similarly, the Canadian reactor has been made available to the Indians and Argentinians largely because it involves no dependence on the United States for enrichment technology. However, external dependence for heavy water will persist unless they have their own plants.

The poorer states will continue to rely upon the United States, France, West Germany, Canada, and the USSR for some time to come. Their demands for reactors and for nuclear technology will almost certainly have to be satisfied from the outside.[5] At least six countries have the potential for producing nuclear explosives in the near future: Argentina, Brazil, Pakistan, South Africa, Taiwan, and Israel.[6] West Germany has recently agreed to sell Brazil not only nuclear reactors but also uranium enrichment facilities and a reprocessing plant.[7] Similarly, France is negotiating the sale of reprocessing plants to South Korea, Pakistan, and Taiwan.[8]

Reprocessing is a critical step because the plutonium can be recycled into new fuel rods or it can be used in nuclear weapons. The United States has held up the $7 billion reactor agreement with Iran over this very issue. The United States seeks to obtain some control over reprocessing; Iran is reluctant to allow such foreign influence. Both France and West Germany have offered Iran a more comprehensive package that may well undermine the United States agreement.[9] The six major countries exporting nuclear equipment are seeking to development guidelines for the transfer of nuclear technology, but so far little has been concluded.[10] Despite frequent disagreements, the development of shared interests is becoming an important feature of nuclear-related transactions.

Shared Interests

There are clearly shared interests in the development of any source of energy in that such activity would expand the amount of energy consumed, decrease pressures on the use of petroleum, diversify the sources of potential political and economic power associated with the control of energy, and give the advanced states a more important role in energy related transactions. Beyond these general communalities, there are specific characteristics of each alternative to petroleum that might enhance the development of shared interests in the West.

Because of the abundance of coal in relatively high grade, everyone has an interest in the development of coal deposits. However, there are many petroleum uses for which coal would simply be an inefficient substitute. Again, international incentives for expanding both availability and use of coal are limited.

Only a small fraction of total energy consumed will draw upon natural gas in the near future and there are few incentives for expanding the exploration of available fields in the West. This situation could, however, change rapidly. The expansion of OPEC influence over natural gas transactions may well provide potential importers with new problems.

It is in the field of nuclear energy that the greatest shared interests exist among the advanced industrial states and the greatest differences between them and the rest of the world. The nuclear states have common interests in developing adequate safeguards for the use and transportation of nuclear energy. The cleavages between developed and underdeveloped states are further reinforced by cleavages between states with nuclear weapons and those without nuclear weapons.

Advanced countries with nuclear weapons, like the United States, USSR, France, and the United Kingdom, are interested in maintaining fairly close control over the expansion and dissemination of this source of energy.

Advanced countries without nuclear weapons, like Japan and West Germany, regard the availability of nuclear power primarily as a source of energy and so far are not willing to accept the costs of using nuclear energy for military purposes or do not see sufficient benefits in so doing.

Less developed countries that do possess the technology for military weapons, such as India and China, regard nuclear capability as one index of power in international politics, and are willing to employ nuclear energy for military purposes.

Finally, countries like Brazil, Argentina, South Africa, Taiwan, Pakistan, and South Korea, namely, those that are less developed and do not possess nuclear weapons, consider the safeguards proposed by the developed states as an attempt to deny them an opportunity to demonstrate their capability in international politics and to restrict access to the status of major power.

There are few shared interests uniting all four groups beyond those of devising safe means of transportation, controlling terrorism, and minimizing the possibilities of accident. Indeed, international cleavage on the issues of developing nuclear energy are likely to persist along these lines for some time to come.

Control

The control of price, regulation, and distribution of alternative sources of energy will undoubtedly pose important economic and political difficulties for all states. It is the many uncertainties about the future price of petroleum that have rendered the availability of alternatives an important policy issue. The question of price, when posed in the context of alternatives to petroleum, highlights further some of the complexities involved.

Price

The price of coal has been steadily increasing due in part to rises in the price of oil. In addition, safety regulations in the United States mines, environmental regulations, and transportation costs all influence the price of coal. The cost component of price differs according to the grade of ore. On balance, however, most of the variables influencing price in the United States are tractable and potentially amenable to governmental regulation or, alternatively, to being shaped by market forces. Other than the power exerted by the coal and environmental lobbies, there are fewer systematic influences that distort market mechanism than in the case of petroleum.

The price of nuclear energy is generally determined by the high capital costs. "Cumulative capital expenditures in the non-Communist world for nuclear power plants and equipment could exceed $250 billion by 1985, with approximately 50 percent of that sum expended in the U.S., 30 percent in W. Europe, 12 percent in Japan, and the remainder in various other countries."[11] The price of uranium is a small fraction of the costs of nuclear energy. Thus, any distortions imposed upon the price of uranium by joint action by major uranium producers would affect the overall price of energy only marginally.

The increase in oil prices has rendered nuclear power economical. The International Atomic Energy Agency has concluded that "if long-term oil prices remain higher than 6 to 7 dollars a barrel, then nuclear plants of 100 megawatts or larger would be competitive with oil-fired power plants."[12] Such assessments have been instrumental in rendering nuclear energy an attractive option for the industrial states.

Distribution

There are no formal mechanisms for either restricting or facilitating access and distribution of coal or natural gas. At present, nuclear power plants are available by the United States to all states that can bear the costs. Recently, nuclear power plants have been employed as an instrument of United States foreign policy as exemplified by the nuclear plans offer to both Israel and Egypt. This sale has been held up due to Israel's stated disinterest. Israel presently has nuclear plants and is reluctant to see Egypt gain a similar advantage.[13]

The possession of nuclear plants is also a way for nations to gain advantage in the nuclear industry. The present export market is controlled by the United States, accounting for 70 percent of total world exports.[14] Canada is seeking to expand her export markets of the CANDU reactor. West Germany and France are also trying to expand their export markets.[15] The distribution of nuclear reactors on a worldwide basis is still subject to strong political constraints, as most of the nonnuclear powers are ready to argue. But the full potentials for employing such transactions as instruments of foreign policy are yet to be fully explored.

Regulation

There are no formal institutional methods for regulating coal, nationally or internationally, nor are there any institutions for the direct regulation of natural gas transactions internationally. In the United States, government control of natural gas prices has potential global implications insofar as low domestic prices create high demand, which may then affect the international market. The International Energy Agency may itself become involved in the regulation of natural gas in the event of another oil embargo. OPEC is also trying to develop mechanisms for regulating transactions among its natural gas exporters. Algeria and Iran are likely to take a major role in the event of an official OPEC posture in this regard.

The dissemination of nuclear technology is regulated in a variety of ways as is the availability of nuclear energy. Bilateral controls are the most common. When Canada made nuclear technology available to India, it insisted on fairly stringent controls.[16] The United States sales to Egypt, Iran, and Israel are also predicated on strong bilateral controls. Such controls are not necessarily effective in limiting the expansion of nuclear technology. The Indian nuclear explosion, for example, indicates that diverting fissionable materials is possible under a system of bilateral controls.[17] However, different bilateral arrangements have different implications. By today's standards, the Canadian-Indian agreement was very weak. Adequate safeguards cannot be developed unless both nations are in agreement about the content, processes, outcomes, and intents of the safeguards. Clearly, there are fundamental differences among the nuclear and some nonnuclear powers in this regard, as there are between the developed and less-developed states.

Safeguards are generally defined as "devices by which control is exercised on all forms of peaceful nuclear activities in order to ensure that no disguised production of nuclear weapons can take place."[18] Existing international safeguards are mandated by the Non-Proliferation Treaty (NPT) and delineated in the International Atomic Energy Agency (IAEA) stipulations. Relevant articles of the Non-Proliferation Treaty read:[19]

> Each non-nuclear-weapon State Party to the Treaty undertakes not to receive the transfer from any transferor whatsoever of nuclear weapons or other nuclear explosive devices or of control over such weapons or explosive devices directly, or indirectly; not to manufacture or otherwise acquire nuclear weapons or other nuclear explosive devices; and not to seek or receive any assistance in the manufacture of nuclear weapons or other nuclear explosive devices. (Article II)
>
> Each non-nuclear-weapon State Party to the Treaty undertakes to accept safeguards, as set forth in an agreement to be negotiated and concluded with the International Atomic Energy Agency in accordance with the Statute of the International Atomic Energy Agency and the Agency's safeguards system, for the exclusive purpose of verification of the fulfillment of its obligations assumed under this treaty with a view to preventing diversion of nuclear energy from peaceful uses to nuclear weapons or other nuclear explosive devices. (Article III-1)

Eighty-three nations have signed the treaty; 23 have signed but have yet to ratify. Both China and France have refused to join, as have Argentina, Brazil, India, Pakistan, Israel, and South Africa. South Korea, Japan, West Germany, and Egypt have signed but have not yet ratified. Jordan, Lebanon, and Tunisia are the three Arab states that have already ratified the treaty; Algeria and Saudi Arabia have never signed, while Iran has both signed and ratified the treaty.[20]

Two perplexing problems continue to confront the international community: first, the question of the rights nations have to develop nuclear weapons capabilities; second, the question of equal rights to access and distribution of such capabilities. The dual problem has been posed as follows: "No matter what the rhetoric, a world in which five or six nations control the weapons technology is by definition discriminatory; a system which leaves all the decision-making in their hands is by definition paternalistic. There is an unfilled need for a more attractive option than either accepting the monopolistic position of the 'nuclear OPEC', or going it alone."[21] The need for such options is viewed differently by different nations.

Prospects for a Uranium Cartel

The prospects for the development of an active uranium cartel appear increasingly plausible, but it is not likely to be governmental. The major producer states—the United States, South Africa, Canada, Australia and Niger—appear too diffuse in their political orientations or economic requirements as to preclude ready agreement among them. Moreover, the Australian government stopped all exports of uranium in 1971. Canada has already committed all its expected production into the 1980s and has announced a new export policy designed to protect its domestic uranium supplies. The United States suspended trade in enriched uranium briefly in March 1975 pending a review of policy. The European response to this move was extremely negative, underlining their perceived necessity of reducing their reliance on the United States. As a result, the United States quickly clarified its policies and exports were resumed. None of these individual moves can be interpreted as a means of raising prices, nor do they appear to harbor any collusive intents.

A prospective uranium cartel is likely to be private, with higher prices as its major if not sole objective. The Uranium Producer's Forum, a group comprised of Britain's Rio Tinto Zinc, Canada's Rio Algom and Denison Mines, Australia's Western Mining, France's Uranex, and an organization of South African Mines called Nuclear Fuels Corporation, control most of the world's production and virtually all production mined for exporting. Even within this group the strength of the individual members is unequal. The Rothschilds of France and England have an interest in nearly every major uranium mine in the world, with controlling interests in the Rio Algom Mines of Canada, which owns the largest uranium reserves in North America, as well as major interests in Rio Tinto Zinc, Anglo-American Corporation, Mokta and Pennaroya Companies.

In the United States 45 percent of the uranium reserves are controlled by

United States oil companies and one company, Kerr-McGee, produces 23 percent of all United States uranium.[22] In 1972 the price of uranium oxide was $6-8 per pound. It is reported that one United States producer has recently offered uranium for delivery in the middle of the next decade at $24 per pound in addition to an annual escalator of 7 percent to be operative immediately.[23]

The concentration of power in a private uranium cartel would be in the hands of a few sellers. Demand is predicted to be sufficiently high to preclude any disagreements about market shares. Risks and costs are ambiguous but do not seem to be very different for different producers. And the buyers are presently disorganized and are likely to remain so in the immediate future. In addition, the cost of uranium is insignificant in comparison to the capital costs of a nuclear power plant. It is estimated that "at $20 per pound, uranium represents about 14% of the cost of a kilowatt hour *vs.* 72% for oil at $12 per barrel. Even with uranium at $50 per pound, about twice the price for early 1980s delivery, nuclear power would still be only as expensive as power from oil when oil costs $5.75 per barrel—one half the current price."[24] This assessment is predicated on relatively low estimates for the cost of a nuclear plant, nonetheless the differentials with petroleum persist.

The market will probably bear prices above cost because demand is expected to be high. Available estimates for demand are calculated prior to the oil embargo of 1973, thus probably underestimating what demand is likely to be. A 1973 study of the Organisation for Economic Co-operation and Development estimated that reactors ordered after 1974 are likely to commit uranium enrichment capacity that does not yet exist.[25] However, uncertainties in the market outlook have led to cancellation of many long-term uranium contracts.

Analysts for the Energy Policy Project of the Ford Foundation dispute the prospects of a uranium cartel, largely on two grounds: first, that differences among the producers are too great to preclude any effective collusion; and second, that there appears to be no concern about a shortage in the foreseeable future.[26] This assessment is short-sighted since it obscures the fact that the lead time for a uranium mine production is eight years. In addition, these analysts draw upon the same data as the 1973 OECD study that argued for the likelihood of a uranium shortage, given doubling demand every five years.[27] In sum, while the prospects of a national cartel of uranium producers is unlikely in the foreseeable future, one of private producers appears increasingly possible.

The symbolic importance of the International Atomic Energy Agency as a worldwide regulatory institution should not overshadow the fact that it performs largely a bookkeeping function. It determines how much nuclear fuel is processed within a country and expects to be informed by individual nations exactly where nuclear fuels are being used. In the event that some nuclear fuel is unaccounted for, the IAEA "operates on the principle that if there is an international system which will give the proper alarm whenever a state is suspected on reasonable grounds of intentional diversion, this in itself should provide sufficient deterrence."[28] At present, the agency is underfunded and its personnel is barely adequate to perform even this limited bookkeeping function.[29] As presently constituted, it cannot be expected to cope with the anticipated growth of nuclear energy even if its jurisdiction is not extended to states that are presently nonnuclear. Both the United States and the United Kingdom have offered to allow the IAEA to inspect nonmilitary facilities, but the agency is insufficiently funded to accept the offer.[30] Attempts are currently being made to rectify this situation.

The weakness of the International Atomic Energy Agency is perhaps best revealed by the fact that the most severe sanction it can impose is to expel a member and call its violations to the attention of the international community and to the Security Council of the United Nations. In the final analysis, there are no international arrangements that can prevent nations from demonstrating their ability to build their own nuclear weapons.[31] The raw materials and the technology both exist and the intent to develop nuclear weapons can always be justified in the name of national sovereignty, punctuated by arguments for national defense.

Alternatives to the Alternatives

The major advantages of solar energy are derived from its virtually unlimited availability with less environmental contamination than other alternatives. But while the radioactivity hazards of nuclear power systems will be avoided, cooling water for steam turbines will be required, thus the potential for thermal pollution will remain although efficiency is known to be low. It is estimated that the maximum contribution of solar power to total energy requirements will not be greater than 20 percent of expected consumption.[32]

Those nations controlling the technology involved would essentially control access to solar energy. Thus, although technology may eventually diffuse, the major cleavages will be along technological lines and the resulting interdependencies technological. As in the case of any alternative to petroleum, solar energy could reduce the United States' demands for Middle East oil, thus making greater supplies available for its allies.

Alternatively, the possibilities for shaping solar technology might increase prospects for community building, if acceptable means of transferring, sharing, or regulating such technology are developed. Inevitably, the poorer nations will not have access to this source of energy, unless it is made available to them by the advanced industrial societies. The resulting global linkages will be along the lines of increasing dependence rather than interdependence as is presently the case with respect to petroleum. There are also possibilities of employing solar—or any advanced—technology as a political instrument, by threatening to withhold access unless certain demands are met. The most critical problem from a global perspective still involves the development of regularized means of interactions and transactions related to access and transmission of solar energy.

Geothermal heat is essentially a form of nuclear energy produced primarily by the decay of radioactive materials in the earth's interior.[33] It is estimated that by 1985 a level of proved recoverable heat reserves could be established in the range of 5-50 billion barrels of oil equivalent. The more important geothermal targets are deep sedimentary basins and shallow magma chambers.[34] But there are major uncertainties regarding the magnitude of recoverable reserves and resource bases. The absence of sufficient investments in research and development has placed strong constraints upon any rapid technological developments. Indeed, there exists no exploratory tool for locating geothermal deposits and existing methods have had limited success. The major obstacles include the need to drill holes of greater depth than is presently possible and the presence of heat transfer problems.[35]

In addition, there are major unresolved questions in some industrial countries pertaining to air pollution resulting from the high sulphur content of steam or other forms of heat that would be brought to the surface. Furthermore, the time required to assess overall environmental implications and handle legal problems would significantly reduce the pace of geothermal exploration and development. Under the optimistic assumption that geothermal sources of energy could be developed on a competitive economic basis in the near future, these would supply no more than 1 percent of anticipated United States energy requirements in 1985. Indeed, there are major uncertainties associated with existing projections of energy to be obtained from geothermal sources.[36] Thus, its total contribution to United States energy uses would be negligible, except perhaps in areas of the West and Southwest where the underlying resource base would make it economically possible to draw upon geothermal energy. Geothermal sources of energy are being used in other countries.

The term "tar sands" refers to hydrocarbon-bearing deposits distinguished from more conventional oil and gas reservoirs by the high degree of viscosity of the hydrocarbon, which cannot be recovered by the same means of oil production. Reservoir energy is minimal, so that some outside form of energy is needed to produce energy from tar sands.[37] There are large tar sand deposits in Canada, Venezuela, and possibly Colombia as well. Deposits in the United States are much smaller and are not expected to yield considerable amounts of energy given present technology or levels of recovery. Given additional technological advances to process usable oil from such deposits, it is likely that both Canada and Venezuela will continue their policies of exportation to the United States. The Canadian deposits will not allow a rapid rate of production by 1985. Technological problems, construction lead time, saturation in the construction industry, and capital requirements will all tend to limit the installation of new plants.[38] On balance, it is expected, therefore, that the rate of production by 1985 will not exceed 1.25MMB/D regardless of rises in the price of alternative sources of energy.[39] Since Canadian tar sands and heavy oil deposits will be the only source of commercial production for this type of energy at least through 1985, it is not anticipated to make any significant contribution to the meeting of energy consumption levels in the United States.[40]

Oil shale is an oil-bearing rock, which may be burned directly and distilled to obtain oil products.[41] World production of shale oil is about 25 million tons per year. This figure does not include production in mainland China; it does, however, allow for the estimate that the USSR is the main producer of shale oil.[42] The United States has extensive reserves of oil shale, which could be marshalled as a viable source of energy. Oil shale deposits in the United States' western areas are estimated to yield possibly 1.8 trillion barrels of crude shale oil. But less than 6 billion barrels of recoverable reserves could be recovered given limitations imposed by construction time and environmental and legal constraints.[43] However, plans to develop these deposits have temporarily been put aside largely because the extraction of oil shale requires large amounts of water to process the oil from shale, and water is extremely scarce in areas where shale is available. In the absence of marked technological developments, it is highly unlikely that this energy source will be used to any great extent in the near future.

Extensive technological developments in producing shale oil may occur as the industry develops and as national priorities are reoriented to take into account the extensive United States reserves. Present bottlenecks in mine and plant organization, in construction, and in the establishment of increased automation must be removed before any significant cost reductions will be possible.[44] There are also considerable ambiguities regarding the legal status of shale lands. Mining claims are yet to be accorded clear legal status. Federal leasing policies will invariably influence the level and rate of production, largely because over 80 percent of oil shale resources are located on federal lands.[45] Again, as national energy priorities are reassessed and appropriate measures taken, such problems might be resolved satisfactorily in a direction that would enhance the potential contribution of shale oil to United States energy needs.

Finally, there is the question of *costs* associated with alternative sources of energy. The difficulties inherent in economic calculations of costs are overshadowed by those involved in calculating environmental, political and social costs. To date, we have only the most rudimentary understanding of the composite cost calculus associated with alternative sources of energy. We have only begun to appreciate the overall costs of reliance on petroleum. Only the vaguest glimpse of the overall costs of different mixes of energy alternatives have yet been made. Even the most sketchy observations may not be warranted, given the state of knowledge of *overall* cost assessments.

Conclusion: The Global Imperative

A comparative assessment of the alternatives to petroleum for the United States and their implications for global interdependence is presented in Table 9-1. It highlights economic and political consequences, some issues pertaining to security of access, possibilities for international cooperation, and potential environmental effects. Some of these inferences are predicated on empirical data, others are speculative; yet, all point to important differences among six different sources of energy.

The development of any alternative to petroleum would, of course, not eliminate the United States' use of oil as a primary source of energy. But it would reduce its dependence on imports for meeting consumption needs. The development of any alternative to petroleum would certainly enhance the United States' position in the world energy system. It would place the United States in a pivotal position: In effect, the United States could become the equivalent of OPEC in the present petroleum market.

While any alternative to petroleum will also ensure United States dominance in energy transactions the economic and environmental costs of this dominance may be extensive. The structure of interdependence in the petroleum system will be replaced by other needs and demands, and ways of satisfying them. Because of the countervailing global effects of alternative energy sources—tending toward cooperation as well as toward conflict—it is important that both energy-exporting and energy-importing nations develop viable means of regulating their transactions and accommodating their respects needs and demands.

The development of alternative sources of energy would almost certainly be undermined by sudden declines in OPEC petroleum prices. These declines could result from changing market conditions or, as is more likely, from a concerted OPEC strategy to reduce incentives for investments in energy-related technology. The oil-exporting nations thus have yet another leverage in their policies toward the oil-importing countries. The irony is that the persistence of high petroleum prices is a necessary condition for the development of alternative energy sources. As long as the oil-consuming nations succeed in persuading OPEC to moderate its price increases, the incentives to increase their own investments in alternative sources of energy will be reduced accordingly.

On balance, however, no matter what sources of energy will be used in the future, in whatever mix or proportion, the management of interdependence will remain the most critical challenge confronting all nations. In the last analysis, the technological and economic features of any energy system will not take precedence over political considerations in the development of national policies for the management of energy demands.

Against this background, the worldwide policy implications of interdependence will continue to revolve around the control of alternative energy sources. The greater the quantity of energy at man's disposal, the more crucial becomes the old Roman query: "*Quis custodiet custodies?*" (Who is to control the controllers?). The question pertains not only to whatever type of international regime or institution might be developed for the control of nuclear weaponry, but more critically, to the regulation, access, and distribution of energy and the technology for generating and applying it.

There are time lags associated with even the most determined efforts to

Table 9-1
Alternative U.S. Energy Systems and Issues in Global Interdependence

	Coal	Natural Gas	Nuclear Fission	Solar	Geothermal	Tar Sands Oil Shale
Political and economic consequences	1. Expansion of total resources 2. Exportable 3. Domestic gains 4. Transport costs 5. Balance of payments reduction	1. Expansion of total energy resources 2. Higher domestic costs 3. Transport costs	1. Expansion of total energy resources 2. High cost 3. High capital use 4. Uranium costs 5. Balance of payments reduction	1. Expansion of total energy resources 2. High cost 3. High capital use	1. Expansion of total energy resources 2. High cost	1. Expansion of total energy resources 2. High cost 3. Exportable
Security of access	1. Nonvulnerable resource	1. Increasingly vulnerable resource	1. Nonvulnerable resource 2. Proliferation potential 3. Terrorist potential	1. Nonvulnerable resource	1. Nonvulnerable resource	1. Nonvulnerable resource
Implications for international cooperation	1. Frees oil resources for allies 2. Technology transfers 3. Divergent allied interests	1. Frees oil resources for allies 2. Increased Soviet trade possible 3. Possibility of cartelization	1. Frees oil resources for allies 2. Divergent allied interests	1. Frees oil resources for allies 2. Technology transfers	1. Frees oil resources for allies 2. Technology transfers	1. Frees oil resources sources for allies 2. Technology transfers
Potential environmental effects	1. Strip mining costs 2. Black lung costs 3. Air pollution costs	1. Transportation hazards	1. Radiation hazards 2. Accident potential 3. Waste disposal 4. Thermal pollution	1. Heat release costs	1. Air pollution costs 2. Land disturbance 3. Water pollution	1. Water use costs 2. Strip mining costs

explore these issues. At the very least, we need to develop means of overcoming incremental and piecemeal approaches to such issues; we need to find ways of avoiding the common processes by which efforts to find solutions to one problem generate other problems, the solutions to which give rise to still further difficulties.

Notes

1. Joseph A. Yager and Eleanor B. Steinberg, *Energy and U.S. Foreign Policy* (Cambridge, Mass.: Ballinger Publishing Co., 1974), p. 334.
2. Ibid., p. 356.
3. Lincoln P. Bloomfield, "Nuclear Spread and World Order," *Foreign Affairs*, Vol. 53, No. 4 (July 1975), p. 750.
4. Mason Willrich and Theodore B. Taylor, *Nuclear Theft: Risks and Safeguards* (Cambridge, Mass.: Ballinger Publishing Company, 1974), pp. 167-168.
5. Yager and Steinberg, *Energy and U.S. Foreign Policy*, p. 351.
6. *Boston Globe*, June 8, 1975.
7. Ibid.
8. *The New York Times*, June 13, 1975.
9. *The New York Times*, June 9, 1975.
10. *The New York Times*, June 18, 26, and 29; and July 20, 1975.
11. Yager and Steinberg, *Energy and U.S. Foreign Policy*, p. 335.
12. *The New York Times*, August 3, 1974.
13. *The New York Times*, December 17, 1974.
14. *Wall Street Journal*, June 24, 1975.
15. *Wall Street Journal*, June 24, 1975.
16. *The New York Times*, May 21 and 23, 1974.
17. *The New York Times*, May 21, 1974.
18. Ryukichi Imai, "Nuclear Safeguards," *Adelphi Papers*, No. 86 (London: The International Institute for Strategic Studies, March 1972), p. 1.
19. Ibid., p. 3.
20. Adlai E. Stevenson, III, "Nuclear Reactors: America Must Act," *Foreign Affairs*, Vol. 53, No. 1 (October 1974), p. 67; George H. Quester, "Can Proliferation Now be Stopped?," *Foreign Affairs*, Vol. 53, No. 1 (October 1974), p. 84.
21. Bloomfield, "Nuclear Spread and World Order," p. 747.
22. James Ridgeway, *The Last Play* (New York: Mentor, 1973), pp. 156 and 161.
23. *Forbes*, "It Worked for the Arabs . . . ," Vol. 115, No. 2 (January 15, 1975), p. 19.
24. Ibid., p. 20.

25. Organisation for Economic Co-operation and Development, *Energy Prospects to 1985* (Paris: Organisation for Economic Co-operation and Development, 1974), p. 151.

26. Yager and Steinberg, *Energy and U.S. Foreign Policy*, p. 21.

27. Organisation for Economic Co-operation and Development, *Uranium: Resources, Production and Demand.* A joint report by the OECD Nuclear Energy Agency and the International Atomic Energy Agency (Paris: Organisation for Economic Co-operation and Development, 1973), p. 21.

28. Imai, "Nuclear Safeguards," p. 11.

29. William O. Doub and Joseph M. Dukert, "Making Nuclear Energy Safe and Secure," *Foreign Affairs*, Vol. 53, No. 4 (July 1975), p. 758.

30. Ibid.

31. Ibid., p. 756.

32. Dietrich E. Thomsen, "Farming the Sun's Energy," *Science News*, Vol. 101 (April 8, 1972), p. 238.

33. Allen L. Hammond, "Geothermal Energy: An Emergency Major Resource," *Science*, Vol. 177 (September 15, 1972), p. 978.

34. National Petroleum Council, *U.S. Energy Outlook* (Washington, D.C.: National Petroleum Council, 1972), p. 229.

35. Ibid., p. 230.

36. Ibid., p. 228.

37. Ibid., p. 225.

38. Ibid., p. 226.

39. Ibid.

40. Ibid., p. 225.

41. Nathaniel B. Guyol, *Energy in the Perspective of Geography* (Englewood Cliffs, N.J.: Prentice-Hall, Inc., 1971), p. 49.

42. Ibid.

43. National Petroleum Council, *U.S. Energy Outlook*, p. 4.

44. Ibid., p. 219.

45. Ibid., p. 206.

Bibliography

Bibliography

Books

Acosta Hermoso, Eduardo. *Analisis Historico de la OPEP.* Merida: Facultad de Economia Universidad de Los Andes, Talleres Graficos Universitarios, 1969.

_______. *La Comision Economica de la OPEP.* Caracas: Editorial Arte, 1971.

Ad Hoc Forum Policy Committee. *Uranium Enrichment.* New York: Atomic Industrial Forum, 1972.

Adelman, M.A. *The World Petroleum Market.* Baltimore: Resources for the Future, The Johns Hopkins University Press, 1972.

American Petroleum Institute. *Annual Statistical Review: 1956-1970.* Washington, D.C.: American Petroleum Institute, 1971.

_______. *Petroleum Facts and Figures.* New York: American Petroleum Institute, 1971.

Armstead, H. Christopher, ed. *Geothermal Energy.* New York: UNESCO, 1973.

Bergsten, C. Fred, ed. *The Future of the International Economic Order: An Agenda for Research.* Lexington, Mass.: D.C. Heath and Company, 1973.

Bhagwati, Jagdish N., and Richard S. Eckaus. *Development and Planning.* Cambridge, Mass.: The M.I.T. Press, 1973.

Bill, James A., and Carl Leiden. *The Middle East: Politics and Power.* Boston: Allyn and Bacon, Inc., 1974.

Bobo, D.L., et al. *A Survey of Fuel and Energy Information Sources.* McLean, Va.: Mitre Corporation, 1970.

Brockett, E.D. *Petroleum Resources Under the Ocean Floor.* Washington, D.C.: National Petroleum Council, 1969.

Calleo, David P., and Benjamin M. Rowland. *America and the World Political Economy.* Bloomington: Indiana University Press, 1973.

Clarke, J.L., and W.B. Fisher. *Populations of the Middle East and North Africa: A Geographical Approach.* New York: Africana Publishing Corporation, 1972.

Congressional Quarterly. *Energy Crisis in America.* Washington, D.C.: U.S. Government Printing Office, 1973.

Cooper, Richard N. *The Economics of Interdependence.* New York: McGraw-Hill Book Company, 1968.

Coplin, William D., ed. *The Analysis of Transnational Policy Issues: A Summary of the International Relations Panels of the 1974 American Political Science Convention.* Ithaca, N.Y.: The Consortium for International Studies Education, 1974.

Darmstadter, Joel. *Energy in the World Economy.* Baltimore: The Johns Hopkins University Press, 1971.

Davis, David H. *Energy Politics.* New York: St. Martin's Press, 1974.

Dawn, Ernest. *From Ottomonism to Arabism: Essays on the Origin of Arab Nationalism.* Bloomington: Indiana University Press, 1973.

DeGolyer and MacNaughton. *Twentieth Century Petroleum Statistics: 1973.* Dallas: DeGolyer and MacNaughton, 1973.

Deutsch, Morton. *Resolution of Conflict: Constructive and Destructive Processes.* New Haven: Yale University Press, 1973.

Duchesneau, Thomas D. *Competition in the U.S. Energy Industry.* Cambridge, Mass.: Ballinger Publishing Company, 1975.

Ebel, Robert E. *Communist Trade in Oil and Gas.* New York: Frederick A. Praeger, 1970.

The Economist Intelligence Unit. *International Oil Symposium: Selected Papers.* London: The Economist Intelligence Unit, 1972.

Elliot, Iain F. *The Soviet Energy Balance: Natural Gas, Other Fossil Fuels, and Alternative Power Sources.* New York: Frederick A. Praeger, 1974.

Evron, Yair. *The Middle East: Nations, Superpowers and Wars.* New York: Frederick A. Praeger, 1973.

Facts on File. *Energy Crisis: Volume 1.* New York: Facts on File, Inc., 1974.

Fellner, William. *Competition Among the Few: Oligopoly and Similar Market Structures.* New York: Alfred A. Knopf, 1949.

Flawn, Peter T. *Mineral Resources.* Chicago: Rand McNally and Company, 1966.

Ford Foundation, Energy Policy Project of the Ford Foundation. *A Time to Choose: America's Energy Future.* Cambridge, Mass: Ballinger Publishing Company, 1974.

Freeman, S. David. *Energy: The New Era.* New York: Vintage Books, 1974.

Garvey, Gerald. *Energy, Ecology, Economy.* New York: W.W. Norton and Company, 1972.

Goffman, Erving. *Strategic Interaction.* Philadelphia: University of Pennsylvania Press, 1969.

Gray, T.J., and O.K. Bashus, eds. *Tidal Power.* New York: Plenum, 1972.

Gunter, Hans, ed. *Transnational Industrial Relations.* London: The Macmillan Press, Ltd., 1972.

Guyol, Nathaniel B. *Energy in the Perspective of Geography.* Englewood Cliffs, N.J.: Prentice-Hall, 1969.

Haas, Ernest B. *Tangle of Hopes: American Commitments and World Order.* Englewood Cliffs, N.J.: Prentice-Hall, 1969.

Haim, Sylvia G., ed. *Arab Nationalism: An Anthology.* Berkeley: University of California Press, 1962.

Hammond, Allen L., William D. Metz, and Thomas M. Maugh. *Energy and the Future.* Washington, D.C.: American Association for the Advancement of Science, 1973.

Harari, Maurice. *Government and Politics of the Middle East.* Englewood Cliffs, N.J.: Prentice-Hall, Inc., 1962.

Hartshorn, Jack E. *Oil Companies and Governments: An Account of the*

International Oil Industry in Its Political Environment. London: Faber and Faber, 1962.

Helfrich, Harold W., Jr., ed. *The Environmental Crisis: Man's Struggle to Live with Himself.* 2 vols. New Haven: Yale University Press, 1970.

Hexner, Ervin. *International Cartels.* London: Sir Isaac Pitman & Sons, Ltd., 1946.

Hirschman, Albert. *National Power and the Structure of Foreign Trade.* Berkeley: University of California Press, 1969.

Hirst, David. *Oil and Public Opinion in the Middle East.* New York: Frederick A. Praeger, 1966.

Hottel, H.C., and J.B. Howard. *New Energy Technology–Some Facts and Assessments.* Cambridge, Mass.: M.I.T. Press, 1971.

Hsiao, Gene T. *Sino-American Detente and Its Policy Implications.* New York: Frederick A. Praeger, 1974.

Inglis, K.A.D., ed. *Energy: From Surplus to Scarcity*? New York: John Wiley and Sons, 1974.

Institute for Contemporary Studies. *No Time to Confuse.* San Francisco: Institute for Contemporary Studies, 1975.

International Bank for Reconstruction and Development. *The Economic Development of Kuwait.* Baltimore: The Johns Hopkins University Press, 1965.

Jacoby, Neil H. *Multinational Oil: A Study in Industrial Dynamics.* New York: Macmillan Publishing Company, 1974.

Jensen, Walter G.W. *Energy and the Economy of Nations.* Henley-on-Thames, Oxfordshire: G.T. Foulis and Co., 1970.

_______. *Energy in Europe, 1945-1980.* London: G.T. Foulis and Co., 1967.

_______. *Nuclear Power.* Henley-on-Thames, Oxfordshire: G.T. Foulis and Co., 1969.

Kapoor, A., and Phillip D. Grub. *The Multinational Enterprise in Transition.* Princeton: The Darwin Press, 1972.

Kerr, Malcolm. *The Arab Cold War, Gamal Abdal Nasir and His Rivals, 1958-1970.* New York: Oxford University Press, 1971.

Khalife, Atef M. *The Population of Egypt.* Cairo: Institute of Statistical Studies and Research, 1973.

Kindleberger, Charles. *The International Corporation*, Cambridge, Mass.: M.I.T. Press, 1970.

Klebanoff, Shoshana. *Middle East Oil and U.S. Foreign Policy: With Special Reference to the U.S. Energy Crisis.* New York: Frederick A. Praeger, 1974.

Kneese, Allen V., and Blair T. Bower, eds. *Environmental Quality Analysis, Theory and Method in the Social Sciences.* Baltimore: The Johns Hopkins University Press, 1972.

Kohnstamm, Max, and Wolfgang Hager, eds. *A Nation Writ Large*? New York: John Wiley and Sons, 1973.

Kramish, Arnold. *Atomic Energy in the Soviet Union.* Stanford, Calif.: Stanford University Press, 1959.

Lacouture, Jean. *Nasser.* New York: Alfred A. Knopf, 1973.

Landen, Robert G. *Oman Since 1856: Disruptive Modernization of a Traditional Arab Society.* Princeton: Princeton University Press, 1967.

Landsberg, Hans M., and Sam H. Schurr. *Energy in the United States.* New York: Randon House, 1968.

Ling, H.C. *The Petroleum Industry of the People's Republic of China.* Stanford: Hoover Institution Press, 1975.

Little, Arthur D. *Energy Policy Issues for the United States.* Cambridge, Mass.: Arthur D. Little, 1971.

Lovins, Amory B. *World Energy Strategies.* Cambridge, Mass.: Ballinger Publishing Company, 1975.

Mallakh, Ragaei el-. *Economic Development and Regional Cooperation: Kuwait.* Chicago: University of Chicago Press, 1968.

Mancke, Richard B. *The Failure of U.S. Energy Policy*. New York: Columbia University Press, 1974.

Marine Engineers' Beneficial Association. *The American Oil Industry.* New York: Marine Engineers' Beneficial Association, 1973.

Martinez, Anibal. *Nuestro Petroleo, Defensa de un Recurso Agotable.* Madrid: Taller de Artes Grafica Minerva, 1963.

McDonald, Robert W. *The League of the Arab States: A Study in the Dynamics of Regional Organizations.* Princeton: Princeton University Press, 1965.

Meadows, Dennis L., et al. *The Limits to Growth.* New York: Universe Books, 1972.

Meadows, Dennis L., and Donella H. Meadows, eds. *Toward Global Equilibrium.* Cambridge, Mass.: Wright-Allen Press, 1973.

Mepple, Peter, ed. *Petroleum Supply and Demand.* London: Institute of Petroleum, 1966.

Mikdashi, Zuhayr. *The Community of Oil Exporting Countries.* Ithaca, N.Y.: Cornell University Press, 1972.

Mikesell, Raymond F., ed. *Foreign Investment in the Petroleum and Mineral Industries.* Baltimore: The Johns Hopkins University Press, 1971.

Ministry of Mines Staff. *Venezuela and OPEC–Documents, Speeches and Venezuelan and World Views Relating to the Antecedents and Creation of OPEC.* Caracas: Imprenta Nacional, 1961.

Mitre Corporation. *Energy, Resources, and the Environment.* Springfield, Va.: U.S. Department of Commerce, 1972.

Monroe, Elizabeth, and Robert Mabro. *Oil Producers and Consumers: Conflict or Cooperation.* New York: American Universities Field Staff, 1974.

Morgenstern, Oskar, Klaus Knorr, and Klaus P. Heiss. *Long Term Projections of Power: Political, Economic, and Military Forecasting.* Cambridge, Mass.: Ballinger Publishing Company, 1973.

Morrison, Warren E. *An Energy Model for the United States.* Washington, D.C.: U.S. Department of the Interior, 1968.

Mosley, Leonard. *Power Play.* Baltimore: Penguin Books, 1974.

Musrey, Alfred G. *An Arab Common Market.* New York: Frederick A. Praeger, 1969.

National Petroleum Council. *Emergency Preparedness for Interruption of Petroleum Imports Into the United States.* Washington, D.C.: National Petroleum Council, 1973.

National Petroleum Council, Committee on Petroleum Resources Under the Ocean Floor. *Petroleum Resources Under the Ocean Floor.* Washington, D.C.: National Petroleum Council, 1969.

National Petroleum Council, Committee on U.S. Energy Outlook. *U.S. Energy Outlook.* Washington, D.C.: National Petroleum Council, 1972.

Neuchterlein, Donald E. *United States National Interests in a Changing World.* Lexington: University Press of Kentucky, 1973.

Nye, Joseph, and Robert Keohane, eds. *Transnational Relations and World Politics.* Cambridge, Mass.: Harvard University Press, 1972.

Odell, Peter R. *An Economic Geography of Oil.* New York: Frederick A. Praeger, 1964.

_______. *Oil and World Power.* Baltimore: Penguin Books, 1970.

Office of the Foreign Secretary, National Academy of Sciences, ed. *Rapid Population Growth.* Baltimore: The Johns Hopkins University Press, 1971.

Olson, Mancur. *The Logic of Collective Action.* Cambridge, Mass.: Harvard University Press, 1965.

Organisation for Economic Co-operation and Development. *Energy Prospects to 1985: An Assessment of Long Term Energy Developments and Related Policies.* 2 volumes. Paris: Organisation for Economic Co-operation and Development, 1974.

_______, *The Growth of Output, 1960-1980. Retrospect, Prospects and Problems of Policy.* Paris: Organisation for Economic Co-operation and Development, 1970.

_______, *Statistics of Energy, 1959-1973.* Paris: Economic Statistics and National Accounts Division, Organisation for Economic Co-operation and Development, December 1974.

_______, *Uranium: Resources, Production and Demand.* A joint report by the OECD Nuclear Energy Agency and the International Atomic Energy Agency. Paris: Organisation for Economic Co-operation and Development, 1973.

Organisation for Economic Co-operation and Development Oil Committee. *Oil: The Present Situation and Future Prospects.* Paris: Organisation for Economic Co-operation and Development, 1973.

Organization of Petroleum Exporting Countries. *Sources of Petroleum Statistical Information.* Vienna: Organization of Petroleum Exporting Countries, 1966.

Osgood, Robert E., et al. *Retreat from Empire: The First Nixon Administration.* Baltimore: The Johns Hopkins University Press, 1973.

Parra, Ramos and Parra. *International Crude Oil and Product Prices, 15 October 1974.* Beirut: Middle East Petroleum and Economic Publications, 1974.

Perez Alfonso, Juan P. *El Pentagono Petrolero.* Caracas: Editorial Revista Politica, 1967.

The Petroleum Publishing Company. *International Petroleum Encyclopedia, 1973.* Tulsa: The Petroleum Publishing Co., 1973.

Potier, Michel. *Energie et Securite.* Paris: Mouton and Co., 1969.

Ramazani, Rouhollah K. *The Persian Gulf: Iran's Role.* Charlottesville: University of Virginia Press, 1972.

Rand, Christopher. *Making Democracy Safe for Oil.* Boston: Atlantic-Little, Brown and Company, 1975.

Ridgeway, James. *The Last Play.* New York: Mentor, 1973.

Rifai, Taki. *The Pricing of Crude Oil: Economic and Strategic Guidelines for an International Energy Policy.* New York: Frederick A. Praeger, 1974.

Riker, William H. *The Theory of Political Coalitions.* New Haven: Yale University Press, 1962.

Robana, Abderrahman. *The Prospects for an Economic Community in North Africa: Managing Economic Integration in the Maghreb States.* New York: Frederick A. Praeger, 1973.

Rocks, Lawrence, and Richard P. Runyan. *The Energy Crisis.* New York: Crown Publishers, 1972.

Rouhani, Fuad. *A History of OPEC.* New York: Frederick A. Praeger, 1971.

Sadik, M.T., and W.P. Snavely. *Bahrain, Qatar and the United Arab Emirates: Colonial Past, Present Problems and Future Prospects.* Lexington, Mass.: Lexington Books, D.C. Heath and Co., 1972.

Safran, Nader. *Egypt in Search of Political Community: An Analysis of the Intellectual and Political Evolution of Egypt 1804-1952.* Cambridge, Mass.: Harvard University Press, 1961.

_______. *From War to War: The Arab-Israeli Confrontation, 1948-1967–A Study of the Conflict from the Perspective of Coercion in the Context of Inter-Arab and Big Power Relations.* New York: Pegasus, 1969.

Sayed, Mustafa El-. *L'Organisation des Pays Exportateurs de Petrole.* Paris: Imprimerie Nationale, 1967.

Sayegh, F.A. *Arab Unity: Hope and Fulfillment.* New York: The Devin-Adain Company, 1958.

Schelling, Thomas C. *The Strategy of Conflict.* Cambridge, Mass.: Harvard University Press, 1960.

Schurr, Sam H., ed. *Energy, Economic Growth and the Environment.* Baltimore: The Johns Hopkins University Press, 1972.

_______, and Paul T. Homan. *Middle Eastern Oil and the Western World: Prospects and Problems.* New York: American Elsevier, 1971.

Scientific American. *Energy and Power.* San Francisco: W.H. Freeman, 1971.

Shaffer, Edward H. *The Oil Import Program of the United States.* New York: Frederick A. Praeger, 1968.

Sharabi, Hisham. *Nationalism and Revolution in the Arab World.* Princeton, N.J.: Van Nostrand Company, 1965.

Sherman, Roger. *Oligopoly: An Empirical Approach.* Lexington, Mass.: Lexington Books, D.C. Heath and Co., 1972.

Shubik, Martin. *Strategy and Market Structure: Competition, Oligopoly, and the Theory of Games.* New York: John Wiley and Sons, 1959.

Simon, Herbert. *Models of Man.* New York, John Wiley and Sons, 1957.

Skolnikoff, Eugene B. *The International Imperatives of Technology: Technological Development and the International Political System.* Berkeley: Institute of International Studies, University of California, 1972.

Smith, Clagett G., ed. *Conflict Resolution: Contributions of the Behavioral Sciences.* Notre Dame, Ind.: University of Notre Dame Press, 1971.

Spanier, John, and Eric M. Uslaner. *How American Foreign Policy is Made.* New York: Frederick A. Praeger, 1974.

Stanford Research Institute. *Patterns of Energy Consumption in the United States.* Washington, D.C.: U.S. Government Printing Office, 1972.

Stephens, Robert. *The Arabs New Frontier.* London: Temple Smith, 1974.

Stephenson, Hugh. *The Coming Clash.* New York: Saturday Review Press,

Stern, R.M. *The Balance of Payments: Theory and Economic Policy.* Chicago: Aldine-Atherton, 1973.

Stobaugh, Robert B. *The International Transfer of Technology in the Establishment of the Petrochemical Industry in Developing Countries.* New York: United Nations Institute for Training and Research, 1971.

Stockholm International Peace Research Institute. *Oil and Security.* New York: Humanities Press, 1974.

Stocking, George. *Middle East Oil: A Study in Political and Economic Controversy.* Nashville: Vanderbilt University Press, 1970.

Strassmann, W.P. *Technological Change and Economic Development.* Ithaca, N.Y.: Cornell University Press, 1968.

Szeto, G.C. *The U.S. Energy Problem.* 2 vols. Washington, D.C.: U.S. Department of Commerce, 1971.

Szyliowicz, Joseph S., and Bard O'Neill. *The Energy Crisis and U.S. Foreign Policy.* New York: Frederick A. Praeger, 1975.

Tahtinen, Dale R. *The Arab-Israeli Military Balance Since October 1973.* Washington, D.C.: American Enterprise Institute, 1974.

Tanzer, Michael. *The Political Economy of International Oil and the Underdeveloped Countries.* Boston: Beacon Press, 1969.

Task Force on Energy of the Subcommittee on Science, Research and Development. *Energy Research and Development.* Washington, D.C.: U.S. Government Printing Office, 1972.

Texas Eastern Transmission Corporation. *Competition and Growth in American Energy Markets, 1947-1985.* Houston: Texas Eastern Transmission Corporation, 1968.

_______. *Energy and Fuels.* Houston: Texas Eastern Transmission Corporation, 1961.

Tucker, Robert W. *A New Isolationism: Threat or Promise?* Washington, D.C.: Potomac Associates, 1972.

Tugendhat, Christopher. *The Multinationals.* New York: Random House, 1972.

_______. *Oil the Biggest Business.* London: Eyre and Spottiswoode, 1968.

United Nations, Statistical Office. *World Trade Annual.* Vol. 2. New York: Walker and Co., 1965-71.

Van Sant, S. *Strategic Energy Supply and National Security.* Springfield, Mass.: Frederick A. Praeger, 1971.

Vatikiotis, P.J. *The Modern History of Egypt.* New York: Frederick A. Praeger, 1969.

Vernon, Raymond. *Sovereignty at Bay: The Multinational Spread of U.S. Enterprises.* New York: Basic Books, 1971.

_______. *The Technology Factor in International Trade.* New York: Columbia University Press, 1970.

Willrich, Mason, and Theodore B. Taylor. *Nuclear Theft: Risks and Safeguards.* Cambridge, Mass.: Ballinger Publishing Company, 1974.

Wu Yuan-li. *Raw Materials Supply in a Multipolar World.* New York: Crane, Russak and Company, 1973.

Yager, Joseph A., and Eleanor B. Steinberg. *Energy and U.S. Foreign Policy.* A report to the Energy Policy Project of the Ford Foundation. Cambridge, Mass.: Ballinger Publishing Company, 1974.

Public Documents

United Nations. Committee on Natural Resources, 1st Session, 1971. *Natural Resources Development and Policies, Including Environmental Considerations. Addendum: Natural Resources–Definitions and Concepts.* E/C.7/2/-Add.9. New York: United Nations, 1971.

_______. *Demographic Yearbook, 1973.* ST/STAT/SER.R/2. New York: United Nations, 1975.

_______. Department of Economic and Social Affairs. *Yearbook of National Accounts Statistics, 1973.* ST/ESA/STAT/SER.0/3/Add.2. New York: United Nations, 1975.

_______. Department of Economic and Social Affairs, Statistical Office. *World Energy Supplies–1955-72.* ST/STAT/SER.J. New York: United Nations Publishing Service, 1957-73.

_______. Economic Commission for Asia and the Far East. *Asian Industrial Development News.* New York: United Nations, no. 6, 1970.

United States Atomic Energy Commission. *Civilian Nuclear Power.* Washington, D.C.: U.S. Government Printing Office, 1962.

_______. *Evaluation of Nuclear Power Plant Availability.* Washington, D.C.: U.S. Atomic Energy Commission, January 1974.

_______. *Survey of U.S. Uranium Marketing Activity.* Washington, D.C.: U.S. Government Printing Office, April 1974.

United States Cabinet Task Force on Oil Import Control. *The Oil Import Question.* Washington, D.C.: U.S. Government Printing Office, February 1970.

United States Congress. House. Committee on Foreign Affairs. *Data and Analysis Concerning the Possibility of a U.S. Food Embargo as a Response to the Present Arab Oil Boycott*, 93rd Cong., 1st sess., 21 November 1973. Washington: U.S. Government Printing Office, 1973.

_______. House. Committee on Foreign Affairs. Subcommittee on Foreign Economic Policy. *Foreign Policy Implications of the Energy Crisis. Hearings before a Subcommittee of the House Committee on Foreign Affairs*, 92nd Cong., 2nd sess., 21, 26, and 27 September and 3 October 1972. Washington, D.C.: U.S. Government Printing Office, 1972.

_______. House. Committee on Foreign Affairs. Subcommittee on Inter-American Affairs. *Hearings–Capital Markets and Economic Development: The Kleinman Plan*, 92nd Cong., 2nd sess., July 1972. Washington, D.C.: U.S. Government Printing Office, 1972.

_______. House. Committee on Interior and Insular Affairs. *Fuel and Energy Resources, Parts 1 and 2. Hearings before the House Committee on Interior and Insular Affairs*, 92nd Cong., 2nd sess., 10-13 April 1972. Washington, D.C.: U.S. Government Printing Office, April 1972.

_______. House. Committee on Merchant Marine and Fisheries. *Growth and Its Implications for the Future*, 92nd Cong., 1st sess., Washington, D.C.: U.S. Government Printing Office, 1 May 1973.

_______. House. Committee on Science and Astronautics. *Energy Research and Development*, 92nd Cong., 2nd sess. Washington, D.C.: U.S. Government Printing Office, December 1972.

_______. Joint Committee on Atomic Energy. *Understanding the "National Energy Dilemma,"* 93rd Cong., 1st sess. Washington, D.C.: U.S. Government Printing Office, 1973.

_______. Joint Economic Committee. *A Reappraisal of U.S. Energy Policy*, 92nd Cong., 2nd sess., 8 March 1972. Washington, D.C.: U.S. Government Printing Office, March 1972.

_______. Joint Economic Committee. Subcommittee on Consumer Economics. *The Gasoline and Fuel Oil Shortage. Hearings before a Subcommittee of the Joint Economic Committee*, 93rd Cong., 1st sess., 1 and 2 May and 2 June 1973. Washington, D.C.: U.S. Government Printing Office, 1973.

_______. Senate. Committee on Finance. Subcommittee on Energy. *Fiscal Policy and the Energy Crisis*, 93rd Cong., 1st sess., 20 November 1973. Washington, D.C.: U.S. Government Printing Office, 1973.

_______. Senate. Committee on Finance. Subcommittee on Energy. *Fiscal Policy and the Energy Crisis. Hearings before a Subcommittee of the Senate Committee on Finance*, 93rd Cong., 1st sess., 27-29 November 1973, Parts 1 and 2. Washington, D.C.: U.S. Government Printing Office, 1973.

United States Congress. Senate. Committee on Foreign Relations. Subcommittee on Multinational Corporations. *Multinational Corporations and United States Foreign Policy, Parts 1-5*, 93rd Cong., 1st and 2nd sess., 1974-75. Washington, D.C.: U.S. Government Printing Office, 1974-75.

_______. Senate. Committee on Foreign Relations. Subcommittee on Multinational Corporations. *U.S. Oil Companies and the Arab Oil Embargo: The International Allocation of Constricted Supplies.* A report prepared by the Federal Energy Administration's Office of International Energy Affairs, 94th Cong., 1st sess., 27 January 1975. Washington, D.C.: U.S. Government Printing Office, 1975.

_______. Senate. Committee on Interior and Insular Affairs. *The Energy Information Act. Hearings before the Senate Committee on Interior and Insular Affairs*, 93rd Cong., 2nd sess., 14-15 February 1974, Parts 1, 2, and 3. Washington, D.C.: U.S. Government Printing Office, 1974.

_______. Senate. Committee on Interior and Insular Affairs. *Federal Charters for Energy Corporations–Selected Materials*, 93rd Cong., 2nd sess. Washington, D.C.: U.S. Government Printing Office, 1974.

_______. Senate. Committee on Interior and Insular Affairs. *Financial Requirements of the Nation's Energy Industries. Hearings before the Senate Committee on Interior and Insular Affairs*, 93rd Cong., 1st sess., March 1973. Washington, D.C.: U.S. Government Printing Office, March 1973.

_______. Senate. Committee on Interior and Insular Affairs. *Fuel Shortages. Hearings before the Senate Committee on Interior and Insular Affairs*, 93rd Cong., 1st sess., 1 February 1973, Parts 1 and 2. Washington, D.C.: U.S. Government Printing Office, February 1973.

_______. Senate. Committee on Interior and Insular Affairs. *Market Performance and Competition in the Petroleum Industry. Hearings before the Senate Committee on Interior and Insular Affairs*, 93rd Cong., 1st sess., 28-29 November 1973, Parts 1 and 2. Washington, D.C.: U.S. Government Printing Office, 1973.

_______. Senate. Committee on Interior and Insular Affairs. *Measurement of Corporate Profits*, 93rd Cong., 2nd sess. Washington, D.C.: U.S. Government Printing Office, 1974.

_______. Senate. Committee on Interior and Insular Affairs. *The National Coal Conversion Act and the National Crude Oil Refinery Development Act. Hearings before the Senate Committee on Interior and Insular Affairs*, 93rd Cong., 1st sess., 10 December 1973. Washington, D.C.: U.S. Government Printing Office, 1973.

_______. Senate. Committee on Interior and Insular Affairs. *National Goals Symposium, Parts 1 and 2*, 92nd Cong., 1st sess., 20 October 1971. Washington, D.C.: U.S. Government Printing Office, October 1971.

_______. Senate. Committee on Interior and Insular Affairs. *Oil and Gas Imports Issues. Hearings before the Senate Committee on Interior and Insular*

Affairs, 93rd Cong., 1st sess., 10-11 and 22 January 1973, Parts 1, 2, and 3. Washington, D.C.: U.S. Government Printing Office, 1973.

_______. Senate. Committee on Interior and Insular Affairs. *Survey of Energy Consumption Projections*, 92nd Cong., 2nd sess. Washington, D.C.: U.S. Government Printing Office, 1973.

United States Department of Agriculture. Economic Research Service. "U.S. Agricultural Exports to Mideast Markets Growing Rapidly," *Foreign Agricultural Trade of the United States*, pp. 14-37. Washington, D.C.: U.S. Department of Agriculture, Economic Research Service, October 1974.

_______. Economic Research Service. "U.S. Agricultural Exports to OPEC Doubled in 1974," *Foreign Agricultural Trade of the United States*, pp. 61-78. Washington, D.C.: U.S. Department of Agriculture, Economic Research Service, March 1975.

United States Department of Commerce. *United States Exports/World Area by Commodity Groupings*, FT 455-72, Annual 1972. Washington, D.C.: U.S. Government Printing Office, 1973.

United States Department of the Interior. *An Energy Model for the U.S.* Washington, D.C.: U.S. Government Printing Office, 1968.

_______. *Mineral Industry Surveys–Petroleum Statement.* Washington, D.C.: U.S. Government Printing Office, 1971–September 1973 (monthly).

_______. *Supplies, Costs and Uses of the Fossil Fuels.* Washington, D.C.: U.S. Government Printing Office, February 1973.

_______. *U.S. Energy: A Summary Review.* Washington, D.C.: U.S. Government Printing Office, 1972.

_______. U.S. Office of Oil and Gas. *U.S. Petroleum through 1980.* Washington, D.C.: U.S. Government Printing Office, 1968.

United States Federal Council for Science and Technology. *Extraction of Energy Fuels.* Bureau of Mines. Open File Report 30-73. Springfield, Va.: National Technical Information Service, September 1972.

United States Federal Energy Administration. *Project Independence.* Washington, D.C.: U.S. Government Printing Office, November 1974.

United States General Accounting Office. *Issues Related to Foreign Sources of Oil for the United States*. B-179411. 23 January 1974 (Mimeographed).

_______. *U.S. Actions Needed to Cope with Commodity Shortages.* Washington, D.C.: U.S. General Accounting Office, 29 April 1974.

United States Office of Science and Technology. *A Review and Comparison of Selected U.S. Energy Forecasts.* Washington, D.C.: U.S. Government Printing Office, 1969.

Papers, Monographs, and Reports

Abir, Mordechai. "Red Sea Politics." *Adelphi Papers*, no. 93 (1972). The International Institute for Strategic Studies, London, U.K.

Ahmad, Yusuf J. *Oil Revenues in the Gulf: A Preliminary Estimate of Absorptive Capacity.* Paris: Organisation of Economic Co-operation and Development, 1974.

Alker, Hayward R., Lincoln P. Bloomfield, and Nazli Choucri. *Analyzing Global Interdependence, Volumes I-IV.* Cambridge: M.I.T. Center for International Studies, 1974.

Amuzegar, Jahangir. "Philosophy, Views and Objectives of the Oil Exporting Countries." Statement before the Advanced Seminar on Energy Economics and Management. Northwestern University, Evanston, Illinois. 24 June 1975 (Mimeographed).

Bergsten, Fred C., and Morton H. Halperin. "International Economics and International Politics: A Framework for Analysis." Paper (Typewritten).

Birks, J. "The Size of the World Offshore Potential." Paper presented at the World Energy Supplies Conference, London, U.K., 18-20 September 1973 (Mimeographed).

Bobrow, Davis B., and Robert T. Kudrle. "Theory, Policy and Resource Cartels." An expanded version of a paper presented to the American Political Science Association, Chicago, August 29-September 2, 1974.

The British Petroleum Company. *BP Statistical Review of the World Oil Industry–1972.* London: The British Petroleum Company, 1973.

Brown, Lester R. "The Changing Face of Food Scarcity." *Communique on Development Issues.* Overseas Development Council. No. 21. Washington, D.C., U.S.A.

Chase Manhattan Bank. *Outlook for Energy in the United States.* New York: Chase Manhattan Bank, 1968.

Choucri, Nazli, and D. Scott Ross (with the assistance of Brian M. Pollins). "Energy Problems and International Politics: A Model of Exchange, Price, and Conflict." A Report prepared for the Project on Long Range Resource Availability in the United States, supported by NSF-RANN (Grant No. GI-34808X). Cambridge, Mass., August 1975.

Commissariat a l'Energie Atomique. *Rapport Annual 1972.* Paris: Synelog, 1973.

Debanne, J.G. "A Pollution- and Technology-Sensitive Model for Energy Supply-Distribution Studies." Milton E. Searl, Resources for the Future, ed. Working Papers for a Seminar on Energy Modelling, 25-26 January 1973.

The Environment Fund. "World Populations Estimates, 1974." Washington, D.C.: The Environment Fund, 1974.

Franssen, Herman T. "Oil and Gas in the Oceans," Summary of a lecture presented at the Naval War College, 27 September 1972 (Typewritten).

Gall, Norman. "Oil and Democracy in Venezuela: Part I–'Sowing the Petroleum'." *Fieldstaff Reports*, vol. XVII, no. 1 (1973). American Universities Field Staff, Inc.

_______. "Oil and Democracy in Venezuela: Part II–'The Marginal Man'."

Fieldstaff Reports, vol. XVII, no. 2 (1973). American Universities Field Staff, Inc.

Hunter, Robert E. "The Energy 'Crisis' and U.S. Foreign Policy." Overseas Development Council. Development Paper no. 14. Washington, D.C., August 1973.

_______. "The Soviet Dilemma in the Middle East, Part I: Problems of Commitment." *Adelphi Papers*, no. 59 (September 1969). The International Institute for Strategic Studies. London, U.K.

_______. "The Soviet Dilemma in the Middle East, Part II: Oil and the Persian Gulf." *Adelphi Papers*, no. 60 (October 1969). The International Institute for Strategic Studies. London, U.K.

Imai, Ryukichi. "Nuclear Safeguards." *Adelphi Papers*, no. 86 (March 1972). The International Institute for Strategic Studies. London, U.K.

Jukes, Geoffrey. "The Indian Ocean in Soviet Naval Policy." *Adelphi Papers*, no. 87 (May 1972). The International Institute for Strategic Studies. London, U.K.

McLachlan, Keith. "Spending Oil Revenues: Development Prospects in the Middle East to 1975." The Economist Intelligence Unit (1972). QER Special no. 10. London, U.K.

Monroe, Elizabeth. *The Changing Balance of Power in the Persian Gulf.* New York: An International Seminar Report, the Center for Mediterranean Studies, American Universities Field Staff, Inc., 1972.

_______, and Robert Mabro. *Oil Producers and Consumers: Conflict or Cooperation.* New York: An International Seminar Report, The Center for Mediterranean Studies, American Universities Field Staff, Inc., 1974.

Muraoka, Kunio. "Japanese Security and the United States." *Adelphi Papers*, no. 92 (1972). The International Institute for Strategic Studies. London, U.K.

Peterson, Peter G. "The Energy Dilemmas" An address concerning President Nixon's Cabinet-Level Domestic Council Review of Energy Strategies, presented to the American Petroleum Institute, The Conrad Hilton Hotel, Chicago, Illinois, 14 November 1972.

Pirages, Dennis C. "Strategic Implications of the Energy Crisis." Presented to the Annual Meeting of the International Studies Association, Washington, D.C., 19-22 February, 1975.

Ramazani, Rouhollah K. "Emerging Patterns of Regional Relations in Iranian Foreign Policy," 1974 (Mimeographed).

Saeki, Kiichi. "Japan's Security in a Multipolar World." *Adelphi Papers*, no. 92 (1972). The International Institute for Strategic Studies. London, U.K.

United States Department of Agriculture. Economic Research Service. "World Monetary Conditions in Relation to Agricultural Trade." Washington, D.C.: U.S. Department of Agriculture, Economic Research Service, May 1975, pp. 1-31.

Varon, Benson, "What are the Opportunities for Raising LDC's Earnings from

Exports of Non-Fuel Minerals through OPEC-Type Cooperation—A Brief Answer." Trade Policies and Export Protections Division, Economics Department, International Bank for Reconstruction and Development. February 11, 1972. (Mimeographed).

Vernon, Raymond. "Multinational Enterprises and International Price Formation." February 11, 1972. (Mimeographed).

Warman, H.R. "The Oil Potential of the North Sea." Paper delivered at the *Financial Times* Conference on the North Sea, Houston, Texas, 14-15 November 1973 (Mimeographed).

Wilcox, Wayne. "Japanese and Indian National Security Strategies in the Asia of the 1970's: The Prospect of Nuclear Proliferation." *Adelphi Papers*, no. 92 (1972). The International Institute for Strategic Studies. London, U.K.

Articles in Journals

Abelson, Philip H. "The Deteriorating Energy Position." *Science*, vol. 185, no. 4148 (26 July 1974), p. 309.

_______. "Energy Conservation." *Science*, vol. 178, no. 4059 (27 October 1974), p. 355.

_______. "Energy Independence." *Science*, vol. 182, no. 4114 (23 November 1973), p. 779.

_______. "Energy and National Security." *Science*, vol. 179, no. 4076 (2 March 1973), p. 857.

_______. "Importation of Petroleum." *Science*, vol. 180, no. 4091 (15 June 1973), p. 1127.

_______. "Increasing World Energy Supplies." *Science*, vol. 182, no. 4117 (14 December 1973), p. 1087.

_______. "Underground Gasification of Coal." *Science*, vol. 182, no. 4119 (28 December 1973), p. 1297.

_______. "The Urgent Need for Energy Conservation." *Science*, vol. 182, no. 4110 (26 October 1973), p. 339.

Adelman, M.A. "Is the Oil Shortage Real?" *Foreign Policy*, no. 9 (Winter 1972-73), pp. 69-107.

Akins, James E. "The Oil Crisis: This Time the Wolf is Here." *Foreign Affairs*, vol. 51, no. 3 (April 1973), pp. 462-490.

Al-Hamad, Abdlatif Y. "Arab Capital and International Finance." *The Banker*, vol. 124, no. 575 (January 1974).

American Academic Association for Peace in the Middle East. "The Energy Problem and the Middle East." *Middle East Information Series*, vol. XXIII (May 1973).

Amuzegar, Jahangir. "The Oil Story: Facts, Fiction and Fair Play." *Foreign Affairs*, vol. 51, no. 4 (July 1973), pp. 676-689.

Auer, Peter L. "An Integrated National Energy Research and Development Program." *Science*, vol. 184, no. 4134 (19 April 1974), pp. 295-301.

Ball, George W. "Trilateralism and the Oil Crisis." *Pacific Community*, vol. 5, no. 3 (April 1974), pp. 335-347.

Barattieri, Vittorio. "The Oil Exporters and the Euromarkets." *Euromoney*, May 1974, pp. 27-28.

Bechtold, Peter K. "New Attempts at Arab Co-operation: The Federation of Arab Republics, 1971–?" *The Middle East Journal*, vol. 27, no. 2 (Spring 1973), pp. 152-173.

Berg, R.R., et al. "Prognosis for Expanded U.S. Production of Crude Oil." *Science*, vol. 184, no. 4134 (19 April 1974), pp. 331-336.

Bergsten, C. Fred. "The Threat from the Third World." *Foreign Policy*, no. 11 (Summer 1973), pp. 102-124.

_______. "The Threat is Real." *Foreign Policy*, no. 14 (Spring 1974), pp. 84-90.

Berry, John A. "Oil and Soviet Policy in the Middle East." *The Middle East Journal*, vol. 26, no. 2 (Spring 1972), pp. 149-160.

Billings, Charles E., and Wayne R. Matson. "Mercury Emissions from Coal Combustion." *Science*, vol. 176, no. 4040 (16 June 1972), pp. 1232-1233.

Bloomfield, Lincoln P. "Foreign Policy for Disillusioned Liberals." *Foreign Policy*, no. 9 (Winter 1972-73), pp. 55-68.

_______. "Nuclear Spread and World Order." *Foreign Affairs*, vol. 53, no. 4 (July 1975), pp. 743-755.

Boulding, Kenneth E. "The Social System and the Energy Crisis." *Science*, vol. 184, no. 4134 (19 April 1974), pp. 255-257.

Brandon, Henry. "Were We Masterful . . .", Part I of "Jordan: The Forgotten Crisis." *Foreign Policy*, no. 10 (Spring 1973), pp. 158-170.

Brzezinski, Zbigniew. "The Balance of Power Delusion." *Foreign Policy*, no. 7 (Summer 1972), pp. 54-59.

_______. "U.S. Foreign Policy: The Search for Focus." *Foreign Affairs*, vol. 51, no. 4 (July 1973), pp. 708-727.

Bupp, Irvin C., and Jean-Claude Deriam. "The Breeder Reactor in the U.S.: A New Economic Analysis." *Technology Review*, July/August 1974.

Buzzard, Rear-Admiral Sir Anthony. "Middle East Guarantees." *Survival*, vol. XIII, no. 12 (December 1971), pp. 416-421.

Calvin, Melvin. "Solar Energy by Photosynthesis." *Science*, vol. 184, no. 4134 (19 April 1974), pp. 375-381.

Campbell, John C. "Middle East Oil: American Policy and Super-Power Interaction." *Survival*, vol. XV, no. 5 (September/October 1973).

Campbell, John F. "Points of Conflict." *Survival*, vol. XIII, no. 8 (August 1971).

Carruth, Eleanore. "The New Oil Rush in Our Own Backyard." *Fortune*, vol. LXXXIX, no. 6 (June 1974), pp. 154-159.

Carter, Anne P. "Applications of Input-Output Analysis to Energy Problems." *Science*, vol. 184, no. 4134 (19 April 1974), pp. 325-329.

Carter, Luther J. "AEC Laboratories Would Be Core of Energy R & D Agency." *Science*, vol. 180, no. 4093 (29 June 1974), p. 1346.

_______. "The Energy Bureaucracy: The Pieces Fall Into Place." *Science*, vol. 185, no. 4145 (5 July 1974), pp. 44-45.

_______. "Jackson Wants Big Energy R & D Effort, a la Apollo." *Science*, vol. 179, no. 4076 (2 March 1973), p. 879.

_______. "Solar and Geothermal Energy: New Competition for the Atom." *Science*, vol. 186, no. 4166 (29 November 1974), pp. 811-813.

_______. "Strip Mining: Congress Moves Toward 'Tough' Regulation." *Science*, vol. 185, no. 4150 (9 August 1974), pp. 513-514.

Castor, Gaylord B. "Gasoline Substitutes." *Science*, vol. 183, no. 4126 (22 February 1974), p. 698.

Chapman, Duane, Timothy Tyrrell, and Timothy Mount. "Electricity Demand Growth and the Energy Crisis." *Science*, vol. 178, no. 4062 (17 November 1972), pp. 703-708.

Chase, R.X. "Economic Analysis and Environmental Quality." *American Journal of Economics and Sociology*, vol. 31, no. 3 (July 1972), pp. 271-282.

Chenery, Hollis B. "Restructuring the World Economy." *Foreign Affairs*, vol. 53, no. 2 (January 1975), pp. 242-263.

Chubin, Shahram. "Iran Between the Arab West and the Asian East." *Survival*, vol. 16, no. 4 (July/August 1974), pp. 172-182.

Conant, Melvin A. "Oil: Co-operation or Conflict." *Survival*, vol. XV, no. 1 (January/February 1973), pp. 8-14.

Conner, W.L.M. "Viewpoint on Oil: Turning Off the Tap." *Middle East International*, no. 6 (September 1971), pp. 17-19.

Cook, C. Sharp, and J. O'M. Bockris. "Hydrogen and Power." *Science*, vol. 180, no. 4084 (27 April 1973), p. 370.

Cooper, Richard N. "The Invasion of the Petrodollar." *Saturday Review*. January 25, 1975.

_______. "Macroeconomic Policy Adjustment in Interdependent Economies." *The Quarterly Journal of Economics*, vol. LXXXIII, no. 1 (February 1969), pp. 1-24.

_______. "Trade Policy is Foreign Policy." *Foreign Policy*, no. 9 (Winter 1972-73), pp. 18-36.

_______, et al. "The Future of the Dollar." *Foreign Policy*, no. 11 (Summer 1973), pp. 3-32.

Cowen, Robert C. "Betting on Solar Power." *Technology Review*, vol. 74, no. 4 (February 1972), pp. 5-7.

_______. "Fusion Power: Ten Years to the Great Decision?" *Technology Review*, vol. 73, no. 3 (January 1971), pp. 6-7.

Dean, Genevieve C. "Energy in the People's Republic of China." *Energy Policy*, vol. 2, no. 1 (March 1974), pp. 33-54.

Demaree, Allan T. "Arab Wealth, As Seen Through Arab Eyes." *Fortune*, vol. LXXXIX, no. 4 (April 1974), pp. 108-119.

Diebold, John. "Why Be Scared of Them?" *Foreign Policy*, no. 12 (Fall 1973), pp. 79-95.

Diebold, William, Jr. "U.S. Trade Policy: The New Political Dimensions." *Foreign Affairs*, vol. 52, no. 3 (April 1974), pp. 472-496.

Doub, William O., and Joseph M. Dukert. "Making Nuclear Energy Safe and Secure." *Foreign Affairs*, vol. 53, no. 4 (July 1975), pp. 756-772.

Duff, Declan. "Why Countries Default." *Euromoney*, May 1974, pp. 43-45.

Dunahm, James T., et al. "High Sulfur Coal for Generating Electricity." *Science*, vol. 184, no. 4134 (19 April 1974), pp. 346-351.

Edsall, John T. "Nuclear Energy." *Science*, vol. 178. no. 4064 (1 December 1972), p. 933 (Letters).

Eliav, Arie. "We and the Arabs." *Foreign Policy*, no. 10 (Spring 1973), pp. 62-67.

Emmett, John L., John Nuckolle, and Lowell Wood. "Fusion Power by Laser Implosion." *Scientific American*, vol. 230, no. 6 (June 1974), pp. 24-37.

Enders, Thomas O. "OPEC and the Industrial Countries: The Next Ten Years." *Foreign Affairs*, vol. 53, no. 4 (July 1975), pp. 625-637.

Essenhigh, Robert H. "Fuel Technology Directory." *Science*, vol. 183, No. 4127 (1 March 1974), pp. 797-798.

Ewald, E. "Energy Alternatives: Now and in the Future." *Edison Electric Institute Bulletin*, vol. 39, no. 2 (March/April 1971), pp. 61-63.

Faltermayer, Edmund. "Clearing the Way for the New Age of Coal." *Fortune*, vol. LXXXIX, no. 5 (May 1974), pp. 215-220.

_______. "The Energy 'Joyride' Is Over." *Fortune*, September 1972, pp. 99-101, 178, 180, 182, 184, 186, 188, 191.

_______. "It's Back to the Pits for Coal's New Future." *Fortune*, vol. LXXXIX, no. 6 (June 1974), pp. 137-138.

Farmanfarmaian, Khodadad, Armin Gutowski, Saburo Okita, Robert V. Roosa, and Carroll L. Wilson. "How Can the World Afford OPEC Oil?" *Foreign Affairs*, vol. 53, no. 2 (January 1975), pp. 201-222.

Field, Michael. "Oil: OPEC and Participation." *The World Today*, vol. 28, no. 1 (January 1972), pp. 5-13.

Finn, Donald F.X. "Geothermal Resources: Prospects for Development." *Science*, vol. 185, no. 4150 (9 August 1974), p. 482 (Letters).

Frank, Helmut J. "Economic Strategy for Import-Export Controls for Energy Materials." *Science*, vol. 184, no. 4134 (19 April 1974), pp. 316-321.

Frankel, Ernst. "The 'Energy Crisis' and U.S. Middle East Policy." *Middle East Information Series*, vol. XXIII (May 1973), pp. 8-16.

Frankel, Paul H. "Prospects of the Evolution of the World Petroleum Industry." *Middle East Information Series*, vol. XXIII (May 1973), pp. 17-25.

Friedheim, Robert L. "The 'Satisfied' and 'Dissatisfied' States Negotiate International Law: A Case Study." *World Politics*, vol. 18 (October 1965), pp. 20-41.

_______. "Energy: President Asks $3 Billion for Breeder Reactor, Fuel Studies." *Science*, vol. 172, no. 3988 (11 June 1971), pp. 1114-1116.

Friedheim, Robert L. "Energy R & D: Slicing the Promised Pie." *Science*, vol. 181, no. 4106 (28 September 1973), pp. 1233-1234.

Gillette, Robert. "AEC Shakes Up Nuclear Safety Research." *Science*, vol. 180, no. 4089 (1 June 1973), pp. 934-935.

_______. "Breeder Reactor Debate: The Sun Also Rises." *Science*, vol. 184, no. 4137 (10 May 1974), pp. 650-651.

_______. "Budget Review: Energy." *Science*, vol. 183, no. 4125 (15 February 1974), pp. 636-638.

_______. "Energy 'Blueprint' Sees Little R & D Impact Before 1985." *Science*, vol. 186, no. 4165 (22 November 1974), p. 718.

_______. "India: Into the Nuclear on Canada's Shoulders." *Science*, vol. 184, no. 4141 (7 June 1974), pp. 1053-1055.

_______. "Nuclear Power in the U.S.S.R.: American Visitors Find Surprises." *Science*, vol. 173, no. 4001 (10 September 1971), pp. 1003-1006.

_______. "Nuclear Reactor Safety: At the AEC the Way of the Dissenter is Hard." *Science*, vol. 176, no. 4034 (5 May 1972), pp. 492-498.

_______. "Nuclear Safeguards: Holes in the Fence." *Science*, vol. 182, no. 4117 (14 December 1973), pp. 1112-1114.

_______. "Nuclear Safety (I): The Roots of Dissent." *Science*, vol. 177, no. 4051 (1 September 1972), p. 771.

_______. "Nuclear Safety (II): The Years of Delay." *Science*, vol. 177, no. 4052 (8 September 1972), pp. 867-871.

_______. "Nuclear Safety (III): Critics Charge Conflicts of Interest." *Science*, vol. 177, no. 4053 (15 September 1972), pp. 970-975.

_______. "Nuclear Safety (IV): Barriers to Communication." *Science*, vol. 177, no. 4054 (22 September 1972), pp. 1080-1082.

_______. "Nuclear Safety: AEC Report Makes the Best of It." *Science*, vol. 179, no. 4071 (26 January 1973), pp. 360-363.

_______. "Oil and Gas Resources: Did USGS Gush Too High?" *Science*, vol. 185, no. 4146 (12 July 1974), pp. 127-130.

_______. "Uranium Enrichment: Rumors of Israeli Progress with Lasers." *Science*, vol. 183, no. 4130 (22 March 1974), pp. 1172-1174.

Gray, Colin S. "The Arms Race Is About Politics." *Foreign Policy*, no. 9 (Winter 1972-73), pp. 117-129.

Grose, Peter. "Israel Awaits the Doves." *Foreign Policy*, no. 10 (Spring 1973), pp. 55-72.

Häfele, Wolf. "Energy Choices that Europe Faces: A European View of Energy." *Science*, vol. 184, no. 4134 (19 April 1974), pp. 360-367.

Hammond, Allen L. "The Big Accelerators: A Progress Report." *Science*, vol. 182, no. 4117 (14 December 1973), pp. 1117-1120.

_______. "Breeder Reactors: Power for the Future." *Science*, vol. 174, no. 4011 (19 November 1971), pp. 807-810.

_______. "Conservation of Energy: The Potential for More Efficient Use." *Science*, vol. 178, no. 4065 (8 December 1972), pp. 1079-1081.

_______. "Dry Geothermal Wells: Promising Experimental Results." *Science*, vol. 182, no. 4107 (5 October 1973), pp. 43-44.

_______. "The Fast Breeder Reactor: Signs of a Critical Reaction." *Science*, vol. 176, no. 4033 (28 April 1972), pp. 391-393.

_______. "Fission: The Pro's and Con's of Nuclear Power." *Science*, vol. 178, no. 4057 (13 October 1972), pp. 147-149.

_______. "Geothermal Energy: An Emerging Major Resource." *Science*, vol. 177, no. 4053 (15 September 1972), pp. 978-980.

_______. "Individual Self-Sufficiency in Energy." *Science*, vol. 184, no. 4134 (19 April 1974), pp. 276-282.

_______. "Solar Energy: A Feasible Source of Power?" *Science*, vol. 172, no. 3984 (14 May 1971), p. 660.

_______. "Solar Energy: The Largest Resource." *Science*, vol. 177, no. 4054 (22 September 1972), pp. 1088-1090.

_______. "Solar Energy: Proposal for a Major Research Program." *Science*, vol. 179, no. 4078 (16 March 1973), p. 1116.

_______. "Solar Power: Promising New Developments." *Science*, vol. 184, no. 4144 (28 June 1974), pp. 1359-1360.

Hammond, Allen L., and Robert Gillette. "AEC Begins Shaping Federal Energy Policy." *Science*, vol. 181, no. 4102 (31 August 1973), p. 827.

Haq, Mahbub ul-. "Employment in the 1970's: A New Perspective." *International Development Review*, vol. XIII, no. 4 (1971), pp. 9-13.

Hartshorn, J.E. "A Diplomatic Price for Oil?" *Pacific Community*, vol. 5, no. 3 (April 1974), pp. 363-379.

_______. "From Tripoli to Teheran and Back: The Size and Meaning of the Oil Game." *The World Today*, vol. 27, no. 7 (July 1973), pp. 291-301.

Hawkes, Nigel. "Energy in Britain: Shopping for a New Reactor." *Science*, vol. 183, no. 4120 (11 January 1974), pp. 57-59.

Haykal, M.H. "Soviet Aims and Egypt."*Survival*, vol. XIV, no. 5 (September/October 1972), pp. 231-235.

Henderson, Hazel. "Ecologists versus Economists." *Harvard Business Review*, vol. 51, no. 4 (July-August 1973), p. 28.

Hirst, Eric, and John C. Moyers. "Efficiency of Energy Use in the United States." *Science*, vol. 179, no. 4080 (30 March 1973), pp. 1299-1304.

Hitti, Said H., and George T. Abed, "The Economy and Finances of Saudi Arabia," *International Monetary Fund Staff Papers*, vol. 21, no. 2 (July 1974), pp. 247-306.

Hoffmann, Stanley. "Will the Balance Balance at Home?" *Foreign Policy*, no. 7 (Summer 1972), pp. 60-86.

Holden, Constance. "Clean Air: Congress Settles for a Restrained Coal Conversion Plan." *Science*, vol. 184, no. 4143 (21 June 1974), pp. 1269-1270.

_______. "Energy: Shortages Loom, But Conservation Lags." *Science*, vol. 180, no. 4091 (15 June 1973), pp. 1155-1158.

_______. "The EPC: Environmental Lobby." *Science*, vol. 182, no. 4115 (30 November 1973), p. 905.

Holden, Constance. "New Energy Message Downplays R & D." *Science*, vol. 180, no. 4085 (4 May 1973), p. 475.

Holden, David. "The Persian Gulf: After the British Raj." *Foreign Affairs*, vol. 49, no. 4 (July 1971), pp. 721-735.

Hollick, Ann L. "Seabeds Make Strange Politics." *Foreign Policy*, no. 9 (Winter 1972-73), pp. 148-170.

Horelick, Arnold J. "The Soviet Union, the Middle East and the Evolving World Energy Situation." *Policy Science*, vol. 6, no. 1 (March 1975), pp. 41-48.

Hottinger, Arnold. "The Depth of Arab Radicalism." *Foreign Affairs*, vol. 51, no. 3 (April 1973), pp. 491-504.

Hoyt, Monty. "Middle East Oil: Hobson's Choice for the West." *Middle East International*, no. 7 (October 1971), pp. 41, 45.

Hub, K.A. "Fast Breeder Reactors." *Science*, vol. 178, no. 4067 (22 December 1972), pp. 1240-1241 (Letters).

Hubbert, M. King. "The Energy Resources of the Earth." *Development Digest*, vol. X, no. 3 (July 1972), pp. 30-38.

Hughes, Thomas L. "The Flight from Foreign Policy," *Foreign Policy*, no. 10 (Spring 1973), pp. 141-156.

Hunter, Robert E. "In the Middle in the Middle East." *Foreign Policy*, no. 5 (Winter 1971-72), pp. 137-150.

_______. "Power and Peace." *Foreign Policy*, no. 9 (Winter 1972-73), pp. 37-54.

Ignotus, Miles. "Seizing Arab Oil." *Harpers*, vol. 250 (March 1975), pp. 45-62.

Ikle, Fred. C. "Can Nuclear Deterrence Last Out the Century?" *Foreign Affairs*, vol. 51, no. 2 (January 1973), pp. 267-285.

Irwin, John N. "The International Implications of the Energy Situation." *The Department of State Bulletin*, vol. LXVI, no. 1714 (1 May 1972), pp. 626-631.

"It Worked For the Arabs . . ." *Forbes*, vol. 115, no. 2 (15 January 1975), pp. 19-21.

Jahn, Edward. "Inexhaustible Energy." *Science*, vol. 180, no. 4084 (27 April 1973), pp. 369-370.

Jones, Lawrence W. "Liquid Hydrogen as a Fuel for the Future." *Science*, vol. 174, no. 4007 (22 October 1971), pp. 367-370.

Kaysen, Carl. "The Computer That Printed Out W*O*L*F*." *Foreign Affairs*, vol. 50, no. 4 (July 1972), pp. 660-669.

Kennan, George F. "After the Cold War: American Foreign Policy in the 1970's." *Foreign Affairs*, vol. 51, no. 1 (October 1972), pp. 210-227.

_______. "To Prevent a World Wasteland: A Proposal." *Foreign Affairs*, vol. 48, no. 3 (April 1970), pp. 401-413.

Keohane, Robert O. "The Big Influence of Small Allies." *Foreign Policy*, no. 2 (Spring 1972), pp. 161-182.

_______, and Joseph S. Nye, Jr. "Power and Interdependence." *Survival*, vol. XV, no. 4 (July/August 1973), pp. 158-165.

Kissell, Fred N., Allan E. Nagel, and Michael G. Zabetakis. "Coal Mine Explosions: Seasonal Trends." *Science*, vol. 179, no. 4076 (2 March 1973), pp. 891-892.

Kleinman, David. "Oil Money and the Third World." *The Banker*, vol. 124, no. 583 (September 1974), pp. 1061-1064.

Kohjima, Sachio. "Deficit Should Be Manageable." *Euromoney*, May 1974, pp. 78-79.

Koide, Yoshio. "China's Crude Oil Production." *Pacific Community*, vol. 5, no. 3 (April 1974), pp. 463-470.

Krasner, Stephen D. "Are Bureaucracies Important?" *Foreign Policy*, no. 7 (Summer 1972), pp. 159-179.

_______. "The Great Oil Sheikdown." *Foreign Policy*, no. 13 (Winter 1973-74), pp. 123-138.

_______. "Oil is the Exception." *Foreign Policy*, no. 14 (Spring 1974), pp. 68-83.

Kubo, Arthur S., and David J. Rose. "Disposal of Nuclear Wastes." *Science*, vol. 182, no. 4118 (21 December 1973), pp. 1205-1211.

Kuczynski, Pedro-Pablo. "The Effects of the Rise in Oil Prices on the Third World." *Euromoney*, May 1974, pp. 37-41.

Landsberg, Hans H. "Low-Cost, Abundant Energy: Paradise Lost?" *Science*, vol. 184, no. 4134 (19 April 1974), pp. 247-253.

Lessing, Lawrence. "Lasers Blast a Shortcut to the Ultimate Energy Solution." *Fortune*, vol. LXXXIX, no. 5 (May 1974), p. 221.

Levy, Walter J. "An Atlantic-Japanese Energy Policy." *Foreign Policy*, no. 11 (Summer 1973), pp. 159-190.

_______. "Oil Power." *Foreign Affairs*, no. 4 (July 1971), pp. 652-668.

_______. "World Oil Cooperation or International Chaos?" *Foreign Affairs*, vol. 52, no. 4 (July 1974), pp. 690-713.

Lewis, Bernard. "Conflict in the Middle East." *Survival*, vol. XIII, no. 6 (June 1971), pp. 192-198.

Lidsky, Lawrence M. "The Quest for Fusion Power." *Technology Review*, vol. 74, no. 3 (January 1972), pp. 10-21.

Lincoln, G.A. "Energy Conservation." *Science*, vol. 180, no. 4082 (13 April 1973), pp. 155-162.

Loomis, Carol J. "How to Think about Oil-Company Profits." *Fortune*, vol. LXXXIX, no. 4 (April 1974), pp. 98-103.

Mallakh, Ragaei el-. "The Challenge of Affluence: Abu Dhabi." *The Middle East Journal*, vol. 24, no. 2 (Spring 1970), pp. 135-146.

_______. "The Economics of Rapid Growth: Libya." *The Middle East Journal*, vol. 23, no. 3 (Summer 1969), pp. 308-320.

Massachusetts Institute of Technology, Policy Study Group of the M.I.T. Energy Laboratory. "Energy Self-Sufficiency: An Economic Evaluation." *Technology Review*, vol. 76, no. 6 (May 1974), pp. 22-58.

Mates, Leo. "Non-Alignment and the Great Powers." *Foreign Affairs*, vol. 48, no. 3 (April 1970), pp. 525-536.

Maugh, Thomas H. II. "Fuel from Wastes: A Minor Energy Source." *Science*, vol. 178, no. 4061 (10 November 1972), pp. 599-602.

_______. "Gasification: A Rediscovered Source of Clean Fuel." *Science*, vol. 178, no. 4056 (6 October 1972), pp. 44-45.

_______. "Hydrogen: Synthetic Fuel of the Future." *Science* vol. 178, no. 4063 (24 November 1972), pp. 849-852.

Mayer, Lawrence A. "Oil, Trade and the Dollar." *Fortune*, vol. LXXXIX, no. 6 (June 1974), pp. 193-201.

Mazur, Allan, and Eugene Rosa. "Energy and Life Style." *Science*, vol. 186, no. 4164 (15 November 1974), pp. 607-610.

McCarthy, John. "Energy and the Environment." *Science*, vol. 183, no. 4128 (8 March 1974), pp. 901-902.

Meadows, Dennis L. "Nuclear Energy and Growth." *Science*, vol. 179, no. 4076 (2 March 1973), pp. 855-856 (Letter).

Meir, Golda. "Israel in Search of Lasting Peace." *Foreign Affairs*, vol. 51, no. 3 (April 1973), pp. 447-461.

Mendelsohn, M.S. "World Money—What Is Not Happening, And Why." *Euromoney*, May 1974, pp. 32-35.

_______. "Laser Fusion: A New Approach to Thermonuclear Power." *Science*, vol. 177, no. 4055 (29 September 1972), pp. 1180-1182.

_______. "Laser Fusion Secrecy Lifted: Microballoons are the Trick." *Science*, vol. 186, no. 4163 (8 November 1974), p. 519.

_______. "Magnetic Containment Fusion: What are the Prospects?" *Science*, vol. 178, no. 4058 (20 October 1972), pp. 291-293.

_______. "Oil Shale: A Huge Resource of Low-Grade Fuel." *Science*, vol. 184, no. 4143 (21 June 1974), pp. 1271-1275.

Meyers, R.A., J.W. Hamersma, J.S. Land, and M.L. Kraft. "Desulfurization of Coal." *Science*, vol. 177, no. 4055 (29 September 1972), pp. 1187-1188.

Mikdashi, Zuhayr. "Collusion Could Work." *Foreign Policy*, no. 14 (Spring 1974), pp. 57-67.

Mikolaj, Paul G. "Environmental Applications of the Weibull Distribution Function: Oil Pollution." *Science*, vol. 176, no. 4038 (2 June 1972), pp. 1019-1022.

Miller, Arnold. "The Energy Crisis as a Coal Miner Sees it." *The Center Magazine*, vol. VI, no. 6 (November/December 1973), pp. 33-45.

Mishan, E.J. "The Postwar Literature of Externalities: An Interpretive Essay." *Journal of Economic Literature*, vol. IX, no. 1 (March 1971), pp. 1-28.

Modesta, Jorg. "The Energy Crisis Facing the U.S." *Middle East International*, no. 20 (February 1973), pp. 13-17.

Moran, Theodore H. "Coups and Costs." *Foreign Policy*, no. 8 (Fall 1972), pp. 129-137.

_______. "New Deal or Raw Deal in Raw Materials?" *Foreign Policy*, no. 5 (Winter 1971-72), pp. 119-134.

Murray, James R., et al. "Evolution of Public Response to the Energy Crisis." *Science*, vol. 184, no. 4134 (19 April 1974), pp. 257-263.

Naumann, Robert J. "Automotive Emission Standards and Fuel Economy." *Science*, vol. 183, no. 4125 (15 February 1974), p. 595.

Netschert, Bruce C. "The Energy Company: A Monopoly Trend in the Energy Markets." *Bulletin of the Atomic Scientists*, vol. XXVII, no. 8 (October 1971), pp. 13-17.

Okita, Saburo. "Natural Resource Dependency and Japanese Foreign Policy." *Foreign Affairs*, vol. 52, no. 4 (July 1974), pp. 714-724.

Othmer, Donald F., and Oswald A. Roels. "Power, Fresh Water, and Food from Cold, Deep Sea Water." *Science*, vol. 182, no. 4108 (12 October 1973), pp. 121-125.

Pachter, Henry M. "Imperialism in Reverse." *Harpers*, vol. 248, no. 1489 (June 1974), pp. 62-68.

Penrose, Edith. "Vertical Integration with Joint Control of Raw Material Production: Crude Oil in the Middle East." *The Journal of Development Studies*, vol. 1, no. 3 (April 1965), pp. 251-268.

Pimentel, David, et al. "Food Production and the Energy Crisis." *Science*, vol. 182, no. 4111 (2 November 1973), pp. 443-449.

Pollack, Gerald A. "The Economic Consequences of the Energy Crisis." *Foreign Affairs*, vol. 52, no. 3 (April 1974), pp. 452-471.

Post, R.F., and F.L. Ribe. "Fusion Reactors as Future Energy Sources." *Science*, vol. 186, no. 4162 (1 November 1974), pp. 397-407.

Potter, Stephen P. "Energy Supply." *Science*, vol. 180, no. 4085 (4 May 1973), p. 446 (Letters).

Quandt, William B. "Algeria: Yes," Part I of "Can We Do Business With Radical Nationalists?" *Foreign Policy*, no. 7 (Summer 1972), pp. 108-131.

Quester, George H. "Can Proliferation Now Be Stopped?" *Foreign Affairs*, vol. 53, no. 1 (October 1974), pp. 77-97.

Rand, Christopher T. "The Arabian Fantasy." *Harper's*, vol. 248, no. 1484 (January 1974), pp. 42-54.

Reed, T.B., and R.M. Lerner. "Methanol: A Versatile Fuel for Immediate Use." *Science*, vol. 182, no. 4119 (28 December 1973), pp. 1299-1304.

Reister, David, and Henry Davitian. "Recoverable Oil and Gas Resources." *Science*, vol. 187, no. 4179 (3 July 1975), p. 790 (Letters).

Remba, Oded, and Anne Sinai. "The Energy Problem and the Middle East: An Introduction." *Middle East Information Series*, vol. XXIII (May 1973), pp. 2-7.

Richardson, John P. "America's Middle East Policy." *Middle East International*, no. 16 (October 1972), pp. 13-14.

Rinehart, John S. "18.6-Year Earth Tide Regulates Geyser Activity." *Science*, vol. 177, no. 4046 (28 July 1972), pp. 346-347.

Robson, Geoffrey R. "Geothermal Electricity Production." *Science*, vol. 184, no. 4134 (19 April 1974), pp. 371-375.

Roe, Keith. "The Promises of Technology." *Science*, vol. 185, no. 4150 (8 September 1974), p. 478 (Letters).

Rose, David J. "Controlled Nuclear Fusion: Status and Outlook." *Science*, vol. 172, no. 3985 (21 May 1971), pp. 797-808.

_______. "Nuclear Electric Power." *Science*, vol. 184, no. 4134 (19 April 1974), pp. 351-359.

Rose, Sanford. "Our Vast, Hidden Oil Resources." *Fortune*, vol. LXXXIX, no. 4 (April 1974), pp. 104-107.

Rothschild Intercontinental Bank. "Coping with the Oil Deficit." *Euromoney*, May 1974, pp. 115-118.

Rouleau, Eric. "Egypt from Nasser to Sadat." *Survival*, vol. XIV, no. 6 (November/December 1972), pp. 284-286.

Ruggie, John G. "Collective Goods and Future International Collaboration." *American Political Science Review*, vol. LXVI, no. 3, pp. 874-893.

_______. "The Structure of International Organization: Contingency, Complexity, and Post-Modern Form." *Peace Research Society, Papers*, vol. XVIII, The London Conference (1971), pp. 73-91.

Sadat, Anwar el-. "Where Egypt Stands." *Foreign Affairs*, vol. 51, no. 1 (October 1972), pp. 114-123.

Safran, Nader. "Arab-Israeli Conflict." *Foreign Affairs*, vol. 52, no. 2 (January 1974), pp. 215-237.

Sagan, L.A. "Human Costs of Nuclear Power." *Science*, vol. 177, no. 4048 (11 August 1972), pp. 487-493.

Sakisaka, Masao. "World Energy Problems and Japan's International Role." *Energy Policy*, vol. 1, no. 2 (September 1973), pp. 100-106.

Schmidt, Helmut. "The Struggle for the World Product." *Foreign Affairs*, vol. 52, no. 3 (April 1974), pp. 437-451.

Schoenbaum, David. ". . . Or Lucky?" Part II of "Jordan: The Forgotten Crisis." *Foreign Policy*, no. 10 (Spring 1973), pp. 171-181.

Seaborg, Glenn T. "For a U.S. Energy Agency." *Science*, vol. 176, no. 4040 (16 June 1972), p. 1189.

Seif, Michael. "Fusion Power: Progress and Problems." *Science*, vol. 173, no. 2999 (27 August 1971), pp. 802-803.

Shapely, Deborah. "Auto Catalyst to Stay for 1975." *Science*, vol. 182, no. 4114 (23 November 1973), p. 809.

_______. "EPA Severs Ties with Industry Research Group." *Science*, vol. 183, no. 4120 (11 January 1974), pp. 60-61.

_______. "Law of the Sea: Energy, Economy Spur Secret Review of U.S. Stance." *Science*, vol. 183, no. 4122 (25 January 1974), pp. 290-292.

Shourie, Arun. "Growth, Poverty and Inequalities." *Foreign Affairs*, vol. 51, no. 2 (January 1973), pp. 340-352.

Shulman, Marshall D. "Toward a Western Philosophy of Coexistence." *Foreign Affairs*, vol. 52, no. 1 (October 1973), p. 35.

Silbey, Franklin R. "Will Arab Oil Change the U.S. Middle East Stance?" *Middle East Information Series*, vol. XXIII (May 1973), pp. 40-52.

Simonet, Henri. "Energy and the Future of Europe." *Foreign Affairs*, vol. 53, no. 3 (April 1975), pp. 450-463.

Squires, Arthur M. "Clean Fuels From Coal Gasification." *Science*, vol. 184, no. 4134 (19 April 1974), pp. 340-346.

Stabler, Charles, and Ray Vicker. "Liquid Assets–Middle East Oil Funds Plan an Increasing Role in Monetary Turmoil." *Middle East Information Series*, vol. XXIII (May 1973), pp. 75-78.

Starr, Chauncey, and R. Phillip Hammond. "Nuclear Waste Storage." *Science*, vol. 177, no. 4051 (1 September 1972), pp. 744-745 (Letters).

Stauffer, Thomas R. "Impact of Middle East Petroleum Operations Upon the U.S. and U.K. Balance of Payments." *Middle East Economic Survey*, vol. XII, no. 31 (30 May 1969), pp. 1-5.

_______. "Oil Money and World Money: Conflict or Confluence?" *Science*, vol. 184, no. 4134 (19 April 1974), pp. 321-325.

Steinhart, John S., and Carol E. Steinhart. "Energy Use in the U.S. Food System." *Science*, vol. 184, no. 4134 (19 April 1974), pp. 307-316.

Stevenson, Adlai E., III. "Nuclear Reactors: America Must Act." *Foreign Affairs*, vol. 53, no. 1 (October 1974), pp. 64-76.

Subba Rao, G.V. "The Predicament of Developing Countries." *Saturday Review*, January 25, 1975, pp. 18-19.

Teller, Edward. "The Energy Disease: Diagnosis and Prescription for an International Ailment." *Harpers*, vol. 250 (February 1975), pp. 16-18.

Teman, A. "An Oil-Based Arab Currency." *Euromoney*, May 1974, p. 30.

"A 30-Year Cycle of Energy Development." *Technology Review*, vol. 73, no. 8 (June 1971), p. 59.

Thompson, A.W., P.R. Cooley, and F.J. Hooven. "Fuel Economy and Emission Controls." *Science*, vol. 184, no. 4136 (3 May 1974), pp. 520-522.

Thomsen, Dietrick E. "Farming the Sun's Energy." *Science News*, vol. 101 (April 8, 1972), pp. 237-238.

Tobias, Andrew. "War–The Ultimate Antitrust Action." *New York*, vol. 7, no. 41 (October 14, 1974), pp. 35-40.

Tucker, Robert W. "Oil: The Issue of American Intervention." *Commentary*, vol. 59, no. 1 (January 1975), pp. 21-31.

Tugendhat, Christopher. "Oil–How to Avoid a Catastrophe?" *The Banker*, vol. 124, no. 576 (February 1974), pp. 101-102.

Turcotte, D.L. "Statistical Thermodynamic Model for the Distribution of Crustal Heat Sources." *Science*, vol. 176, no. 4038 (2 June 1972), pp. 1021-1022.

Varon, Benson, and Kenji Takeuchi. "Developing Countries and Non-Fuel Minerals." *Foreign Affairs*, vol. 52, no. 3 (April 1974), pp. 497-510.

Venu, S. "Oil Prices and the Indian Economy." *Euromoney*, May 1974, pp. 105-107.

Vernon, Raymond. "The Multinational Enterprise: Power versus Sovereignty." *Foreign Affairs*, vol. 49, no. 4 (July 1974), pp. 736-751.

Verrier, A. "Oil and Regional Development." *Middle East International*, no. 7 (October 1971), pp. 39-40.

Wade, Nicholas. "Raw Materials: U.S. Grows More Vulnerable to Third World Cartels." *Science*, vol. 183, no. 4121 (18 January 1974), pp. 185-186.

_______. "Windmills: The Resurrection of an Ancient Energy Technology." *Science*, vol. 184, no. 4141 (7 June 1974), pp. 1055-1058.

Walsh, John. "Britain and Energy Policy: Problems of Interdependence." *Science*, vol. 180, no. 4093 (29 June 1973), pp. 1343-1347.

_______. "British Choose Own Reactor for Nuclear Power Program." *Science*, vol. 185, no. 4150 (9 August 1974), p. 511.

_______. "European Community Energy Policy: Regulation or Mainly Information?" *Science*, vol. 184, no. 4142 (14 June 1974), pp. 1158-1161.

_______. "Problems of Expanding Coal Production." *Science*, vol. 184, no. 4134 (19 April 1974), pp. 336-339.

Weinberg, Alvin M. "Global Effects of Man's Production of Energy." *Science*, vol. 186, no. 4160 (18 October 1974), p. 205.

_______. "Nuclear Energy." *Science*, vol. 178, no. 4064 (1 December 1972), pp. 933-934.

_______. "Social Institutions and Nuclear Energy." *Science*, vol. 177, no. 4043 (7 July 1972), pp. 27-34.

Weinhold, J. Frederick. "Nonnuclear Energy for Development." *Science*, vol. 180, no. 4083 (20 April 1973), p. 324.

Wilson, Carroll L. "A Plan for Energy Independence." *Foreign Affairs*, vol. 51, no. 4 (July 1973), pp. 657-675.

Wilson, Richard. "Tax the Integrated Pollution Exposure." *Science*, vol. 178, no. 4057 (13 October 1972), pp. 182-183.

Winsche, W.E., K.C. Hoffman, and F.J. Salzano. "Hydrogen: Its Future Role in the Nation's Energy Economy." *Science*, vol. 180, no. 4093 (29 June 1973), pp. 1325-1332.

Wohlstetter, Albert. "Japan's Security: Balancing After the Shocks." *Foreign Policy*, no. 9 (Winter 1972-73), pp. 171-190.

Wolf, Martin. "Solar Energy Utilization by Physical Methods." *Science*, vol. 184, no. 4134 (19 April 1974), pp. 382-386.

Yergin, Daniel. "The [Economic Political Military] Solution." *The New York Times Magazine*, 16 February, 1975, p. 10.

Zakariya, Hasan. "Some Analytical Comments on OPEC's Declaratory Statement of Petroleum Policy." *Middle East Economic Survey*, 14 February 1969.

Zombanakis, Minos. "Arab Funds and the Markets." *The Banker*, vol. 124, no. 581 (July 1974).

Index

Index

About the Authors

Nazli Choucri is Associate Professor of Political Science at the Massachusetts Institute of Technology. She received the B.A. from American University (Cairo) and the M.A. and Ph.D. from Stanford University. She is author of *Population Dynamics and International Violence: Propositions, Insights, and Evidence* (1974) and co-author (with Robert C. North) of *Nations in Conflict: National Growth and International Violence* (1975). Professor Choucri's current research interests center on problems of public policy in developing countries.

Vincent Ferraro is a graduate student in the Department of Political Science at M.I.T. He received the B.A. from Dartmouth College (1971) and the M.I.A. from Columbia University (1973). His Ph.D. thesis is entitled "Resource Cartels and International Politics: The Cases of Petroleum and Copper."

About the Authors